FAMINE
AS A GEOGRAPHICAL PHENOMENON

III

FAMINE

AS A GEOGRAPHICAL PHENOMENON

Edited by

Bruce Currey and Graeme Hugo

D. Reidel Publishing Company

A MEMBER OF THE KLUWER ACADEMIC PUBLISHERS GROUP

Dordrecht / Boston / Lancaster

IV

Library of Congress Cataloging in Publication Data

DATA APPEAR ON SEPARATE CARD.

ISBN 90-277-1762-1

Published by D. Reidel Publishing Company
P.O. Box 17, 3300 AA Dordrecht, Holland

Sold and distributed in the U.S.A. and Canada
by Kluwer Academic Publishers,
190 Old Derby Street, Hingham, MA 02043, U.S.A.

In all other countries, sold and distributed
by Kluwer Academic Publishers Group,
P.O. Box 322, 3300 AH Dordrecht, Holland

Printed in FR Germany

V

The GeoJournal Library

Series Editor: Wolf TIETZE

Vol. 1.: Famine as a Geographical Phenomenon

Contents

VI

The GeoJournal Library

Series Editor: WOLF TIETZE

About the Cover: (Courtesy of Andrew Little and Reg Brook) The Map of Food Crises during the 1970's portrays, by country, the years in which there were mentions of actual or potential food stress situations in the New York Times. The contents analysis was carried out by Heidi Neitz and Krystyna Kowalski with the Food Crisis Management Group. The Australiancentered equidistant projection was designed by the South Australian Institute of Technology. – The woodcut inset is by Albrecht Dürer (1471–1528) and shows the four horsemen of the Apocalypse – Christ, war, *famine*, and death (see Editorial)

Editorial

Famine as a Geographical Phenomenon

Famines have been an integral part of the historical development of civilisation. In the Latin American countries of Nicaragua and Mexico famine was worshipped as a deity [1]. In South Asia it features in the Ramayana [2]. The earliest oral histories in the Western World tell us that Pandora let famine out of her box which contained the evils associated with technological development [3]. Later in Biblical times St. John saw famine as part of the apocalypse [4]. In the final quarter of the 20th century, nine countries each year are still reported as suffering a food crisis (see front cover) and the famines of Kampuchea, Ethiopia, Uganda, the Sahel and Southern Africa still seem to be part of our civilisation.

Famine is a community crisis; a syndrome with webs of causation through which communities lose their ability to support marginal members who consequently either migrate in families because of lack of access to food, or die of starvation or starvation related disease. Famines are regional scale phenomena which result from the complex concatenation of spatial processes like deforestation, and events like the sudden sales of grain for the elites from public granaries before an election. The impact of famine ramifies through society changing everything from the socio-economic structure to political power, from international food policies to immigration policies, and from viral transmission to rural development.

The geographer's training and perspective is particularly appropriate not only in the elucidation of the causes and impact of famines but also in approaching the problems of managing famines. Applied geographical work has a significant input to make in developing long and short term strategies to ameliorate the effects of famine, to minimise the probability of their recurrence and to develop famine warning systems. Many of these problems are inherently geographical and geographers have a responsibility to make their knowledge available outside the narrow coterie of academics.

Nevertheless, famine has never been a central focus for geographical literature. The fact that Aristippus found no famine affected villages on the sands of Rhodes may have influenced Clarence Glacken to omit it from his magnum opus of man's relations with the environment: *Traces on the Rhodian Shore* [5]. The "Natural Hazards Research" paradigm, centered in the ethereal heights of Boulder, Colorado, has given famine minimal attention, although Wisner [6] and Mbithi [7], working in Africa, have made useful individual contributions. Possibly there is a tragedy for Geography as a discipline, in that Michigan's former geography department powerhouse in the mid-1960's — a group headed by John F. Kolars, with John Nystuen, Melvin Marcus, Rhoads Murphey and Waldo Tobler — submitted a proposal entitled FEED (Famine Evaluation and Early Detection) [8] for US funding only to have it rejected. Now, almost two decades later and despite the recession in research funding, it might possibly be accepted, but the Geography Department no longer exists. Presently, there is no International Geographical Union Commission, or Working Party, on famine. A recent section on famines in *Progress in Human Geography* [9] quoted no work by geographers. Perhaps it is time for some geographical introspection and action.

Although unfocussed, geographers nevertheless have a tradition of confronting famine. On 12th December 1873, Sir H. Bartle E. Frere, President of the Royal Geographical Society, lectured the Society of Arts on the topic "Impending Bengal Famine: How it will be met, and how to prevent future famines in India" [10]. In the early 1920's Mallory in China [11], Chassigneux in Indochina [12], and Renner in the Sahel [13], each developed a similar famine preventive theme. Today, professional geographers working and writing in an administrative capacity in famine situations, continue the action orientation. Hugh Brammer in Bangladesh [14], working with the Ministry of Agriculture, has written and advised on how to reduce vulnerability to famine. Geoffrey Last, in the Ministry for Education in Ethiopia, has tried to involve schools in the national famine warning system [15].

Our academic tradition is spotty and often historical in nature because of the availability of data, e.g. Cousens' work on the demographic impact of the Irish Famine [16,17,18], Pfister in Switzerland [19], Walton in Scotland [20], and Brooke in Tanzania [21,22]. Unfortunately, the two most popular books (de Castro's *Geography of Hunger* [23] and Dando's *Geography of Famine* [24]) are distanced from the pragmatic realities of famine, the former by the burning emotion of ideology and the latter by emotionless data from chronicles embedded in a computer data base.

The famines of the early 1970's have spawned a new group of academic geographers. Some are associated with the International Africa Institute and the International Disaster Institute in London. Others include Jean Copan's Sahelian group in Paris [25], together with those individuals fortunate enough to be funded on foreign field work for dissertations: Watts [26] and van Apeldoorn in Nigeria [27], Wisner in East Africa [6], Wood in Ethiopia [28] and Currey in Bangladesh [29]. They have worked amidst famine conditions and know the fear, emotion and apprehension which seldom appears in government reports.

Had Peter Kropotkin [30] been a Bengali landless labourer or Bill Bunge [31] been a Kampuchean peasant, more young geographers may have been encouraged to explore actively the problem of famine. Data difficulties, ethical dilemmas, and lack of a conceptual model would then have disappeared rapidly. Those who have proposed "triage" policies, or puffed on pipes as they mused about rearranging the deck-chairs on the sinking "Titanic", have never been personally involved with famine. "Dire scenes of horror, which no pen can trace, nor rolling years from memory's page efface" 32).

This first edition of *GeoLibrary* is specifically aimed at geography students. There is no order to the articles such as might occur in a book or conference proceedings. They are a collection of papers written by individuals, many of whom have been connected, sometimes in a visiting capacity, with the Multidisciplinary Famine course or the Food Crisis Management Group at The Flinders University of South Australia. Some Geography Departments, like that of Pennsylvania State University, incorporate famine into their lower level courses. The University of Hull has a famine component in its biogeography course, Arizona State University has a geography course on food and famine, and the University of Hawaii includes famine within a course on hazards. The University of California, Berkeley has just begun a new Geography Course entitled Food and Famine. In the developing world, both Adolfo Mascarenhas in Tanzania 33) and Nazrul Islam in Bangladesh 34) confront their students with the issues of famine. Would not every country in the modern world prone to food crises *(see front cover)* surely benefit by having famine as an integral part of their introductory geography programme?

Although the authors are from a range of disciplines, each article refers to famine as a geographical phenomenon as befits the problem. They have attempted to see famine as part of the developmental process. Where others have already paved the way, such as the historian Lillian Li's conference on *Famine in China* at the Fairbank Centre in 1980 35), the economic historians Michael Drake's and Jean Francois Bergier's conference on *Famine in History* at Vevey 36) in 1981, and the joint venture between the International Disaster Institute and the London School of Tropical Medicine and Hygiene for their conference on *Famine and Food Emergencies* in London in 1982 37), we have looked elsewhere. Even so, we have unfortunately left many interesting branches of the geography of famine, such as the biogeography of famine foods, still to be explored. In our opinion, the greatest research lacuna remains the need to listen to local knowledge, to view famines from the perspective of the victims, as did the Bangladesh Rural Advancement Committee's *Peasant Perceptions of Famine 38)*.

Graeme Hugo leads off with a broad ranging review of the short and long-term demographic impacts of famine, a field that is much more geographical in scope than previous definitions of famine (in terms of starvation mortality) have suggested. He begins by linking famine to demographic theory and ends by highlighting avenues for future research by demographically trained geographers. Victims of famine seldom have voices, but Meng-Try Ea, formerly a geography lecturer in Pnomh Penh and now a Kampuchean refugee who lost most of his family amidst the tragedy, culls through the myriad of conflicting reports to provide a vived descriptive account of the contemporary tragedy of Cambodia in a famine associated with war. He emphasises the over-riding importance of the political factors. The association of famine with war may become increasingly prevalent in the latter part of the 20th century. Just as Kampuchea has seen famine in a land renowned for its abundance, this has increasingly become a common theme in famine studies. David Watts discusses the reasons for famine amidst plenty in the Caribbian,where development in the form of an imposed agricultural system has been a major variable in causing famine. Brian Murton uses local records in Southern India to examine the geographical patterns of famine before the British drew up their extensive Famine Codes. Lance Brennan follows on, detailing the political intrigue involved in establishing the 1878-80 Famine Commission which in turn led to the compilation of the Indian Famine Codes. Mehtabunisa Ali, a Bengali geographer, highlights the role of women in the famines of Bengal, astutely questioning the real status of women at times of famine, as seen from an Asian perspective. Peter Gould and Annik Rogier give linear programming a new lease of life for first year students in their didactic article based on the African Sahel situation. Robert Snow takes a humanistic approach to learning about relief. He asks a series of new questions about the potential impact of famine relief using the example of the Turkana in north west Kenya. Finally, Bruce Currey provides a management approach for putting short term famine relief in a long term development context. We considered adding an annotated bibliography on famine at the end of this collection but, lest our prejudices show, we commend the reader to the world bibliography on famine [39] which our group has produced, and to the extensive references at the end of most of the articles.

This first edition of *GeoLibrary* has been made possible through the invited efforts of the international contributors, together with support from Flinders University staff members Susan Blackwell, Reg Brooks, Heather Bushell, Mary Cherin, Joy Davis, Jean Lange, Andrew Little, Sue Stack and Debbie Whisson. Particular thanks go to our sub-editor Bryan Mellonie, a writer historian.

Bruce Currey
Graeme Hugo
Geography Discipline
The Flinders University of South Australia
Bedford Park, SA 5042, Australia

Notes:

1) The Deities, Visitot in Nicaragua and Apizteotl in Mexico.

2) The Ramayana, Ayodhyakanda, Ch. 100, p. 374.

3) Interpretation and translation of the introduction of Hesiod's Works and Days by Wayne Bledsoe, Visiting Professor in the School of Social Sciences, Flinders University, South Australia and Professor of History, University of Missouri — Rolla.

4) Four Horsemen of the Apocalpyse. "Revelations 6.1−8. The rider on the white horse has many interpretations — one is that he represents Christ; the rider on the red horse is war; on *the Black Horse* is famine and on the pale horse, death". The Columbia Encyclopaedia, Third Edition, Columbia University Press, 1963, p. 751.

5) Glacken, C.J.: Traces on the Rhodian Shore. University of California Press, Berkeley 1967.

6) Wisner, B.G.: The Human Ecology of Drought in Eastern Kenya, Ph.D. University, Clark University. University Microfilms Order No. CCN78-49268, Ann Arbor, Michigan 1978.

7) Mbithi, P.M.: Famine Crises and Innovation: Physical and Social Factors Affecting New Crop Adoptions in the Marginal Famine Areas of Eastern Kenya. Department of Rural Economy and Extension, Makerere University, Kampala, Uganda. Paper Number 52, 1967.

8) Kolars, J.F. et al.: Feed (Famine Evaluation and Early Detection) Proposal to Office of Naval Research ORA-65-684-PBI. The University of Michigan, Ann Arbor, Michigan 1965.

9) Harriss, B. and Harriss, J.: Development Studies. Progress in Human Geography 6,4 p. 587, 1982.

10) Frère, Sir H.B.E.: On the impending Bengal famine: how it will be met, and how to prevent future famines in India — a lecture delivered before the Society of Arts. December 12, 1873, John Murray, London 1874.

11) Mallory, W.H.: China: Land of Famine. American Geographical Society. New York 1926.

12) Chassigneux, E.: La lutte contre la famine en Annam. L'Asie Francaise. 70−73, March 1923.

13) Renner, G.T.: A famine zone in Africa. The Sudan. Geographical Review, 16, 583−396 (1926)

14) Brammer, H.: Disaster Preparedness, Planning, Precautionary and Rehabilitation Measures for Agriculture. Dacca. January 1975.

15) Last, G.C.: Relief and Rehabilitation and the Education System. Working paper. Government of Ethiopia. Addis Ababa 1975.

16) Cousens, S.H.: Regional death rates in Ireland during the great famine, from 1846 to 1851. Population Studies, 14,1, 55−74 (1960)

17) Cousens, S.H.: The regional pattern of emigration during the great Irish famine, 1846−1851. Transactions and Papers of the Institute of British Geographers No. 28, 119−134 (1960)

18) Cousens, S.H.: The regional variation in mortality during the great Irish famine. Proceedings of the Royal Irish Academy 63, Section C (3), 127−149 (1963)

19) Pfister, C.: The Little Ice Age: Thermal and Wetness Indices for Central Europe. Journal of Interdisciplinary History X,4, 665−696 (1980)

20) Walton, K.: Climate and famines in north east Scotland. Scottish Geographical Magazine, 68,1, 13−21 (1952)

21) Brooke, C.: The heritage of famine in central Tanzania. Tanzania Notes and Records 67, 167−176 (1967)

22) Brooke, C.: Types of food shortages in Tanzania. Geographical Review, 57,3, 333−357 (1967)

23) de Castro, J.: The Geopolitics of Hunger. Monthly Review Press, New York (1977)

24) Wisner, B.: Review of "The Geography of Famine", by W.A. Dando, Halstead Press, New York. Review — Progress in Human Geography 6,2, 271−275 (1982)

25) Copans, J.: Editor, Secheresses et Famines du Sahel. Librairie Francois Maspero, Paris 1982.

26) Watts, M.J.: A Silent Revolution: The nature of famine and the changing character of food production in Nigerian Hausaland. Vols. I and II. Ph.D. Dissertation, University of Michigan. University Microfilms International Order No. CCN80-47855, Ann Arbor, Michigan 1979.

27) van Apeldoorn, G.J.: Perspectives on drought and famine in Nigera. Allen and Unwin, London 1981.

6

28) Wood, A.P.: The Resettlement of Famine Victims in Illubor Province, Ethiopia. African Mobility Project. Working Paper Number 28. University of Liverpool 1976.
29) Currey, B.: Mapping Areas Liable to Famine in Bangladesh. Ph.D. Dissertation, University of Hawaii. University Microfilms International Order No. CCN80-12253, Ann Arbor, Michigan 1979.
30) Kropotkin, P.: What geography ought to be. The Nineteenth Century, 18, 940−56 (1885)
31) Bunge, W.: The Geography. The Professional Geographer, 25, 331−7 (1973)
32) Shore, J.: Poem in the Memoir of the Life and Correspondence of John Lord Teignmouth by his Son. Vol. i, pp. 25, 26, 8vo. London, 1843.
33) Mascarenhas, A.C. (Ed.): Journal of the Geographical Association of Tanzania, Special Number: Studies in famines and food shortages, VIII, October. Dar-es-Salaam (1973)
34) Centre for Urban Studies: Squatters in Bangladesh Cities: A Survey of Urban Squatters in Dacca, Chittagong and Khulna. 1974. Centre for Urban Studies. Dacca 1976.
35) Li, L.M.: Coordinator, Workshop on Food and Famine in Chinese History. John K. Fairbairn Center for East Asian Research, Harvard University, August 5th−25th. Several papers from this workshop were later published together in the Journal of Asian Studies, XLI, 4, pp. 685, August 1982.
36) Drake, M. and Francois-Bergier, J.: Coordinators, Famine in History Symposium. Alimentarium, Vevey, Switzerland, 2nd−4th July 1981.
37) International Disaster Institute and the London School of Hygiene and Tropical Medicine, Famine and Food Emergencies conference report in Disasters 6,3, 159−162 (1982)
38) Bangladesh Rural Advancement Committee: Peasant Perceptions: Famine. Bangladesh Rural Advancement Committee. Dacca. July 1979.
39) Currey, B., Ali, M. and Khoman, N.: Famine: A First Bibliography. Available from the Office of Foreign Disaster Assistance, Agency for International Development, Washington, DC, pp. 347, 1981.

The Demographic Impact of Famine: A Review

Hugo, Graeme J., Senior Lecturer in Geography, School of Social Sciences,
The Flinders University of South Australia, Bedford Park, South Australia, 5042, Australia.

Abstract: The aim of this paper is to review and integrate current knowledge relating to the demographic consequences of famine. Initially the role ascribed to famine in some major population theories is summarized and a conceptual framework for examining demographic adjustments to famine is put forward. The remainder of the paper takes the three basic processes of mortality, fertility and population movement in turn and discusses evidence of how they are influenced by the onset of famine. An attempt is made to draw out general tendencies with respect to both the immediate and longer term responses and to the complex interrelationships and interactions between the demographic processes themselves. Finally some suggestions are made regarding the necessity for more focussed research into the demographic effects of famine and the likely benefits of such work to both theory and applied work in developing famine warning systems.

Introduction

After reviewing a large number of authoritative definitions of famine Alamgir (1978) concluded that famine is "a general state of prolonged food grain intake decline per capita giving rise to a number of sub-states (symptoms) involving individuals and the community as a whole which ultimately lead, directly or indirectly, to excess deaths in the country or region". Most definitions of famine contain such explicit references to its demographic impact. It is somewhat surprising therefore that our understanding of the relationships between demographic processes and famine is extremely limited. These complex relationships are of particular interest not only to the demographer seeking to develop theories of fertility and mortality change but also to population geographers in their search for understanding and explanation of changes over space-time in population growth and composition. There is no well developed body of theory which we can draw upon to provide a conceptual framework for examining the complex inter-relationships between demographic processes and famine. The limited and somewhat scattered literature is predominantly of an empirical, case study type and there is a pressing need to develop an adequate theoretical framework for considering these inter-relationships. As a small initial step in this direction the aim of this paper is to review and integrate current knowledge relating to the demographic effects of famine. In the space available the review is necessarily selective but there has been an attempt to ensure that the major thrusts of existing research are represented.

Demographic research into famine is dominated by studies of its impact on mortality so that it is not surprising that the few attempts to incorporate the impact of famine in demographic theories have related to mortality changes. An initial section of this paper summarizes the role ascribed to famine in some major demographic theories. However as Chen and Chowdhury (1977) have pointed out, famine "is a complex syndrome of multiple interacting causes, diverse manifestations, and involving all three demographic variables – mortality, fertility and migration". Accordingly, subsequent sections of the paper take each of the basic demographic processes in turn and review some of the ways in which they have been influenced by famine.

Famine and Demographic Theory

Famine of course was an element in one of the earliest theories which was instrumental in the establishment of demography as the scientific study of population – that of Thomas Malthus. Famine was one of the major "positive" checks which, according to Malthus, kept growth of population from outstripping expansion of the means of subsistence to support that population. An interesting sidelight on Malthusian population theory which illustrates the complexity of the demographic study of famine has been discussed by Ambirajan (1976). He argues that, since most members of the Indian civil service during the second half of the nineteenth century had been trained in Britain, they were strongly influenced by Malthusian views. In particular, Malthus' conclusion from his analysis that the poor in any society were improvident and had no right to be sustained, Ambirajan argues, provided not only the intellectual basis for the Indian colonial administration's long run perspective about Indian famines but also buttressed their largely negative approach to famine relief in the short run. One of Ambirajan's (1976) quotations of contemporary writers will suffice to illustrate how a demographic theory by shaping administrators' attitudes toward famine relief may in itself have some influence on the demographic impact of famine.

The rapid succession of devastating famines has no doubt been providently intended as a correcting influence to thin the population of this inconvenient heavy growth by one heavy blow, and in this respect calamities may not be without their use.

One group of theories, which are somewhat connected with Malthusian theory, are those which deal with the spatial and temporal manifestations of the recurrent demographic crises (of which famine was a major type along with natural disasters, the outbreak of disease and military activity) which characterized pre-industrial societies. Woods (1982) has summarized this set of theories relating to demographic crises which he defines as situations when the number of deaths exceeds the number of births by a substantial amount over a relatively short period of time. A recent publication of the International Union for the Scientific Study of Population provides examples of major demographic crises drawn from a wide variety of contexts (Charbonneau and La Rose 1980). Woods (1982) identifies three general forms of time series of the incidence of demographic crises and he suggests that spatial comparison of such time series offers a means of elaborating a theory which will account for both the causes and the incidence of demographic crises.

The crisis mortality associated with famine is of course a major factor in the high and fluctuating levels of mortality which characterize the pre-modern society in the familiar demographic transition theory. In the classical statement of the theory as put forward by Notestein (1945) the entire transition is initiated in a society by a decline in mortality which is associated in part with a greatly reduced incidence of famine due to development of more adequate food production technology and greater availability of the means for famine relief, especially better transport. With the falls in mortality which follow the whole rationale for maintenance of very high fertility rates is removed. However, Notestein argues, there is a lag in the decline in fertility because the age-old economic and social institutions imbedded in society could not be changed immediately. Hence the emergence of the new ideal of the small family awaited the obsolescence of these institutions which occurs gradually under the pressures of industrialization and urbanization. Hence in the traditional version of the theory the amelioration of crisis mortality via reduced incidence of famine is ascribed a crucial triggering role in the ultimate transition from stable high fertility to the stable low fertility characterizing most contemporary developed nations. This classical "forcing" model, however, is accepted by few contemporary demographers and the most widely accepted reformulation of fertility transition theory which has been undertaken during the last decade (Caldwell 1982) does not postulate major mortality decline as a necessary pre-condition of fertility decline, nor does it imply that such a mortality decline initiates a series of changes which inevitably will bring about a transition to low fertility.

Omran (1971) has elaborated upon the inter-relationships between famine and changing patterns of mortality as societies undergo social and economic changes in developing what he refers to as the "epidemiologic transition". He postulates that societies tend to pass through this transition in which there are three relatively well-defined stages, each of which are characterized by not only particular levels of mortality but specific patterns of cause of death. The three stages in the transition from high and fluctuating mortality to relatively stable low mortality are an age of "pestilence and famine", one of receding pandemics when mortality declines progressively and epidemic peaks get less frequent and less catastrophic and a final stage when degenerative diseases are dominant. Omran specifies three ways in which the epidemiologic transition develops − a classical, Western model in which famines and pandemics receded gradually, an accelerated transition model exemplified by Japan and a contemporary or delayed model typical of most Third World countries where mortality has been "artificially" reduced since World War II largely via imported (often internationally sponsored) initiatives.

Conceptualizing the Demographic Impacts of Famine

The preoccupation with the impact of famine in increasing regional death rates and in depressing overall population growth rates is such that the demographic impact of famine is frequently interpreted as its mortality impact. There are, however, some exceptions. Sorokin (1942, Chapters 5 and 6) was one of the earliest writers to systematically summarize the effect of famine upon mortality, fertility, marriage, migration and mobility and to consider some historical theories relating to famine-demographic processes inter-relationships. However he, like most other subsequent commentators, concentrated upon theories relating famine to mortality.

While it is apparent that famine's role in periodically increasing mortality levels is central to several demographic theories, there are virtually no theories which relate famine to the other major demographic processes of fertility and migration. In subsequent sections of this paper, however, it is shown that population growth rates in regions experiencing famine (particularly in the post World War II period) are often more affected by the famine's impact upon population movement and fertility than that upon mortality. Tab 1 summarizes the major demographic responses to famine and draws attention to some important conceptual distinctions which should be made at the outset. Responses and impacts to famine can and do take many and varied forms – socio-cultural, economic, physiological and political as well as demographic. The varied nature of the impacts of famine can be appreciated from the fact that the famine of the 1970's in Ethiopia had a major role in the toppling of a 2,000 year old monarchy (Dirks 1980). The typology in Tab 1, while it stresses the demographic responses to famine, attempts to place the subject of adjustment to food shortage in a wider context by listing some other types of responses, although these may have strong inter-relationships with demographic responses (e.g. dietary adjustments also influence mortality and fertility). In particular, it is necessary to differentiate short- and long-term adjustments. The mortality, fertility and migration changes which occur in immediate response to the onset of famine often are quite different in both type and degree to those which are ultimately made as individuals and groups adopt strategies to ensure their survival in the long term. This will be considered in some detail later but one example of this distinction which is developed by Bongaarts and Cain (1981) can be quoted here to illustrate this. They show that in many cases the short term fertility response is a decline in the birth rate some nine months following the onset of famine. However, in the long term the response may be higher levels of fertility because children are seen as a form of insurance in a high risk environment created by the famine.

Tab 1 also makes a distinction between demographic responses which occur *in situ* and those which involve individuals and groups leaving the famine affected area. The former responses may involve changes in mortality and fertility patterns which are inter-related with physiological and dietary changes, local changes in employment and the degree of outside assistance received. Clearly a rational response to famine is to move elsewhere and it will be shown later that famine-impelled migrations are of considerable significance. However, the importance of non-permanent migration in this context is often overlooked. Such moves may in fact represent a compromise between an *in situ* and *ex-situ* adjustment, in that there is no intention of settling outside of the home area but some members are temporarily sent out to earn cash or collect food for remitting back, thus ensuring the survival of the group in the home area.

Each type of response listed in Tab 1 can occur at a range of levels and be influenced by decision making at those various levels. It is possible of course to distinguish between individual and group responses.Within the latter we can recognize adjustments made by nuclear families, extended families, kinship groups, villages, clans, tribes, regional groups, nations etc. Significant decision makers can be individuals, various informal and formal leaders and groups, as well as administrators at many levels (including international). It should also be noted that, although the various responses are listed separately in Tab 1, any group can and usually will make more than one type of adjustment as part of an overall strategy to survive the famine. More importantly, we should stress that each type of response

Tab 1 Typology of community and individual responses to famine with special emphasis on demographic responses.

Short Term Adjustments

	In Situ Adjustments				Ex Situ Adjustments	
Dietary	Increased Mortality	Reduced Fertility	Employment	Outside Assistance	Temporary Movement	Permanent Movement
- Lack of food - Less nutritious food - Different types of food - Kill wild animals or domestic animals - Malnutrition - Weight loss - Organized fasting within households	- Infanticide - Greater incidence of infectious disease - Malnutrition - Excess deaths among vulnerable groups (aged, infants etc.) - Socio-economic and spatial differentials	- Abortion - Abstinence - Delayed marriage - Increased divorce - Prolonged lactation - Reduced fecundity - Lowered frequency of intercourse	- Seek off farm work - Farm and graze new areas	- Remittances from Family living elsewhere - Government and international aid	- Nomadic herding - Commuting migration - Seasonal migration - Contract migration - Rural-urban movement	- Emigration - Rural-urban migration - Settlement in new agricultural area

Long Term Adjustments

	In Situ Adjustments				Ex Situ Adjustments	
Dietary	Increased Mortality	Reduced Fertility	Employment	Outside Assistance	Temporary Movement	Permanent Movement
- Lack of food - Less nutritious food - Different types of food - Smaller stature	- Infanticide - Greater incidence of infectious disease - Malnutrition - Excess deaths among vulnerable groups (aged, infants etc.) - Socio-economic and spatial differentias	- Increased due to "insure" against crisis - Reduced due to lower mortality - Reduced due to lower fecundity	- Seek of farm work - Farm and graze new areas	- Remittances from family living elsewhere - Government and international aid	- Establish regular seasonal migration pattern - Establish regular cyclic migration pattern	- Emigration - Rural-urban migration - Settlement in new agricultural areas

is inter-related in often complex ways with other types of response, as for example was suggested earlier with respect to long term higher fertility being a response to the high risk of death associated with famine crises.

Problems and Availability of Data

A major obstacle to the student of famine demographic interrelationships is the dearth of appropriate and accurate data. Understandably the collection of demographic data frequently is accorded low priority in societies experiencing a famine. As Dirks (1980) has pointed out:

> While the biology of starvation has been analyzed in considerable detail, there exists little systematic knowledge about social behaviour. This imbalance has been attributed to certain stumbling blocks impeding field study: chaotic conditions, the priority of the relief mission, the repugnance of seeking data amidst human suffering.

Field studies of famine rarely cover the full cycle of the first onset of food shortage through the various phases of adaptation and the postfamine period. In fact demographic field studies of famine are rare. Some of the best studies of the impact of famine have been by anthropologists who happen to have been working in a community when it is struck by famine. Firth (1959) revisting the site of his well-known study of Tikopian culture saw it under famine conditions and thus was able to clearly point out the changes brought about by food shortage. Caldwell (1975), in his review of the Sahelian drought, says that demographers have been remiss in not mounting appropriate field studies during recent famines. Such studies will almost always require the development of new and innovative approaches and will be confronted by considerable logistic difficulties. However, detailed and carefully conducted studies of the demographic impact of famine are likely to be very fruitful, not only in terms of insights that may lead to future amelioration of suffering caused by famine, but also in terms of insights into how demographic processes undergo change.

Many of the countries which have experienced famine in recent years do not have well established and accurate registration systems. Moreover, where such systems are in place the conditions which prevail during a famine make it likely that registration will be disrupted and subject to under-recording. Hence conventional data sources are frequently not available to the demographer studying famine affected areas. This has necessitated the use of less conventional sources, some examples of which are given in Tab 2 and the results of which are reported in later sections of this paper. These approaches have included analyses of grain prices to establish levels of food shortage and malnutrition to match against mortality data (Post 1976) and reports of street deaths to establish changing mortality levels (Currey 1978).

It is paradoxical that some of the best work on the demographic impacts of famine which utilizes the most imaginative and innovative analysis and interpretation of a wide variety of sources has been completed by historical demographers. Several especially those concerned with European famines (e.g. Drake 1968, Gille 1949) make careful and imaginative use of a range of data of variable completeness and accuracy, official reports, contemporary accounts and other sources, several of which are listed in Tab 2. In some parts

Tab 2 Types of sources used in studying the demographic impact of famine and some examples

Data Type	Examples of Sources	Impact Described Mortality	Fertility	Migration
Anthropological Case Study	Faulkingham and Thorbahn (1975)	x	x	x
Retrospective Cohort Studies	Stein et al. (1975)	x	x	
Longitudinal Demographic Survey	Chen and Chowdhury (1977), Ruzicka and Chowdhury (1978,1979)	x	x	x
Censuses	Sen (1980), Smout (1979), Cousens (1960a and b), Klein (1973)	x	x	x
Participant Observation	Sorokin (1942,1975)	x	x	x
Ethnographic Accounts	Firth (1959)	x	x	x
Burial/Baptismal/Marriage Records	Connell (1955), Swann (1980), Smout (1979), Currey (1978)	x	x	
Reports and Memoirs of Administrators	Fisher (1927), Singh (1975), McAlpin (1979), Ambirajan (1976)	x	x	x
Cross Sectional Sample Surveys	Biellik and Henderson (1981), Cain (1981), Mahalanobis et al. (1946)	x	x	x
Medical Studies	Stein et al. (1975)	x	x	
Journalistic Works	Clarke (1978), Glantz (1976)	x	x	x
Historical Works	Woodham Smith (1962), Smout (1979)	x	x	x
Vital Statistics	Post (1976), Gille (1949), McAlpin (1979), Lee (1981)	x	x	
Literary Sources	Drake (1968)	x	x	
Food Prices	Drake (1968), Post (1976), Dymond (1981), Currey (1978)	x		
Field Visits	Birks (1978), Caldwell (1975)	x	x	x
Parish Registers	Swann (1980)	x	x	
Hospital and Medical Records	Swann (1980)	x	x	
Mortality Projection	Sen (1980)	x		

Tab 3 Vital events and migration recorded in the Matlab Demographic Surveillance System 1974 and 1975 (Source: Ruzicka and Chowdhury 1978)

Event	1974 No.	Rate Per 1000	1975 No.	Rate Per 1000	Change (%)
Mid-year Population	263,807	—	259,194	—	− 1.8
Live Births	11,316	42.9	7,622	29.4	− 32.6
Deaths	4,362	16.5	5,393	20.8	+ 23.6
Infant Deaths (per 1000 births)	1,559	137.8	1,462	191.8	− 6.2
Inmigration	2,875	10.9	6,054	23.4	+110.6
Outmigration	5,242	19.9	14,127	54.5	+169.5
Natural Increase	6,954	26.4	2,229	8.6	− 67.9
Loss due to Migration	2,367	− 9.0	8,073	−31.1	+241.1
Total Population Change in last year	+ 4,587	17.4	− 5,844	−22.5	—

of Europe (especially Scandinavia) vital statistics are available back to the eighteenth century, but in others literary accounts have been judiciously used. Drake (1968), for example, reconstructs patterns of mortality during the Irish famine of 1840–41 largely from the files of Faulkner's Dublin Journal.

Tab 2 summarizes and gives examples of some of the major sources of data utilized by researchers in examining the demographic impact of famine. It is by no means exhaustive but gives an indication of the enormous range of materials that have been mined by demographers with varying degrees of success. There can be no doubt that demographers, as Caldwell (1975) points out, have missed many data collection opportunities with respect to the impact of famine. It is also true that the lack of appropriate data has been a major obstacle to the development of generalizations and theory linking famine and mortality, fertility and migration.

There is a recent notable exception to the picture painted above of a dearth of demographic data in famine prone areas which can be used to illustrate how famines invariably produce major changes in the basic demographic processes. The Cholera Research Laboratory in Dacca, Bangladesh have been maintaining a demographic surveillance system (Matlab) since the mid 1960's in some 228 villages containing some 120,000 people. In 1974 widespread flooding in Bangladesh, including much of the study area, destroyed both the major and minor rice crops causing a famine. The Matlab vital registration data for 1974 and 1975 thus constitute an excellent continuous record of the demographic effects of the famine. Tab 3 shows the changes which occurred in mortality, fertility and migration over the famine period. It shows a substantial increase in mortality rates, especially among infants, a significant decline in the crude birth rate and a huge increase in both in and out migration. The latter is of course indicative of a high rate of population turnover due to circular migration, but the extent of net migration loss also more than trebled in 1974–5. The Bangladesh case and several others will be discussed in some detail below where separate sections are devoted to the examination of the impact of famine upon mortality, fertility and migration.

The Impact of Famine on Mortality

Despite the fact that mortality is seen as one of the major effects of and is an integral part of many definitions of famine, there is surprisingly little data available to precisely quantify the impact of famine on mortality rates – even for the famines of the 1970's. Historical records of famines in pre-industrial societies usually paint pictures of death on a massive scale and the low rates of population growth in pretransitional and early demographic transition societies testify to the high wastage of life associated with famine. Sorokin (1942) has demonstrated the horrific loss of life caused by historical famines suggesting that death rates in affected areas sometimes reached 200, 500 or 800 for every thousand population compared with normal rates of 10 to 30. In the Soviet famine of 1921 he maintains that regional death rates reached 600/1000. Prior to the great famine of 1846–51 Ireland was within the early stages of the demographic transition with its population increasing from 6.8 to 8.2 million between 1821 and 1841. It has been estimated (Cousens 1960b) that some 800,000 persons, or nearly a tenth of the national population lost their life during the five year period as a direct result of the famine. As with all famines, this excessive mortality was not only brought about by outright starvation. Famine-induced malnutrition leaves the population relatively defenceless against, and increases their susceptibility to, any infections that they may encounter. Hence although the recorded cause of death may be an infectious disease, famine and malnutrition are usually the more fundamental cause. This relationship is well demonstrated in the fact that in the United Kingdom of the sixteenth and seventeenth centuries typhus was known as "famine fever".

The latter point until recent years assumed a degree of orthodoxy in the literature. Sorokin (1942) for example stated that

... most of the major famines have been followed by various epidemics. Up to the last few centuries the history of epidemics is almost wholly a history of famine sickness.

Recent writers, however, have challenged the existence of such a simple nutrition-epidemic relationship. Post (1976), for example, set out to establish whether or not famine was primarily responsible for typhus and plague epidemics in nineteenth century Europe. He concluded that it was not on the basis of the fact that some regions had very high grain prices but little epidemic typhus, while other areas had lower prices but rampant typhus. Others, on the other hand, suggest that such findings do not resolve whether or not there was any connection between typhus and nutritional levels. Appleby (1977) says that too many factors were operating at the same time to permit one to isolate the nutrition-typhus relationship and he goes on to point out that the famine-epidemic relationship is not simply based upon low nutrition levels weakening human resistance to typhus. In addition, at times of famine . . .

... people were on the move, seeking food where it could be found, usually in the cities where charitable resources were greater than in the countryside. These wandering poor probably helped diffuse the disease and also added to the crowding in the cities where the typhus flourished. People were also less energetic during food shortages. They bathed less often and were less concerned with cleaning their lice-infested clothes.

There is then a continuing debate, especially among historians and historical demographers, as to the nature and significance of famine-nutrition-disease-epidemics-mortality relationship.

In examining the mortality impact of contemporary famines, the concept of "excess deaths" has been found useful. This is "the number of deaths over and above those that would have occurred if previous nutritional conditions had prevailed: (Bongaarts and Cain 1981). One study which makes detailed estimates of excess mortality due to famine is that of Sen (1980). He makes several reasonable corrections to the existing mortality data for the Bengal famine of 1943 and concludes that the total figure for excess mortality associated with that famine was some 3 million. Hollingsworth (1975) has developed a formula which produces an index which enables the intensity or severity of a crisis to be determined. This index takes into account the size of the total population at risk, the proportion that died and the duration of the crisis.

However, accurate measurements of excess deaths are few and far between. Frequently there is a reliance upon indirect evidence. Currey (1978), for example, presents data from a Muslim burial society in Dacca showing a fourteenfold increase in the number of unclaimed dead bodies of the poor found in the city's streets during the 1974−1975 famine. Caldwell (1975) has drawn on a wide variety of sources in his examination of mortality associated with the Sahel famine of the early 1970's. He shows that although local food production was halved during the drought his fieldwork indicated clearly that world newspaper headlines of the crisis such as "six million facing starvation" and "100,000 die of starvation" had no basis in fact whatsoever. His estimate of excess mortality over the entire Sahel during 1970−74 was no more than quarter of a million. In contrast to the 1913−14 famine which was a major killer, Caldwell (1975) is convinced that the publicity of massive death rates hid the vital truth that . . . "The real lesson was not how easily man succumbed to the drought but how tenacious he was in managing his survival." He suggested that people survived in the Sahel through a wide range of adaptations including the eating of plants of little food value not exploited in normal years, the killing of wild animals as well as domestic stock, improved road transport bringing in food from the South as well as international aid and especially through a wide range of migration strategies.

Caldwell's findings are supported by a village study conducted in 1973−74 in the heart of the famine affected areas of the Sahel in Niger. Faulkingham and Thorbahn (1975) found high levels of malnutrition among woman and children, but rigorous methods used to collect data on deaths showed no discernible increase in mortality levels during the famine period. They attributed this to a series of adaptations similar to those discussed by Caldwell and listed in Tab 1. This should not, however, be taken as being universal for Africa. Beillik and Henderson's (1981, 1333) sample survey in the South Karamoja area of Uganda hit by famine in 1980 showed that 21 per cent of the population in the survey villages had died during 1980 "mostly from starvation". The impact of this drought-induced famine however, was greatly exacerbated by a complete breakdown of civil order. Indeed, it seems that in most cases where there has been a massive loss of life associated with modern famines, civil chaos has been an important contributory factor. Modern famines do not appear to have taken the massive toll of lives that they did prior to World War II and in general they have had little discernible impact on mortality levels at a national level. This, however, is partly a reflection of the fact that "normal" death rates in famine prone areas are very high. Moreover, adaptations made in the Sahel and elsewhere may not be readily available in future crises. Caldwell (1975) cautions that his findings about Sahel famine mortality should not be misunderstood.

The drought was immensely distressing: it caused pain and sickness; it broke up households and herds and it forced many to sell treasured articles. But it did not cause massive erosion of human numbers and it did not halt population growth.

It would appear however that elsewhere, especially in South Asia, excess mortality may be more significant. Alamgir (1980) has estimated excess death during the 1943 Bengal famine at 2 million and those in Bangladesh in 1974−75 at 1.5 million. The latter is supported in the Matlab data referred to earlier. Tab 2 shows a sharp increase in mortality rates, especially of infants, at the onset of the famine. Ruzicka and Chowdhury (1978) charted the changes in mortality quarter by quarter throughout the crisis period and their findings can be summarized as follows:

1)   Mortality rates responded to the food shortage immediately increasing by almost 50 % in the third quarter of 1974.

2)   In the succeeding two quarters the rates were double those in early 1974.

3)   Over the next three quarters there was a gradual reduction, but by the end of 1975 they

still remained 40 % above "normal". Hence recovery is not instantaneous due to longer term impacts of deterioration of nutritional status.

4) The trend of infant mortality is identical to that of general mortality, albeit at substantially higher levels.

Bongaarts and Cain (1981) have suggested that the distinct phases of mortality response identified above are general to all famines, but they suggest in their model that a year or more after the famine mortality levels will in fact be lower than "normal" because of a Darwinian selection of the least vulnerable subgroups in the population during the famine period. This does not appear to have been the case in the Bengal famine of 1943. Sen's (1980) careful analysis of the mortality asssociated with that famine suggests that large numbers of excess deaths were recorded for several years after the famine due to the epidemics associated with the famine.

One area of mortality-famine relationships which has been particularly neglected by demographers is the differential mortality impact upon particular sub-groups in the population and in various sub-regions in the area affected by famine. Best documented is the fact that excess deaths appear to be particularly visible for infants and children. Infant mortality rates, already high in "normal" years, often soar as protein calorie malnutrition increases and birthweight declines. The Matlab Bangladesh study showed a 70 % increase in the Infant Mortality Rate (IMR) at the peak of the 1974−5 famine to a level of 529 deaths per 1000 live births (Ruzicka and Chowdhury 1978). A study of the 1980 famine in Karamoja, Uganda measured the IMR at 607 (Biellik and Henderson 1981). However, older children are also very vulnerable and the 1980 Ugandan study found death rates of 305/1000 for children aged 1 to 4 years and 171 for those aged 5−17 years compared to 140 for the population aged over 18 years.

Nutrition studies of children in famine affected areas are somewhat difficult to interpret since the severe wastage of life of malnourished children means that these studies are often of a selected group of survivors. However, Tab 4 shows that despite this there has been a very high prevalence of acute malnutrition recorded among children in recent African famine affected populations.

Tab 4[a] Prevailence rates of acute malnutrion[b] in recent african drought related famines

Location	Year	Prevalence of Malnutrition (%)
Ethiopia	1974	15.9
Chad	1974	22.5
Mali	1974	10.7
Mauritania	1974	9.9
Upper Volta	1974	9.1
Zaire	1978	8.7
Uganda	1980	4.8

[a] Source: Biellik and Henderson, 1981

[b] Percentage of children less than 80 % of reference median weight for height

Children subjected to prolonged low calorie and protein diets have reduced resistance to disease and they are greatly at risk in famine situations. One Bangladesh study followed children aged 1—4 years prospectively for 18 months during the 1971—72 famine and found that out of 1000 children classified as malnourished at the outset of the study, 860 survived the 18 months compared to 970 of 1000 normally nourished children. In fact death rates among children aged 1—4 and 5—9 years are generally accepted as a more sensitive indicator of famine than infant mortality (Chen and Chowdhury 1977).

Bongaarts and Cain (1981) point out that the mortality associated with a severe famine can substantially alter local and regional age compositions with a greater concentration in the young and middle adult years at the expense of older and especially younger age groups. The elderly make up only very small proportions of the total populations of Third World nations, but they too are especially vulnerable to excess mortality in times of severe food shortage (Chen and Chowdhury 1977). The additional nutritional demands placed upon pregnant and lactating woman will expose them to greater risk of death in famine situations (Bongaarts and Cain 1981). In some societies also preference may be given in intra-family distribution of food to particular sub-groups and expose the least favoured sub-groups to higher mortality risk. For example, the practice that males are fed before females may be associated with higher mortality levels among female children in Bangladesh during famine years.

Less is known about spatial and socio-economic differentials in famine related mortality. Where the selective impact of mortality is discussed it is usually not supported with data and often is based upon hunch, apparently logical deduction, prejudice and anecdote. The following quotation (Sorokin 1942) is fairly typical of the pre World War II literature when eugenics was very much in vogue:

So far as rigor is concerned the selective role of famine and pestilence is on the whole, somewhat positive. Those who are constitutionally weaker naturally succumb in greater measure than the strong. Moreover the more intelligent elements are in a position to take greater precautions against infection during epidemics than those who are mentally less endowed. Again the upper and middle classes are, as a rule, better situated to resist the ravages of both pestilence and famine. Finally, since the upper, professional and middle classes exhibit a lower criminal rate than the depressed strata of population, and since the latter are generally weaker economically, the selective role of famine and epidemics tends to militate against the survival of the ethically inferior elements.

There is no doubt, however, that the horror of famine mortality falls disproportionately on the poor and landless. Chen and Chowdhury (1977) for example report the results of a Bangladesh case study showing that the 1975 Crude Death Rate among landless families was three times higher than that for families with three or more acres ($\geq$ 1.21 ha) of land. The death rate among children aged 1—4 years was 86.5/1000 for landless families and 17.5 for landed families with more than 3 acres (1.21 ha). It is also clear that in the excess mortality associated with the 1943 Bengal famine the most affected groups were agricultural labourers (Mukherji 1965). Studies of inter-regional differences in the mortality impact of famine are few. Indeed existing studies predominantly relate to historical famines with Cousens' (1960a) study of the 1846—51 Irish famine and Swann's (1980) analysis of the demographic impact of famine during the 1780's in Northern Mexico being good examples. The latter found significant variations in famine-related mortality between urban and rural settlements and within major towns. Greenough (1980) shows that during the 1943—1944 Bengal famine the urban minority suffered much less than the rural majority. That spatial variations in famine mortality are not simply a reflection of inter-regional differences in the severity of the famine has ben shown in an analysis of the 1943 Bengal famine (Sen 1980), and research into these differentials in areas more recently affected by famine is needed.

Greenough (1980) makes some interesting observations concerning the differential impact of famine in his study of victims of the 1943−44 Bengal famine. An important response to that famine he argues was to turn to a patron for assistance and the critical period of the famine begins when these patrons exhaust their resources and can no longer support their clients. Then households are thrown back on their own resources and within the household "distinctions begin to be made between those who are more and those who are less deserving of survival". Greenough shows how incidence of separation of spouses and the sale of and abuse of children increased during the famine.

A study of major importance of the impact of famine was that carried out following the Bengal famine of 1943 by the Indian Statistical Institute (Mahalanobis et al. 1946). This sample survey of 15,769 households can be regarded as representative of the entire Bengali population (Greenough 1980). The researchers constructed a destitution index and found that fishermen, agricultural labourers, paddy huskers, craft and transport workers suffered the greatest incidence of destitution. The main cause of destitution was given as the death of the principal income earner of the household.

The Impact of Famine on Fertility

A distinction of importance here is that between fecundity (a predisposition or latent capacity for reproducing) and fertility (the demonstrated capacity of women for reproducing). Our main emphasis here is on the later. There is some debate in the literature relating to the effects of malnutrition on fecundity. Bongaarts (1980) concludes in his summary of the evidence that "malnutrition can impair the function of the human reproductive process. This effect is strongest and most evident in famine and starvation . . ." However, he suggests that moderate chronic malnutrition has only a minor effect on fecundity although this has been challenged in some respects by Frisch (1982). Stein and others (1975) in their study of fertility in the Dutch famine of 1944−5 conclude that starvation had a direct and current effect on fecundity. They concluded in their study which had an exemplary methodology that the marked downturn in fertility "stemmed in part from a reduced capacity of couples to reproduce" (Stein et al. 1975) and not simply a result of changed sexual behaviour.

In examining fertility responses to famine it is especially necessary to differentiate between short term and longer term adjustments. Most studies show an initial continuation of birth rates at pre-famine levels with a decline occurring some nine months after the onset of the famine. Again the most conclusive evidence comes from Bangladesh. Langsten (1979) has used econometric techniques of lag analysis to demonstrate clearly in the Bangladesh context an association between food shortage (reflected in increased food prices) and an immediate response in conceptions reflected in substantial fertility declines 9−10 months later. Similarly the Matlab study monitored the effect of the time lag between conception and delaying the direct response of birth rates to the 1974 famine (Ruzicka and Chowdhury 1978). High Crude Birth Rates (CBR) were maintained during the last two quarters of 1974 (40.3/1000 and 50.3/1000) but these fell dramatically in the first two quarters of 1975 to 34.3 and 21.9. Thereafter there was a slow recovery but by the end of 1975 the CBR was still only 31.7. However, the 1976 CBR of 43.3 (Ruzicka and Chowdhury 1979) would suggest that recovery of pre-famine fertility patterns was complete. Currey's (1978) data for a single famine affected village shows a similar pattern with very few births being recorded between 9 and 15 months after the onset of famine.

There has long been a recognition that the sequence outlined above for Bangladesh has wider and more general applicability. Sorokin (1942), writing four decades ago, maintained that the "movement of the birth rate during calamities also exhibits a fairly uniform pattern varying in detail according to the magnitude of the catastrophe." Indeed the sequence which he outlines is similar to that considered above. The very careful study of the fertility patterns of the 1944—5 Dutch hunger winter also had very similar findings (Stein et al. 1975) and at the height of the famine births were reduced to one-third the expected number. Bongaarts and Cain (1981) have put forward a specific model of this sequence. Their model is one of decline in birth rates beginning nine months after the onset of the famine reaching a low point nine months after the end of the crisis, with the extent of decline being directly proportional to the severity of the famine. The conception rate recovers quickly and the interval of depressed fertility is followed by one of "excess fertility" due to an abnormally low percentage of women who are pregnant or anovulatory due to breastfeeding. The birth rate then exceeds pre-famine levels for up to three years and the "excess fertility" only partly compensates for the preceding deficit.

The reasons for the short term decline in births in famine situations are fairly well understood. As with mortality change, malnutrition plays a critical role. There is a decrease in fecundity when the nutritional value and quantity of food consumed falls below minimal levels and women stop ovulating and male sperm mobility and longevity are reduced (Bongaarts 1980, Zeitlin et al. 1982). Moreover, in times of famine there is likely to be increased foetal wastage due to the deteriorating condition of mothers, while women may breastfeed children for longer periods and in so doing prolong post-partum amenorrhea. Mondot-Bernard (1977) has reviewed much of the literature examining the relationships between nutrition and fertility and she stresses the importance of prolonged breast feeding in curtailing fertility. Moreover she concludes that malnutrition would appear to prolong the duration of amennorhea only among lactating women. She also points, however, to the complex interactions of nutrition and fertility with another demographic variable — child and infant mortality. Because malnutrition is also largely responsible for excess mortality among children she argues that this may in turn cause an *increase* in fertility because the death of the child will result in a termination of breast-feeding and hence probably of amennorhea, also the parents may desire to replace the deceased child with another. Bongaarts and Cain (1981) list several other factors contributing to the deficit in conceptions . . .

1) A decrease in fecundity due to psychological stresses associated with the crisis
2) Lower frequency of intercourse due to decline in libido, general weakening of adults and separation of spouses associated with temporary migrations in response to the famine
3) An increase in voluntary birth control through contraception, abstinence or abortion

4) Postponement of marriage.

An excellent discussion of famine-induced fertility decline in Bangladesh in 1974−5 has been prepared by Ruzicka and Chowdhury (1978). They demonstrate the significance of postponement of marriage but also show that in the Matlab villages divorces and separations doubled in response to the crisis and this clearly would have had a depressing impact on fertility. Their analysis also shows that the extent of reduction in fertility was fairly similar in all ages and occurred independent of parity.

Several writers stress the importance of postponement of marriage as a major factor in fertility reduction during famines (e.g. Sorokin 1942, 95). Connell (1955, 82−3) in his consideration of the impact of the Irish famine maintains that

Of all the casualties of Irish social life in the decades after the Famine, one of the most significant was marriage . . . Many of the characteristics of social and economic life in the two generations before the Famine depended on the readiness with which men and women in the early twenties or younger could arrange to marry . . .

He shows that after the famine not only were marriages postponed but the initiative of arranging marriage moved away from young people to fathers, and it became customary for a couple to marry only when they were assured of adequate land to support a new family.

The discussion here has been based heavily upon Bangladesh. Caldwell's study of the Sahel contains little reference to the impact of the drought on birth rates other than to suggest that it may have fallen marginally because of the enforced separation of husbands and wives by outmigration of one partner to earn money to support the family (1975, 48). Faulkingham and Thorbahn (1975) found that the already high birth rates prevailing prior to the drought in their study village in Niger were maintained and even enhanced during the crisis.

As is the case with mortality we have little or no information on spatial or socio-economic differentials in the pattern of fertility response to famine. The scattered evidence suggests that it is the poor and landless who most reduce their rate of conception during famine (e.g. Ruzicka and Chowdhury 1978). The excellent data available to Stein and others (1975) in their study of the impact of famine in 1944−5 in the Netherlands allowed some careful analysis of the differential impact of the famine on fertility of particular groups. They concluded that "Famine effects on fertility and presumably fecundity were most marked among the labouring classes. Older women of higher parity were more affected than younger women of lower parity . . ." (Stein et al. 1975).

Thus the limited data available suggests that in the short term famine has little impact on fertility "partly because the deviations from normal levels are smaller than changes in the death rate and and partly because the birth rate deficit is compensated by a period of excess births" (Bongaarts and Cain 1981). However, what of the long term reponse to famine? Classical demographic transition theory would suggest that in traditional societies the long term response to famine is high levels of fertility. It is argued that this is necessary insurance to guard against the high risk of a mortality crisis depriving parents of all their children and hence of their major means of support in old age. A similar position is taken by Bongaarts and Cain (1981), and Cain (1981) who argue that the ever present threat of famine creates a demand for risk insurance which an investment in children partially satisfies. In this way the threat of famine is a prop supporting continued high fertility and rapid population growth and impeding social and economic development. Thus, they suggest, the longer term fertility response may ultimately have more tragic consequences than the immediate suffering caused by famine. Cain (1981) has made detailed field studies of villages in two regions with harsh environments with high risk of famine and food shortage – one in India, the other in Bangladesh. In the former region this risk has been neutralized by development of capital markets and public relief employment and Cain suggests that this has resulted in the region having low and declining fertility. In the Bangladesh study area, on the other hand, no such cushions against risk have been developed so, Cain argues, the value of children as risk insurance remains high as does fertility.

A somewhat different perspective is provided by Faulkingham and Thorbahn (1975). In speculating about the future of their famine-affected study village in Niger, they conclude that while the drought had no discernible impact on population growth it may have a lagged effect in *reducing* fertility in the future. This, they postulate, is due to the fact that during the four year drought young children experienced very high le els of protein calorie malnutrition which may have a residual effect in reducing their fecundity when they reach adult age. Clearly there are inter-relationships between the fertility and mortality responses to famine as well as complex linkages to other non-demographic responses and this is an area in which our understanding is very limited. The importance of examining the interaction of demographic variables when considering the effects of famine is frequently preached but unfortunately little practised, not only with respect to fertility and mortality inter-relationships but also their interactions with a third type of demographic response – that of population movement.

The Impact of Famine on Population Movements

The response of leaving a famine-affected area on a permanent or temporary basis and moving to an unaffected area would seem eminently rational and indeed this has been and remains a most important survival strategy adopted during times of famine. Yet our knowledge of the numbers involved in such movement during modern as well as historical famines is minimal and we have little understanding of the particular conditions under which moves of particular types are or are not undertaken, or the short and long term impacts of these moves on areas of origin and destination as well as the movers themselves. It is clear from the literature, however, that famine related population mobility has taken a wide variety of forms and that it has not only had the short term impact of enabling large numbers of people to survie famines but had considerable longer term consequences for economic and social change as well as reshaping patterns of population distribution.

Famine impelled population movements have in common that they are not part of the "normal" pattern of life of residents of the famine affected areas and that they are triggered by the exceptional circumstances of the onset of severe food shortage. As Sorokin (1942, 106) puts it, "In contradiction to the gradual, orderly and voluntary character of migration and mobility in normal times catastrophes render these processes sudden, violent, chaotic, largely involuntary and essentially tragic." Such moves, however, can be meaningfully differentiated along several other dimensions:
1) The degree of permanency of the move

2) The distance of the move
3) Whether the move involves crossing a significant cultural or political boundary
4) Whether the move involves all or part of the basic family unit
5) Whether the move involves a transfer between rural and urban areas
6) Whether there is a significant change in the occupation of the mover (e.g. transfer from a rural to an urban job or from the traditional to the modern sector)
7) The degree of age/sex and socio-economic selectivity of movement.

Historically migration has been one of the most important ways in which people have coped with famine. Sorokin (1942) discusses the "mapless migration of wandering hordes created by European famines." In France during several eighteenth century famines such *emigrés* numbered as many as 1 million. In West Java, Indonesia records from the sixteenth century, when the dominant cultivation system was a dry field one (ladang), show that periodic crop failures initiated substantial temporary and, to a lesser extent, permanent, mass movement of population to nearby agricultural areas not affected by the crisis (Hugo 1980). As was the case in Europe many such migrations resulted in the colonization of new agricultural areas. These failures were largely eliminated during the last century by the widespread adoption of a more reliable wet rice cultivation system (sawah). However, in 1977 an infestation of brown leaf hopper *(wereng)* once again caused widespread crop failure and food shortage and initiated substantial temporary population movements, for example from the agricultural areas of the north coast into the metropolitan area of Jakarta (Sacerdoti 1977).

A very different pattern of migration was associated with the Irish famine of 1846−51 (Cousens 1960b; Lees and Modell 1977). Migration *within* Ireland was remarkably restricted. Early in the crisis there were reports of the towns of Cork and Galway being besieged by beggars and the main roads to Cork had to be blocked to keep out the hordes of paupers in search of food and shelter. As is the case in contemporary Third World nations with a colonial heritage, there was little industrial or urban development so that large numbers of Irish rural dwellers couldn't make the simple adjustment of migrating to the city when the effects of crop failure were felt. Consequently most migrants settled in either Britain or the United States. As Lees and Modell (1977) have pointed out, this famine migration initiated a massive social as well as demographic change in that most migrants left Irish rural areas for British or American cities and had to change their way of life to adapt not only to an alien country but also to an alien urban environment. The scale of the emigration was substantial − in the five years following the severe failure of the potato crop in 1846 the total Irish population was reduced by some two million from its total of 8.5 million and at least half of this loss was due to net emigration. Cousens' (1960b) study of the regional pattern of net migration loss shows that in half of the counties the net loss amounted to more than 12.5 % of the 1841 population. It is interesting to note that these areas of heavy net migration loss tended to be areas with somewhat lower mortality − pointing again to the significance of inter-relationships between the major demographic processes when considering adjustment to famine.

Turning to recent famines in Third World countries, there is clear evidence from a wide range of contexts that permanent and temporary population movements have been the most widespread and significant of contemporary adjustments to famine. A recent collection of studies has demonstrated that both survival and living standards in the Sahel have long depended to a considerable degree upon the possibility of migration (Colvin et al. 1981). However, Caldwell (1975) maintains that the 1970—74 Sahelian drought produced unprecedentedly large scale population movements, often of a type not known at all during "normal" seasons. The movement was predominantly from north to south and frequently involved migrants crossing international boundaries, such as that from Mauritania to Mali and Senegal, that from Mali to Senegal, Ivory Coast, Upper Volta, Dahomey, Togo, Nigeria and Ghana, that from Upper Volta to Ivory Coast, Ghana, Dahomey and Togo and that from Niger to Nigeria and Sudan. As with many other population movements in Sub-Saharan Africa, the presence of international boundaries (often the legacy of a colonial heritage rather than a reflection of geographical or cultural homogeneity) is frequently no barrier to famine migration. For example, the 1976 census in Senegal showed that 7 % of the national population were foreign born while in the Gambia the figure was 11 % (Colvin 1981a). During the famine there was even movement into Ghana which has a very restrictive immigration policy.

Unfortunately measurement of these movements in the Sahel is almost totally lacking. Caldwell (1975) criticizes the failure of demographers to devise innovatory techniques to measure famine movements and there were very few case studies of migration during the drought. However, he is able to point out some of the major features of the Sahel famine migrations. Obviously much of the temporary migrations were focussed on refugee camps. Shorter distance local rural migrations involving an eventual return to drought affected areas when conditions have improved were probably the most substantial type of movement in numerical terms. Particular attention has been concentrated upon movement to cities and towns which have been the focus of much famine migration. For example, Colvin's (1981a) analysis of Senegalese census data shows "that the drought did indeed swell urban populations, beginning with the small outlying cities, then progressing by steps to the regional capitals and finally to Dakar". There has been some debate about the permanency of these famine impelled rural-urban displacements, but it is clear that much of the urbanization arising out of the famine was permanent. Sow (1981), for example, argues that in Senegal the drought served as a catalyst but not the original cause of all the migration. This contemporary rural-urban flow is not universal and in some famines marked depopulation of large cities occurred. Sorokin (1942) says that the Russian famine of 1921—22 caused a depopulation of Moscow and Leningrad from 1.8 and 2.4 million to 1 million and 740,000 respectively between 1917 and 1920.

Caldwell (1975) notes that rural to urban migration during the drought in the Sahel was particularly pronounced among nomadic groups and suggests that when totally displaced from their normal pattern of life nomads tended to not go into sedentary agriculture but to take the leap from nomadism to urban employment. The mobility responses to famine of nomadic groups, however, take a variety of forms. Caldwell makes a clear distinction between the famine induced migrations of the nomads and the sedentary farmers of the Sahel. Many of the nomads moved with their herds in stages southward, gradually eating and selling their herds and eventually seeking a livelihood in cities. Sedentary farmers on the other hand generally moved longer distances in a single move, directly to towns and cities (especially those where they had friends or relatives), or to refugee camps. Birks' (1978) study of the impact of drought on nomadic mountain pastoralists in Oman identified two major types of movement among the responses:

1) Movement of an entire group and their herds from an area where water and/or pasture resources are no longer adequate to another which can support them. Most cover only short distances within tribal boundaries and 48 per cent of the groups studied by Birks had moved in this way.

2) Movement of the menfolk to work as migrant labourers in the modern cities and industries of the Gulf of Oman and Saudi Arabia. Most of these migrants, however, were from families who as a result of the drought "were admitting defeat; men were departing to gain an alternative income to replace that which they used to derive from their herds . . ." (Birks 1978).

The first type of movement in response to drought involves a maintenance of the traditional pastoral way of life, but the second is permanently eroding it and establishing a pattern of households being dependent on remittances from their male members employed in the modern sector outside of the mountain region.

Studies among sedentary agriculturalists in the Sahel drought affected area indicate that much of the mobility initiated was temporary (e.g. Sow 1981) and did not involve the displacement of entire families. In the village study in southern Niger referred to earlier, Faulkingham and Thorbahn (1975) found that as the drought progressed the proportion of males aged between 15 and 44 years working outside the village (especially in the cities of Lagos, Kano and Abijan) rose from one third to three quarters. Caldwell (1975) reports a study of Upper Volta showing that almost all adult males, except for old men, left their homes to seek work in Abijan during the 1973 dry season. Clearly, the emphasis on studies of individuals in many studies of migration decision making would be misplaced in these circumstances. The survival strategy of the household is for the head to send one or more members of the family out of the home area on a permanent or temporary basis to earn money elsewhere for the support of the home-based family. Thus the family (however defined) is the critical unit of analysis (Hugo 1983) in examining population mobility adjustments to famine. Family and kinship linkages can also be critical in that mobility may be more readily seen as a survival strategy by families with relatives and friends already established in places not influenced by famine. Certainly the existence of such linkages will shape the direction of migration. Colvin's (1981b) review of Senegal and Gambia suggests that the "universal use of extended family hospitality" in cities by migrants forced out of famine afflicted rural areas minimized the suffering of many immediate victims of the famine and much of this migration thus remained invisible to officials and planners until revealed by 1976 census figures. Kinship, family and other social linkages were also important in initiating non-institutional flows of assistance (money, food etc.) from areas not directly affected by the famine (especially cities) toward families and friends living in famine areas (Caldwell 1975).

While it is clear that much of the unprecedented movement impelled by the Sahelian drought was temporary in nature, it is apparent that in many areas it has produced a more or less permanent redistribution of population (Colvin 1981b). This is typical of many "forced" migrations in which the movers may initially have intentions of returning to the area which they have been forced to leave but over time this intention is eroded away due to a failure of conditions to improve at the origin or the fact that the movers establish themselves economically and socially at the destination so that they perceive they are better off there. The familiarity with alternative opportunities at locations away from the home place may in fact in the long term not only initiate significant social changes due to changes in aspirations etc. but also encourage permanent settlement elsewhere or set in motion a pattern of seasonal or regular temporary migration outside of the home place to augment family income from local sources. Hence a migration initially triggered by a food shortage may and often does produce a wider more permanent social and demographic change in the longer term.

McAlpin (1979) in her study of the reduction in mortality associated with crop failures in Western India between 1870 and 1920 concludes that this was due partly to changes in the economy which made it possible for agriculturalists to survive even severe crop failures by earning income from wage labour. Participation in wage labour in agriculture or in private or public construction projects was found to be of growing significance throughout the period. He shows that in some districts "seasonal migration, either to other rural places or to urban areas, had become a way of life for communities" and quotes one official as reporting "Emigration was encouraged in every possible way and saved the situation. I have never seen so severe a famine attended with so little human distress . . . To these classes of petty cultivators, a bad season only means an earlier exodus" (McAlpin 1979, 155).

The Bangladesh famine of 1974−75 also initiated a substantial migration response. Currey (1979) shows in his case study a clear association between the onset of famine and outmovement from the village. Ruzicka and Chowdhury (1978) explain that outmigration was an almost immediate response to the onset of food shortage in the Matlab villages. The data in Tab 2 indicate that between 1974 and 1975 the net migration loss from Matlab villages more than trebled from 2,367 to 8,073 and the net outmigration rate increased from 9 to 31 per 1,000. However, it will also be noticed that although there was a 170 % increase in outmigration, inmigration increased by 111 %. Thus while the region experienced a net loss there was a substantial population turnover indicating that temporary outmigration in response to famine was also of significance. In a study of response to drought in Northeastern Brazil, Brooks (1971) distinguishes not so much between temporary and permanent migration but between what he calls "micro" and "macro" migrations. The former refers to short distance movements to the nearest place of refuge from starvation, usually an adjoining rural region or small town, and it is implied that such movements are usually of short duration, involving hurried decision making and little planning. Macro migration is mass flight from the disaster area involving longer distances and more permanent displacement from the migrant's native soil.

In China famine has historically been a frequent occurrence. In densely populated Shantung province for example famines were recorded at a little over one every decade during the pre-revolutionary period (Howard 1929). These famines induced significant population movements even during the early years of the revolutionary period. The bad harvests of 1953 and 1954 for example saw a massive unauthorized movement of rural dwellers from affected areas into cities where they created serious problems (Aird 1960).

Little is known about the selectivity of famine migration, although it is clear that those sub-groups in the population who are most affected by the crisis are likely to be over-represented among migrants. In ancient Rome the mass expulsion of foreigners was a favoured initial measure taken to alleviate the effects of actual or imminent famine (Sorokin 1942). This will usually mean the poorest segment of the population who do not have the reserves of capital or food to cope with the shortages. As the period of famine is extended or its effects are intensified, other things being equal, it could be anticipated that this socio-economic selectivity would decrease. Initially families with contacts outside the region, due to prior migration of family members, are more prone to move because the certainty with which they can expect assistance at the destination is much greater than those having no such linkages. Temporary outmigration is usually selective of males, especially young adult men who are sent out to earn money to send back to their families, although with increased severity of the famine both the age and sex selectivity of movement is progressively reduced.

Separation of spouses by migration is typical of many famine situations. Greenough's (1980) study of the 1943–44 Bengal famine produces anecdotal and survey evidence to demonstrate the importance of permanent and temporary separation of husbands and wives in families rendered destitute by the famine. This not only took the form of a man leaving because he could no longer provide for his wife but also of men asking their wives to leave and seek subsistence elsewhere. Greenough reports a survey of destitutes in Calcutta which found that many were abandoned wives, many of whom became prey to sexual exploitation.

Population mobility associated with famine can and has brought about major short term and long term redistributions of population and it is somewhat surprising that it has not been studied very closely by demographers. It is assumed that most such movement is "forced" and hence self-explanatory but this does not explain why some regions, groups or individuals opt for a survival strategy involving population mobility and others experiencing the same famine conditions do not. Closer examination of the conditions under which particular types of population mobility survival strategies are and are not adopted as responses to environmental stress thus should be rewarding not only in the context of the study of famine but in furthering our understanding of population movement generally. However, it is clear from the above that the significance of famine-related population mobility goes far beyond enabling huge numbers of people to survive a famine as vitally important as that is. It also goes beyond the reshaping of population distribution patterns in both the short and long terms, which also is of major significance. Population movements which are either caused totally by the onset of famine or which are the product of a large number of interacting forces among which the famine is the triggering factor or the "final straw that broke the camel's back" can have considerable significance in hastening or even initiating significant social and economic change. We know little of what these effects are, but it is apparent that the movement of people on a temporary or permanent basis into new areas involves to a greater extent mixing with different ethnic, cultural and socio-economic groups, exposure to new and different ideas, attitudes and ways of doing things, participation in different forms of employment and levels of income and exposure to different levels and types of consumption. This confrontation with very different ways of life may not only influence the famine migrant's ultimate decisions about where they should settle but also reshape their thinking and behaviour in a whole range of significant areas regardless of whether they relocate or return to their homeplace after the crisis has passed. Some have suggested that the disruption associated with famine migrations frequently and seriously undermines family unity and other traditional institutions and initiates swift transformation of social institutions and the emergence of radically different social forms (Sorokin 1942).

Conclusions

This has been a necessarily brief overview of some of the relationships between the three main demographic processes and famine. However, each of these processes cannot be considered to operate in a mutually independent way. Several interaction effects have been mentioned earlier and others are reviewed in the literature (e.g., Chen and Chowdhury 1977; Bongaarts and Cain 1981). Studies of the response to famine which focus only upon mortality, fertility or migration run the risk of severe misinterpretation. One need only take the example of migration — extensive population movement may counterbalance the impact of famine upon mortality levels by reducing local food shortages through reduction of the number of local consumers as well as via inflow of remittances. Moreover, since the migration is selective of young adults, especially young men, it is probable that the reduction in the proportion of the local population made up of fecund couples as well as the enforced separation of spouses, will produce a temporary lowering of local fertility. There may also be longer term implications with migrants being the initiators of social change leading to a general lowering of fertility. Response to famine is inherently complex and multi-faceted and it is also important to view demographic responses in the context of other *in situ* and *ex situ* adjustments which can be made by individuals, groups or nations, some of which are indicated in Tab 1.

It is clear from this review that demographers have generally neglected the response to famine as a field of study and there is much to be done in measuring the impact upon mortality, fertility and migration, let alone unravelling the complexities of their causes and consequences. It is with respect to the latter that population geographers can make a worthwhile contribution. Their spatial perspective is not only of relevance in the neglected study of population mobility associated with famine, but also in the analysis of the spatial and socio-economic differentials that exist with respect to the effects of famine on mortality, fertility and migration. Our knowledge in these areas is extremely limited and identifiction of the precise nature of those differentials and, more importantly, understanding the processes shaping them is sorely needed.

Pleas for further research such as that presented above are of course commonplace in review papers, but it would appear that in this case there is considerable justification. This stems not only from the benefits which may accrue for planning and implementation of disaster intervention programmes and policies, but also from the perspective of deepening our understanding of the basic demographic processes so that we can move toward more comprehensive theoretical formulations relating to changes in mortality, fertility and population movement. With respect to the policy implications of research, it is almost self-evident that examination of the demographic effects of famine and the sub-groups in the population who are affected disproportionately by famines can be of utility not only in designing appropriate short and long term interaction strategies but also in focussing them on those sub-groups who have the greatest vulnerability and need. Drought and other disasters causing severe food shortages are going to recur but as Kates (1981) points out, "there is nothing necessary about its human impacts ... loss of life from natural hazard can be diminished even in the absence of needed development or social reconstruction, although the task is made much harder in societies indifferent to marginal groups." There is thus a need to draw out the lessons for disaster security from examination of responses and adjustments to famines of the past.

Precise identification of demographic responses to famine may also have some utility in developing famine warning systems. As Chen and Chowdhury (1977) point out, many demographic indicators are responsive to crisis only after it has already occurred, whereas earlier warning signals are needed. Nevertheless, it may be that even quite small changes in infant mortality levels or population mobility patterns in some areas may be harbingers of the impending onset of famine. When used in combination with other indicators they may be useful in making possible the mobilization of appropriate resources to ameliorate the human effects of the famine. The identification of model patterns of mortality and fertility change associated with famine by Bongaarts and Cain (1981) has considerable potential utility in disaster intervention programmes. Close examination of the demographic impacts of a famine crisis may also, as Chen and Chowdhury (1977) demonstrate, highlight longer term problems which exist in a region or nation in a more muted form during normal times and hence direct greater attention and resources toward their amelioration. From an academic perspective it would also appear that examination of the mortality, fertility and population mobility responses to famine crises may be productive of insights into and understanding of the nature of changes in those processes under particular conditions an their causes and consequences for social change and economic development. It may assist in the identification and generalization of the conditions under which these processes do or do not undergo change.

References

Aird, J.S.: The present and prospective population of mainland China. Pp. 93–140 in Milbank Memorial Fund. Population Trends in Eastern Europe, the USSR and Mainland China. Milbank Memorial Fund, New York 1960.

Alamgir, M.: Towards a theory of famine. University of Stockholm, Institute for International Economic Studies Seminar Papers 103, 53 pp. (1978)

Alamgir, M.: Famine in South Asia. Oelschlager, Gunn and Hain, Cambridge 1980.

Appleby, A.B.: Famine, mortality and epidemic disease, a comment. Economic History Review 30, 3, 508–13 (1977)

Ambirajan, S.: Malthusian population theory and Indian famine policy in the nineteenth century. Population Studies 30, 1, 5–14 (1976)

Biellik, R.J. and Henderson, P.L.: Mortality, nutritional status and diet during the famine in Karamoja, Uganda 1980. Lancet 8259:1330–3 (1981)

Birks, S.: The mountain pastoralists of the Sultanate of Oman: reactions to drought. Development and Change 9, 71–86 (1978)

Bongaarts, J.: Does malnutrition affect fecundity? A summary of evidence. Science 208, 564–9 (1980)

Bongaarts, J. and Cain, M.: Demographic Responses to Famine. The Population Council, Center for Policy Studies Working Papers No. 77 (1981)

Brooks, R.H.: Human response to recurrent drought in Northeastern Brazil. Professional Geographer 23, 1, 40–45 (1971)

Cain, M.: Risk and insurance: Perspectives on fertility and agrarian change in India and Bangladesh. Population and Development Review 7, 3, 435–74 (1981)

Caldwell, J.C.: The Sahelian Drought and Its Demographic Implications. Overseas Liaison Committee, American Council of Education Paper No. 8 (1975)

Caldwell, J.C.: Theory of Fertility Decline. Academic Press, New York 1982.

Charbonneau, H. and La Rose, A.: The Great Mortalities: Methodological Studies of Demographic Crises in the Past. Ordina, Liege 1980.

Chen, L.C. and Chowdhury, A.K.M.A.: The dynamics of contemporary famine Pp 409–423. In: Proceedings of International Union for the Scientific Study of Population. Population Conference Mexico 1977. Ordina, Liege 1977.

30

Clarke, T.: The Last Caravan. Putman, New York 1978.

Colvin, L.G.: Senegal, in: Colvin, L.G. et al. The Uprooted of the Western Sahel. Pp. 83−112, Praeger, New York 1981.

Colvin, L.G.: Migration and public policy in the Senegambia. In: Colvin, L.G. et al. The Uprooted of the Western Sahel. Pp. 317−343, Praeger, New York 1981.

Colvin, L.G. et al.: The Uprooted of the Western Shel. Praeger, New York 1981.

Connell, K.H.: Marriage in Ireland after the famine: The diffusion of the match. Journal of the Statistical and Social Inquiry Society of Ireland 19, 82−103 (1955)

Cousens, S.H.: Regional death rates in Ireland during the Great Famine from 1846 to 1851. Population Studies, XIV, 1, 55−74 (1960a)

Cousens, S.H.: Regional patterns of emigration during the Great Irish Famine 1846−51. Transactions of the Institute of British Geographers 28, 119−124 (1960b)

Currey, B.: The famine syndrome: its definition for relief and rehabilitation in Bangladesh. Ecology of Food and Nutrition 7, 87−98 (1978)

Currey, B.: Mapping Areas Liable to Famine in Bangladesh. Ph. D. Dissertation, University of Hawaii, UMI No. 8012253.

Dirks, R.: Social responses during severe food shortages and famine. Current Anthropology 21, 1, 21−44 (1980)

Drake, M.: The Irish Demographic Crisis of 1740−1791. T.W. Moody (ed.) Historical Studies IV. Pp. 101−124, Routledge and Kegan Paul, London 1968.

Dymond, D.: The Famine of 1527 in Essex. Local Population Studies 26, 29−40 (1981)

Faulkingham, R.H. and Thorbahn, P.F.: Population dynamics and drought: a village in Niger. Population Studies XXIX, 3, 463−77 (1975)

Fisher, H.H.: The Famine in Soviet Russia (1919−1923). Macmillan, New York 1927.

Firth, R.: Social change in Tikopia. Macmillan, New York 1959.

Frisch, R.E.: Malnutrition and fertility. Science 215, 1272−3 (1982)

Gille, H.: The demographic history of the Northern European countries in the eighteenth century. Population Studies III, 3−65 (1949)

Glantz, M.: The Politics of Natural Disaster: The Case of the Sahel Drought. Praeger, New York 1976.

Hollingsworth, T.H.: A formula for assessing the relative severity of population crises. International Journal of Environmental Studies 7, 119−22 (1975)

Howard, H.P.: Population pressure and the growth of famine in China. Chinese Economic Journal 2, 24, 471−474 (1929)

Hugo, G.J.: Population movements in Indonesia during the colonial period. In: J.J. Fox et al. (eds) Indonesia: Australia Perspectives. Pp. 95−132, Research School of Pacific Studies, Australian National University, Canberra 1980.

Hugo, G.J.: Population Mobility and Wealth Transfers in Third World Societies with Particular Reference to Indonesia. Papers of the East West Population Institutes, 1983.

Kates, R.W.: Drought Impact in the Sahelian-Sudanic Zone of West Africa. A Comparative Analysis of 1910−15 and 1968−74. Centre for Technology, Environment and Development, Clark University, Worcester 1981.

Klein, I.: Death in India, 1871−1921. Journal of Asian Studies XXXII, 4, 639−59 (1973)

Langsten, R.: Agricultural crisis and short term fertility response in Bangladesh. Paper presented to annual Meeting of the Population Association of America, Philadelphia 1979.

Lee, R.: Short term variation: vital rates, prices and weather. In: E.A. Wrigley and R.S. Schofield. the Population History of England 1541−1871. Pp. 356−401, Edward Arnold, London 1981.

Lees, L.H. and Modell, J.: The Irish countryman urbanized: a comparative perspective on the famine migration. Journal of Urban History 3, 4, 391−408.

McAlpin, M.B.: Death, famine and risk: the changing impact of crop failures in Western India 1870−1920. Journal of Economic History XXXIX, 1, 143−187.

Mahalonobis, P.C.; Mukherjea, R. and Gnosh, A.: A sample survey of the after effects of the Bengal Famine of 1943. Statistical Publishing Society, Calcutta 1946.

Mondot-Bernard, J.M.: Relationships Between Fertility, Child Mortality and Nutrition in Africa. Development Centre of the OECD 1977.

Mukherji, K.: Agriculture, Famine and Rehabilation in South Asia. Visva Baharati, Santiniketan 1965.

Notestein, F.W.: Population: the long view. in: T.W. Schultz (ed.) Food for the World. Pp. 36−57 Chicago University Press, Chicago 1945.

Omran, A.R.: The epidemiologic transition: a theory of the epidemiology of population change. Milbank Memoria Fund Quarterly 49, 509−38 (1971)

Post, J.D.: Famine, mortality and epidemic disease in the process of modernization. Economic History Review 24, 1, 14−37 (1976).

Ruzicka, L.T. and Chowdhury, A.K.M.A.: Demographic Surveillance System − Matlab. Volume Four. Vital Events and Migration 1975. Cholera Research Laboratory, Dacca, Bangladesh (1978).

Ruzicka, L.T. and Chowdhury, A.K.M.A.: Demographic Surveillance System − Matlab. Volume Five. Vital Events and Migration 1976. Cholera Research Laboratory, Dacca, Bangladesh (1979)

Sacerdoti, G.: Help for Java's drought victims. Far Eastern Economic Review 98, 43, 48−9 (1977)

Sen, A.K.: Famine mortality: a study of the Bengal Famine of 1943. in: E.J. Hobsbawn et al. (eds) Peasants in History. Pp. 144−220 Oxford University Press, Calcutta, 1980.

Singh, K.S.: The Indian Famine 1967. Peoples Publishing House, New Delhi 1975.

Smout, T.C.: Famine and famine relief in Scotland in: L.M. Cullen and T.C. Smout (eds) Comparative Aspects of Scottish and Irish Social and Economic History. Pp. 21−31, John Donald, Edingburgh.

Sorokin, P.A.: Man and Society in Calamity: The Effects of War, Revolution, Famine, Pestilence Upon Human Mind, Behaviour, Social Organization and Cultural Life. E.P. Dutton and Co., New York 1942.

Sorokin, P.A.: Hunger as a Factor in Human Affairs. University of Florida Press, Gainsville, 1975.

Sow, F.: Migration to Dakar. in: L.G. Colvin et al. (ed) The Uprooted of the Western Sahel. Pp. 204−243, Praeger, New York.

Stein, Z., Susser, M., Saenger, G. and Marolla, F.: Famine and Human Development: The Dutch Hunger Winter of 1944/45. Oxford University Press, New York 1975.

Swann, M.M.: The demographic impact of disease and famine in late colonial Northern Mexico. Geosciences and Man XXI, March 21, 97−109.

Woods, R.: Theoretical Population Geography, Longmans, London 1982.

Zeitlin, M.F. et al: Nutrition and Population Growth: The Delicate Balance. Oelgeschlager, Gunn and Hain, Cambridge 1982.

War and Famine: The Example of Kampuchea

Ea, Meng Try, Population Council Research Fellow, Department of Demography,
The Australian National University, Canberra, ACT 2600, Australia.

Abstract: War-induced famines have severely reduced the population of Kampuchea during the 1970's. The different policies of successive governments in Pnomh Penh and those of external governments have sought to establish political power and national security, but have ridden rough-shod over food security for the Kampuchean population.

Incomplete information from a variety of sources is certainly imprecise but sufficiently accurate to corroborate the repeated rupture of Kampuchean communities. Politics and war also affected the relief response which is now declining and can never fully relieve the emotive tragedy.

Introduction

"When I'm old I want to be a farmer, I want to grow rice in Cambodia, I also want to draw — no guns, no tanks, but trees, animals and mountains, anything, but no guns, no tanks". — Thik, 13 years of age.

"In my family, we speak sometimes about the past, but not too often, beause all of us, we want to forget the past. We do not think about the future either, because we do not know what the future will be".   Ek Son. 10 years of age.
In Chroniques Cambodgiennes, racontéés par des enfants réfugiés à travers le mot et l'image (as told by children refugees through word and pictures) 1980.

These voices of the young victims of Kampuchea in the 1970's reflect the tragedy of the past and the uncertain hopes of the future. The juxtaposition of the wish to grow rice and the wish for no guns or tanks epitomises the nexus between food security and political security. This article describes the waves of politics affecting access to food which have swept through Kampuchea in the last decade and their effect on nutrition and hopes for this new decade.

Demographers, historians, and anyone studying subsistence crises in Kampuchea, must be struck by the food shortages in that country during the 1970's and, more particularly, those which occurred in 1975 and 1979. The 1975 crisis was directly responsible for the deaths of some 50,000 people: in the latter the number was much higher. One source estimated that three million Kampucheans (almost half of the entire population) were at risk of dying from hunger towads the end of 1979[1] (New York Times 12th Aug. 1979). Although the situation presently seems to have returned to relative normality the consequences from ten consecutive years of food shortages are likely to be felt for some time to come. In any case, the future may well be marked by tragedy, since Kampuchea is by no means immune from famine (Richardson 1982), a situation aggravated by prolonged political instability with military intervention.

34

The Crises

While reasons for a shortage of food in Kampuchea can be attributed historically to natural disasters and over-population, the main causes during the last decade are to be found in political crises and military action. Following the coup d'état of March 1970, the country was at war until April 1975. Throughout this particularly troubled period, rice, Kampuchea's principal crop and the staple diet of the majority Khmer population, became increasingly scarce as agricultural production fell. Tab 1 illustrates the extent by which rice crops in various provinces declined between 1969/70 and 1972/73, overall production falling by 73 % after three years of warfare.

Tab 1 Estimated paddy rice production (000 tonnes) by Kampuchean province 1969/70–1972/73

	1969/70	Production 1970/71	1971/72	1972/73	Decrease (%)
Battambang	709	611	245	334	− 53
Kampot	226	136	165	30	− 87
Kandal	216	162	172	127	− 41
Kompong Cham	347	330	238	91	− 78
Kompong Chhnang	141	156	121	77	− 45
Kompong Speu	183	119	136	69	− 62
Kompong Thom	184	175	71	3	− 98
Prey Veng	532	242	355	na	...
Pursat	204	216	111	75	− 63
Siemreap	352	263	175	136	− 61
Svay Rieng	280	161	99	na	...
Takèo	300	148	238	78	− 74
Koh Kong	...	na	na	na	...
Kratié	...	na	na	na	...
Mondulkiri	...	na	na	na	...
Oddar Meanchey	...	na	na	na	...
Preah Vihear	...	na	na	na	...
Ratanakiri	...	na	na	na	...
Stung Treng	...	na	na	na	...
(The last seven provinces)	140	na	na	na	...
	3814	2732	2126	1020	− 73

Sources: Economic Data Book, Khmer Republic, January 1975

It should be noted that the short-fall was particularly severe in Kompong Thom, Kampot, Kompong Cham, and Takèo provinces (Fig 1) which had been the scene of fierce and constant fighting since the beginning of hostilities. Production in Svay Rieng and Prey Veng also fell dramatically, but the seriousness of the military situation during 1972/73 was such that the government was unable to make even a provisional estimate of rice

Tab 2 Rice production and trade 1969–1973 (000 tonnes)

	1969	1970	1971	1972	1973
Production[a]	3813	2732	2126	953	655
Exports[b]	166	180	40		
Imports[b]				138	300

[a] The production of paddy is based on the crop data of 1969–70 which ended at the end of March 1970.
[b] Calendar year

Sources: Economic Data Book, 1975; Porter and Hildebrand, 1976; Shawcross, 1980.

Tab 3 Paddy rice production and bomb tonnage 1969–1976 (000 tonnes)

Years	Paddy Rice Production	Index	Bomb Tonnage	Index
1969	3813	100	...	
1970	2732	72	67[a]	100
1971	2126	56	109	162
1972	953	25	106	158
1973	655	17	258[b]	385

[a] From March 1968 to December 1970.
[b] From 27th January to 15th August.

Sources: Centre for International Studies, 1971; Shawcross, 1980; US Senate Hearing, 1973.

crops in these two provinces. Yields from Stung Treng, Mondulkiri, Ratanakiti, and Kratié in the north-east of Kampuchea, an area less involved in the war, remained low by comparison with other parts of the country due to the nature of the soil which is not well suited to the cultivation of rice.

Although the loss was less important in effect than that of rice, secondary crop production also declined. The cultivation of maize, for example, dropped from 150,000 t in 1972 to 73,000 t in 1973, a decrease of 49 %. In the same period, maize production fell from 23,000 tonnes to 15,000 t. (Economist Intelligence Unit 1980)

The 1972/73 paddy rice crop provided food for only 60 % of the Kampuchean population, based upon a daily average consumption of 420 grams per person. To remedy the deficit, the Lon Nol government imported rice from American Aid: 150,000 t in 1972, 300,000 t in 1973, and the same tonnage in 1974. By way of contrast, in more peaceful times during the 1960's, Kampuchea used to export rice, the annual average exported at that time being 250,000 t. The figures in Tab 2 indicate the transformation which occurred between 1969 and 1973. The decrease in production between 1972 and 1973 was associated with the American bombing (some 250,000 t from January to mid-August) of fertile, heavily populated areas in the centre and south-east of Kampuchea, the association being evident in Tab 3 and Fig 1.

36

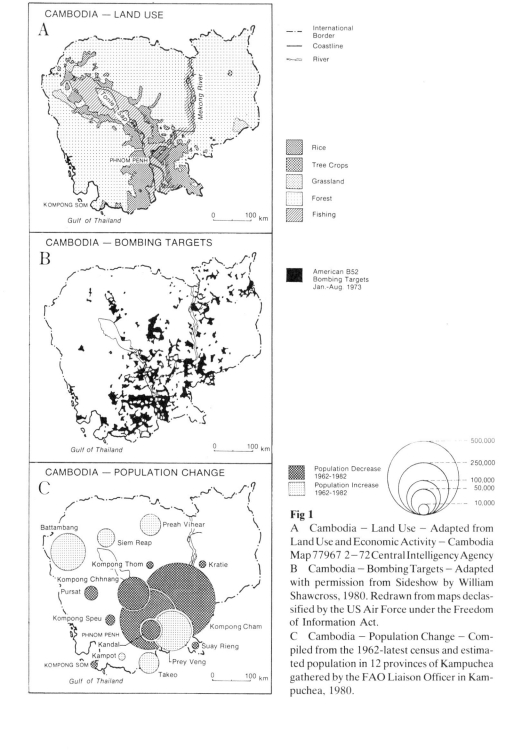

CAMBODIA — LAND USE

A

Tonle Sap

Mekong River

PHNOM PENH

KOMPONG SOM

Gulf of Thailand

0   100 km

---·— International Border
——— Coastline
〜〜 River

Rice

Tree Crops

Grassland

Forest

Fishing

CAMBODIA — BOMBING TARGETS

B

Gulf of Thailand

0   100 km

American B52
Bombing Targets
Jan.-Aug. 1973

CAMBODIA — POPULATION CHANGE

C

Battambang

Preah Vihear

Siem Reap

Kompong Thom

Kratie

Kompong Chhnang

Pursat

Kompong Speu

Kompong Cham

PHNOM PENH

Kandal

Suay Rieng

Kampot

Prey Veng

KOMPONG SOM

Takeo

Gulf of Thailand

0   100 km

500.000

250.000

100.000
50.000

10.000

Population Decrease
1962-1982
Population Increase
1962-1982

Fig 1

A   Cambodia – Land Use – Adapted from Land Use and Economic Activity – Cambodia Map 77967 2 – 72 Central Intelligency Agency

B   Cambodia – Bombing Targets – Adapted with permission from Sideshow by William Shawcross, 1980. Redrawn from maps declassified by the US Air Force under the Freedom of Information Act.

C   Cambodia – Population Change – Compiled from the 1962-latest census and estimated population in 12 provinces of Kampuchea gathered by the FAO Liaison Officer in Kampuchea, 1980.

The Difficulties

In spite of the steady increase in imported cereals, the average national dietary intake, in terms of calorie value, continued to drop (Tab 4).

Tab 4   Calorie and protein intake of Kampucheans 1961–1965, 1972, 1973, and 1974

Year	Total	Calories Vegetable Origin	Animal Origin	Total	Proteins (grams) Vegetable Origin	Animal Origin
1961–1965	2161	2037	124	52.9	41.5	11.4
1972	2190	2080	109	51.5	43.2	8.3
1973	2180	2075	104	50.7	42.9	7.8
1974	1884	1783	101	44.4	36.9	7.5

Source: FAO Year Book, 1976

Taking into account the destruction caused by hostilities and the consequent necessity to import cereals, it is difficult to believe that the calorie levels for 1972 and 1973 exceeded those for the period 1961–1965, particularly for resident urban inhabitants and peasants who had left their landholdings to seek work and food in towns or cities.

The intensity and frequency of the food crises can best be understood by reviewing the price movements of rice, the staple diet of most Kampucheans, and other foodstuffs. As indicated by Fig 2 in contrast with later substantial increases, the cost of food rose relatively little in Phnom-Penh during the first two years of the war. At that stage, the hostilities had not greatly disturbed agriculture, systems of transport, nor communications. Cereals were generally available throughout the country. Limited amounts were still being exported.

Towards the end of June 1972 rice prices began to rise sharply, however, continuing upwards to such an extent that they quickly exceeded the capacity of all but the wealthy to purchase it. While the fundamental cause of the price increase was the scarcity of rice (in turn the result of deliberate American strategies to disrupt agricultural production), there were other reasons which contributed significantly to the supply crisis both at that time, and later (Baczynskyj 1972). Fear, speculation, anarchy and corruption each played a part in maintaining price levels that placed the staple beyond the reach of those who needed it most, a situation which continued despite the cessation of American bombing in 1973, and massive imports and improved agricultural production during 1974 and 1975.

As if the wartime suffering and hardship were not enough, the very fabric of Kampuchean society had also been devastated. Unemployment was high, trade virtually ceased, industrial production declined, and the cost of living soared. Social conflict reached endemic proportions as individual Kampucheans struggled to survive against a backdrop of inefficiency and maladministration (Steinbach and Steinbach 1976). Demoralisation within the civil service

38

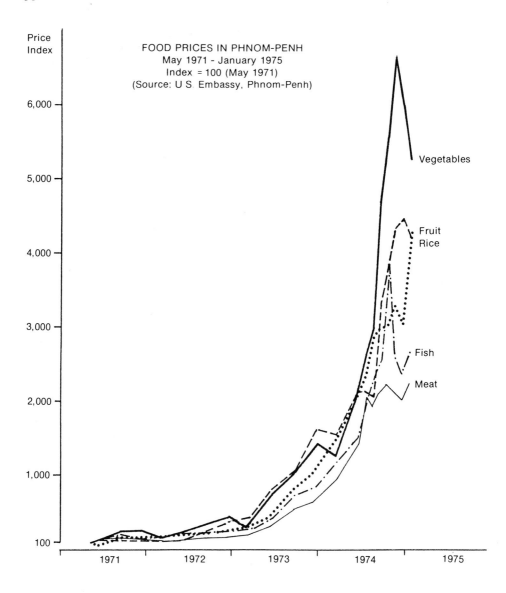

Price
Index

FOOD PRICES IN PHNOM-PENH
May 1971 - January 1975
Index = 100 (May 1971)
(Source: U S Embassy, Phnom-Penh)

6,000

5,000

Vegetables

4,000

Fruit
Rice

3,000

Fish

2,000

Meat

1,000

100

1971   1972   1973   1974   1975

Fig 2 The rapid rise in food prices amidst war and its aftermath. Compared with the even higher price of vegetables, US aid, subsidies, and the availability of some local rice, may have prevented even higher rice prices. Even the May 1971 index prices were probably double those of "normal peacetime" prices after a year of warfare.

and armed forces was rife. The Lon Nol government, using the limited resources at its disposal, concentrated upon the defence of towns and cities. Not surptisingly, the national budget reflected disintegration of the country's economic infrastructure, as Tab 5 shows.

Tab 5   Economic and financial indicators of the Khmer Republic 1969–1973

Indicators	1969	1970	1971	1972	1973
Trade Balances					
Export (a)	66,1	39,8	13,3	8,3	15,0
Import (a)	−99,2	−68,6	−55,1	−65,5	−42,0(b)
National Budget (c)					
Military	1523	5362	10872	19024	26073
Civil	6568	6494	6957	13171	22461
Total	8091	11856	17829	32195	48534
Revenue	7070	4811	4931	6223	12500
Deficit	1021	7045	12898	25972	36034
Money Supply	6150	11580	17310	22941	30185

(a) FOB $ US millions.
(b) For the first six months of the year.
(c) Million riels.

Sources: National Bank, Cambodia

The decline in purchasing power and grossly inflated food prices severely affected the health of many Kampucheans, particularly the poor who lived from day to day, earning little or nothing. Malnourished, poorly housed, and lacking adequate intake of calories and protein, refuges were the first to succumb to weight loss, digestive disorders and infectious diseases. As conditions deteriorated, their resistance lowered and epidemics spread. Cholera, tuberculosis and dysentery were common place. Doctors and hospitals were unable to provide even minimal standards of treatment, so acute were the shortages of trained staff, hospital beds and medicines. Commenting upon the effects of the food crises during 1974 in Phnom-Penh, a medical practitioner observed.

"... large numbers of children ... are currently suffering severe nutritional damage ... I saw there − the only times I have seen it in Indochina − cases of kwashiorkor in infants ..." (Hearing, 93rd Congress, US Senate, 18 July, 1974). Similar observations were made by other paediatricians in the city (Leslie 1975).

The Famine of 1975

Changes in the political and military situation in Kampuchea during 1975 did little to ease the food crises. For the bulk of the population, one set of difficulties and problems was, in effect, replaced by another. As the strategic situation of the Phnom-Penh authorities worsened, the supplies of rice for the city deteriorated further. The fight to control the Mekong River (the principal supply artery from Saigon to Phnom-Penh) and intensified bombing of Pochentong Airport by communist forces, marked the beginning of the famine.

According to official estimates, the population of Phnom-Penh in 1973 required 770 t of rice per day to feed the city's inhabitants (US Congress 1975). In February and March 1975, the daily airlifted supply had dropped to 440 t (Porter and Hildebrand 1976). Between 1973 and 1975, however, the population of the city had been increased by an influx of refugees. Whatever its consequences from a political perspective, the fighting between ideologically opposed factions aggravated what was already a precarious nutritional situation for the simple reason that it resulted in even less rice for more people. To make matters worse, the reduced supply resulted in a 40 % increase in the cost of rice. In no more than 12 weeks, the price rose from 240 riels/kg in December 1974 to 340 riels/kg by February 1975 (Economist Intelligence Unit 1980). Since the purchasing power of the majority of the city's inhabitants was such that they were able to buy very little of anything, it is not unreasonable to conclude that their ability to purchase what was available, was as much responsible for the horror of the famine as the diminished supply of their staple diet.

There was a dramatic rise in the number of deaths attributable to famine during the last three months of the Lon Nol regime. In the nutrition centre at Tuol Kauk (a suburb of Phnom-Penh), for example, not only was there a significant increase in child admissions but the proportion of these who subsequently died also increased: from 12 % during the period June − September 1974 to 20 % in December of the same year. One month later, in January 1975, the proportion had reached 36 % (Porter and Hildebrand 1976). In February the death rate was 40 % of all admissions to the Catholic Relief Services Children's Centre. Both institutions reported that the majority of deaths occurred within 24 hours of admission. In addition, many deaths probably occurred among those who were refused admission because of the lack of facilities to cope with the emergency (Steinbach and Steinbach 1976).

Medical observers remarked upon the extent and degree of malnutrition among children. In March 1975, the occupants of one children's ward were found to have an average weight loss of 40 %. In another, during the same period, 90 % of the occupants were diagnosed as suffering from severe nutritional deprivation. Porter and Hildebrand (1976) calculated that during the same month, 250 people died from hunger in the city each day. The total number of deaths for the year was estimated to be almost 80,000 (Porter and Hildebrand 1976).

To this excess mortality must be added the population (particularly children) on which the effects of malnutrition has left permanent medical and physical injuries, a point noted by a medical doctor present during the 1975 food crisis:

"This generation is going to be a lost generation of children. Malnutrition is going to affect their numbers and their mental capacities. So, as well as knocking of a generation of young men, the war is knocking off a generation of children".

(Leslie 1975)

By January 1975, the attempts by the Lon Nol government to intervene in the food crisis were completely paralysed. Speculation, looting, fear and corruption brought the distribution of food to a virtual standstill. Most of Kampuchea's shops and restaurants were either closed or destroyed. The last remnants at the nation's health service structure collapsed when, three months later, the government capitulated to the revolutionary forces. Almost immediately, the new leadership decided to evacuate entire populations to rural areas of Kampuchea where, it was said, they could find food and cultivate the land.

It was a drastic decision. Many of its consequences brought additional suffering and hardship to those already weakened from months of malnutrition. Some four million inhabitants of towns and cities suddenly found themselves forced to make what was often a long and difficult journey to settlement camps in the country (Fig 3). Conditions under which they travelled were frequently no better than those they had left. Several unofficial sources quoted high mortality rates among children, the elderly, the sick and the wounded before those who did survive eventually reached their destination. En route, medical care and hygiene facilitis were almost non-existent.

When the Lon Nol government fell, American aid ceased, bringing to an end relief supplies of imported rice. Despite immediate difficulties imposed by an acute shortage of food, the new administration under Pol-Pot implemented a course of action based upon policies which, in the long term, it was hoped would lead to national independence and self-determination. In theory, programmes of re-education and reallocation of resources would revolutionise Kampuchean political and economic structures. The situation was so acute, however, that in practice such goals could only be achieved through continuing deprivation (at least for a period) of a people and a nation ravaged by war and war-induced famine.

Fig 3 Yos Vun (13 years) has portrayed the forced evacuation of urban populations to rural areas. Adapted from Chroniques Cambodgiennes, Fédération National des Associations de l'Unesco, Japan, 1980.

42

Crises during the 1975 — 1978 Revolution

At the time of the Pol-Pot revolution, the seriousness of the food situation throughout Kampuchea was compounded by an almost complete absence of accurate information. What details were available were often fragmentary, and contradictory in nature. It can, however, be said with certainty that improvements in agricultural production coincided with major works programmes imposed upon the country's population by what was virtually forced labour (Fig 4). Following the slogan "with water you have rice: When you have rice yuo have everything", the adult population was mobilised *en masse* in elevating dykess, building dams, digging reservoirs and irrigation channels. According to official information, some 6 million hectares of land were considered suitable for cultivation. During 1977, 400,000 ha were irrigated for all season use. In 1978, the figure rose to 700,000 ha.

The 1975 crops, while good in themselves, were inadequate for the needs of Kampuchea's population due to the extent of damage to agricultural areas caused by the war. In contrast, the rice harvest in 1976 was much improved, being sufficient to feed the nation (nearly 8 million inhabitants), and provide a small surplus of 150,000 t for export. The crops in 1977 and 1978 were not so bountiful, however, due to the effects of flooding and hostilities against the Vietnamese (Leifer 1980).

Testimony by refugees from Kampuchea have not always supported official claims and statistics of the Pol-Pot regime. Depending upon their credibility, it seems that

Fig 4 Chea Soksan (12 years) portrays forced labour in the rural areas of Kampuchea. Adapted from Chroniques Cambodgiennes, Fédération Nationale des Associations de l'Unesco, Japan, 1980.

pronouncements about improved transportation, organised co-operatives and bumper yields omitted to mention the small scale or localised famines occurring in the same period. No reference was made, for example, to the hardship and privation experienced during 1976–1978 by town dwellers sent to work in the mountainous regions of Pursat and Battambang, considered the granary of Kampuchea. Often severely affected by their enforced evacuation in 1975, it seems they again suffered from food shortages and malnutrition in their new location.

The new classless society of Pol-Pot was certainly different. There was little or no money. Everybody worked, ate and lived in cooperatives. Production, distribution and consumption were fixed by *L'Angkor Loeu* (the Supreme Organisation), who confined the actiity of local authorities to planning and supervising the planting, harvesting and allocation of the rice crop. Food crises which occurred under the new administration were, however, due more to the poor management, incompetence and overzealous authoritarianism of revolutionary officials, than they were to Lon Nol's destructive war efforts and the American bombing. Except for model co-operatives producing rice for the army, government leaders, and workers involved in major works programmes, the rice production targets set by Pol-Pot in 1977 were seldom reached. While the population at large was encouraged to believe that good revolutionaries always economised to the last grain of rice, it seems that those directing its distribution failed at times to practice what they preached. The regime, for the most part relying upon violence and terror to administer its policies, alienated much of the population and thereby lost what control it might otherwise have had over distribution and consumption. Ideological and political crises between pro-Vietnamese commands and pro Pol Pot-Khmer Rouge clans worsened an already difficult situation, one consequence of which was that while workers in some areas continued to die from hunger and disease, those in others managed to live and eat reasonably well.

It is difficult, if not impossible, to know how many Kampucheans died as a result of Pol-Pot's "pure and hard" revolution. Available data, being at best fragmentary and ambiguous, does no more than reflect upon the causes and effect of man's inhumanity to man.

The 1979 Famine

In January 1979, Vietnamese troops invaded Kampuchea and occupied Phnom-Penh. Soldiers of Pol-Pot retired to the mountainous regions in the north-east of the country, near the border with Thailand, from where they commenced resistance fighting. Because the harvesting of the crops coincided with the Vietnamese invasion, the 1978–1979 yield of rice was not as abundant as it would otherwise have been. Stocks in the Pol-Pot co-operative granaries were soon exhausted and in some cases, were squandered. The new pro-Vietnamese regime, attempting to console the population by destroying or discrediting any heritage from the previous administration, did little to intervene. According to some estimates, the Khmer Rouge resistance fighters took with them between 10 and 20 % of the year's crop at the time of their retreat (Zasloff 1980). Had they not done so, and had more normal conditions prevailed at the time of harvest, it is possible that there would have been sufficient stocks of rice to feed the entire Kampuchean population for three months.

While difficulties associated with the shortage of food in Kampuchea received mention in a diplomatic review from Bangkok as early as March, world opinion was not alerted until July when, following a visit to Kampuchea, representatives of UNICEF and the International Red Cross drew attention to the plight of the population. This was soon followed, in the media by photographic evidence of their suffering. Two months later, an American satellite report revealed that no more than 5–10 % of cultivatable land in Kampuchea had been sown for rice crops. On this basis, it was calculated that 2.25 million Kampucheans would be at risk of death from starvation during the forthcoming winter.

The International Red Cross and UNICEF predicted that assistance would be required to the value of $ US 110 million, the sum needed to provide the Khmer population with 165,000 t of rice, 15,000 t of sugar and 8,000 t of oil over a period of six months. The World Food Program forecast assistance of 150 t of rice per day for the 300,000 refugees in various settlement camps, a figure calculated on the basis of a daily requirement of 500 grams of rice per person. Other sources placed the total Kampuchean daily need at 1,000 t of rice for at least 6 months to provide immediate relief against the famine. By combining these and other estimates, it was said that 2,500 t per day would be required over a period from 16 months to 2 years to enable the entire population to return to normal health.

On 9th November, the United Nations decided to grant aid to the value of $ US 210 million, thus providing the necessary financial assistance. The problem then became one of distribution created by logistic and political difficulties. On 23rd November, 1979, for example, the Heng Samrin government received 9,950 t of rice, yet only 446 t were actually distributed, the reason given was the lack of suitable transport.

In general, the international aid which eventuated, was poorly distributed. In refugee settlements, supplies often went directly to camp leaders who sold or bartered rice and other commodities, instead of giving them away as the donors intended. Rather than distributing relief supplies to the interior of the country where the need was greatest, a significant proportion was allocated to civil servants and to military personnel in lieu of wages, because currency, (suppressed under the Pol-Pot administration) was not re-introduced until March 1980. What distribution there was varied according to region and the category of persons to whom it was made. In Phnom-Penh, civil servants and their families received allocations of 13 kg for adults, with half that amount for children, in lieu of monthly salaries. By way of contrast, suburban inhabitants received only 7 or 8 kg representing a daily intake of 270 grams. In rural areas, relief was as meagre as it was irregular. Because of the distance from relief distribution points, many inhabitants in the border area between Kampuchea and Thailand were obliged to buy or barter food from neighbouring Thai provinces whose populations were better fed.

1979 saw the most catastrophic famine in the history of the Khmer people. A refugee reported that the province of Battambang was „almost empty", the only people left in the villages being the elderly and beggars. Everyone else had gone because "they were afraid of dying from hunger" *(Le Matin (Paris), 6. Nov. 1979)*. According to official sources, the mortality rate of those hospitalized in Phnom-Penh during 1979 varied between 25 and 76 %. In the provinces, it was undoubtedly higher.

Those who lived in the mountains under the control of Khmer-Rouge soldiers suffered even more. Unable to cultivate rice, they lived on maize and manioc. The resulting dietary deficiency was the direct cause of extreme rates of mortality and sickness. The

Tab 6 Primary causes of death at Sakeo Field Hospital

Causes	Number of deaths	Percentage
Malaria	38	26
Pneumonia	26	18
Malnutrition	20	15
Diarrhoea	16	11
Premature Death	11	7
Other causes	33	23

Sources: Glass, et al., Lancet, 19 April 1980

International Red Cross and UNICEF estimated that two-thirds of the inhabitants in areas controlled by the Khmer-Rouge suffered from malaria, 80 % were undernourished, and one out of every two children died within a year of birth. In the refugee settlements in Thailand, the principal causes of mortality were almost entirely the direct consequences of famine. Tab 6 shows the causes of the 144 deaths which occurred during the 28 day period at the Sakeo camp hospital between 8th November, 1979 and 5th December, 1979.

There is, however, no doubt that the massive international aid programmes mounted by foreign governments and relief agencies managed to avert a catastrophe in spite of the logistic and political difficulties which they encountered[1].

Conclusion

Food crises in Kampuchea during the 1970's had their origins in the political and military events of the decade. While the fall of the Pol-Pot regime, the Vietnamese occupation and decisions of the Heng Samrin administration have resulted in more abundant agricultural production, a substantial decline in international aid since 1981 continues to concern both the Phnom-Penh authorities and those responsible for the aid programmes. Surface area cultivation for the 1979−1980 season was 700,000 ha which produced 400,000 t of rice. In 1980−1981, 1,500,000 ha were cultivated, the harvest being 750,000 t of rice (Office of Special Relief Operations 1980). The target set for 1981−1982 was a production of 850,000 t but, due to flooding and drought in the months of September and October, the crop only yielded 690,000 t (Wain 1981), a decrease of 8 % by comparison with the previous year's achievement. Actual famine conditions have receded, but international assistance remains a pre-requisite for the survival of the Kampuchean population.

Economic assistance alone will not, however, resolve Kampuchea's difficulties. For as long as warfare remains the response to ideological crises like those in the seventies, agricultural production will continue to be insufficient to provide even subsistence levels of nutrition. Armed hostilities continue to prevent or disrupt the cultivation and harvesting of the nation's rice crops, and risk of famine in Kampuchea remains. The situation is therefore one in which both moral and material issues must be considered. Short term military and political victories, favouring this or that ideology, will only be defeats, if those who survive them, do not have enough to eat.

For the time being, politics in Kampuchea are at an *impasse*. As with previous administrations, a major concern of the Heng Samrin authorities is the provision of sufficient food for continued survival of Kampucheans. Forecasted subsistence crises and diminishing international aid make the outlook a bleak one for a nation and people already devastated by war and famine.

Notes

1) See also:

1. Southeast Asia Refugee Crisis. Hearing before the Subcommittee on East Asia and Pacific Affairs of the Committee on Foreign Relations, United States Senate. Ninety-Sixth Congress, September 27, 1979, Washington 1980.

2. 1979 – Tragedy in Indochina: War, Refugees, and Famine, Hearings before the Subcommittee on Asian and Pacific Affairs of the Committee on Foreign Affairs, House of Representatives. Ninety-Sixth Congress, First Session, Washington, 1980.

3. Cambodian Famine and US Contigency Relief Plans. Hearing before the Subcommittee on Arms Control, Oceans, International Operations and Environment of the Committee on Foreign Relations, United States Senate, Ninety-Sixth Congress. First Session, November 1979, Washington 1980.

4. Cambodian Relief A Report to the Committee on Foreign Relations United States Senate. October 1980, Washington 1980.

5. Food Aid to Cambodia. Hearing before the Subcommittee on Foreign Agricultural Policy of the Committee on Agricultural, Nutrition, and Forestry, United States Senate. Ninety-Sixth Congress, First Session, November 19, 1979, Washington 1980.

6. 1980 – The Tragedy in Indochina Continues: War, Refugees, and Famine, Hearings before the Subcommittee on Foreign Affairs, House of Representatives. Ninety-Sixth Congress, Second Session, Washington 1980.

7. Kampuchea – An Assessment of Current Information. November 5, 1979, International Disaster Institute (London).

8. Kampuchea Update. December 11, 1979, International Disaster Institute, London.

9. Becker, Elizabeth: The Politics of Famine in Cambodia. Washington Post (18 November 1979).

10. Shawcross, William: The End of Cambodia? The New York Review, (1980).

11. Cambodia's Long Path Back, Nature, 281, (1979).

12. The Cambodian Picture Becomes Clearer, Nature, 282 (1979).

13. Kampuchea's Shattered Agriculture is on the Way to Recovery, World Agricultural Report (1981)

14. Holt, Julius: The Kampuchean Emergency, Food Policy (1980).

15. Kershaw, Roger: Multipolarity and Cambodia's Crisis of Survival. Southeast Asian Affairs 1980, Institute of Southeast Asian Studies, Heineman Asia.

16. Nations, Richard: Battle for the Hearts and Stomachs, FEER (December 7, 1979).

17. Starvation, Deathwatch in Cambodia, Time (November 12, 1979).

References

Baczynskyj, B.: Socio-cynicism, Far Eastern Economic Review, 24. (1972)

Centre for International Studies: The Air War in Indochina, A Preliminary Report, Cornell University, Ithaca, 1971.

Chroniques Cambodgiennes. National Federation of Unesco Associations in Japan. UNAAER, Paris, pp. 65, 1980.

Economist Intelligence Unit. Quarterly Economic Review of Indochina: Vietnam, Laos, Cambodia. Annual Supplement, 1980.

Food and Agricultural Organisation. Production Yearbook, Vol. 30, FAO Rome 1976.

Glass, R.I., Nieburg, P., Cates, W., Davies, C., Russbach, R., Nothdurft, H., Peel, S., Turnbull, R.: Rapid Assessment of Health Status and Preventative Medicine Needs of Newly Arrived Kampuchean Refugees Sa Kaeo, Thailand. Lancet 1, 868 − 872 (1980)

Government of the Khmer Republic. Economic Data Book, Phnom-Penh, 1975.

Leifer, M.: Kampuchea 1979: From Dry Season to Dry Season. Asian Survey XX, 1, 33 − 41 (1980)

Leslie, J.: Children Victims in Phnom-Penh: Starvation Claims Thousands in War, Los Angeles Times (24th March 1975)

Fruits of Victory Bitter for Hanoi. New York Times (12th August 1979)

Office for Special Relief Operations. Report of the Food Assessment Mission to Kampuchea, W/P0604, FAO Rome, 1980.

Porter, G. and Hildebrand, G.: Cambodia: Starvation and Revolution. Monthly Review Press, New York, 1976.

Richardson, M.: Aid with No Labels. Far Eastern Economic Review. (5th February 1982)

Shawcross, W.: Sideshow: Kissinger, Nixon and the Destruction of Cambodia, Fontana, London, 1980.

Steinbach, J. and Steinbach, J.: Phnom-Penh Libéré. Editions Sociales, Paris 1976.

United States Senate Committee Hearing. Bombing in Cambodia. Hearing before the Comittee on Armed Services, United States Senate, First Session (July and August), Washington 1973.

United States Senate Committee Hearing: Humanitarian Problems in Indochina, Ninety Third Congress, Second Session, Washington DC (18th July 1974)

US Congress: Supplement Assistance for Cambodia. Calendar No. 52, 94th Congress, 1st Session, Washington 1975.

Wain, B.: Life in Kampuchea Improves, But More Problems Lie Ahead, Asian Wall Street Journal (14th December 1981)

Zasloff, I.J.: Kampuchea: A Question of Survival. American Universities Field Staff. Reports Series. Hanover 1980.

Cycles of Famine in Islands of Plenty:
The Case of the Colonial West Indies in the Pre-emancipation Period

Watts, D., Senior Lecturer, Department of Geography, The University of Hull, Hull HU6 7RX, UK

Abstract: The West Indies provide good examples of tropical islands which, while inherently capable of providing a well-balanced, adequate diet for a large population, can nevertheless become vulnerable to famine if an inappropriate cultivation system is imposed on them. In examining contrasts in food production between aboriginal and European food-producing systems, evidence that the latter could create cycles of famine in particular islands is assessed. Famine in the West Indies generally gave rise to increased death rates and a substantial emigrant outflow.

Tropical islands, with their apparent superfluity of vegetative, animal and soil resources, are not normally regarded as areas which are vulnerable to famine: indeed, the common image is one of a bounteous serendipity. Recent discussion of modern famine (e.g. Spitz, 1976; Franke and Chasin 1980) has tended to ignore island situations, concentrating rather on the chronic and prolonged food shortages experienced in continental regions such as the Sahel and Somalia in Africa, Cambodia and Bangladesh in Asia. Within the last decade, evidence for the periodic existence of famine within tropical island milieus has also been compiled. Handy and Handy (1972) have suggested that Pacific region indigenes were constantly anxious about the possibility of famine prior to European contact, and Currey (1980) has proposed that many Pacific islands have an inherent susceptibility to famine which is no less prevalent now than in pre-contact days. Also, Schmitt (1970) has indicated that since European contact in Hawaii, famines recurred there, on average, every 21 years.

It is my contention that famine was experienced in the West Indies group of islands too at fairly regular intervals during the colonial period. Surprisingly, this feature of Caribbean socio-economic life has been largely ignored by previous writers. The onset of famine in this region, as elsewhere, is linked to a complicated set of physico-environmental, biological and socio-economic circumstances, detailed below, the absence of any one being sufficient to prevent or substantially alleviate the consequences and duration of the famine period. Although the circumstances varied from island to island, the customary sociological complements to the onset of famine were an increase in the rate of mortality, and outmigration.

Environmental Conditions

Nothing in the physical or biological framework of the West Indies suggests that famine should have been a problem for settlers in the region. The islands lie largely within the tropics along a broad arc from the western tip of Cuba to the south-eastern shores of Trinidad, a distance of some 4000 km (Fig 1), and within them there is great diversity not only of size (Tab 1) but also of landforms, geology and relief. The four largest islands, termed the Greater Antilles, are Cuba, Hispaniola (including the present states of Haiti and the Dominican Republic), Jamaica and Puerto Rico. In each, fertile limestone and alluvial lowlands are to be found. As well, there are rugged mountain ranges, the peaks of which rise to 3175 m in Hispaniola (Pico Duarte), 2275 m in the Blue Mountains of Jamaica, 1972 m in the Sierra Maestra of Cuba, and 1065 m in the central mountains of Puerto Rico. Most of the other islands are small in size. The Bahamas group consists of over 1000 coral limestone islands, the majority dry, with land surfaces lying only a few meters above sea-level. Except for the composite island of Guadeloupe, the Lesser Antilles are usually less than 40 km across. An inner chain comprises roughly-circular volcanic islands which rise steeply up to a central peak while a discontinuous outer chain is formed of low-lying islands with a coral limestone base. The three islands which stand separately in the southeast of the region — Barbados, Trinidad and Tobago — all have links with South American geological structures, although much of Barbados is covered by Pleistocene deposits of coral limestone.

Under natural circumstances, the geological, climatic and soil conditions are all favourable for the development and support of an immensely varied, rich flora and fauna. Most soils, whether developed from coral limestone, volcanic material or, as in the case of Trinidad and Tobago sedimentary or metamorphosed rocks, are potentially very fertile, although some are susceptible to severe erosion if the vegetation cover is removed. The islands lie within the Trade Wind zone. Temperatures are constantly high except for the occasional winter cold spell in the north of the Bahamas. Mean annual precipitation totals range from 1000 to 1500 mm on most coastal or low land, but may reach 2500 mm on the windward sides of major mountain ranges or volcanic peaks. In contrast, they may fall as low as 500 mm in rain shadow districts, such as southern Hispaniola. Everywhere, distinctive dry and wet seasons prevail. The region has a tropical seasonal climate, in which the dry season, occurring during the first part of the year, may last from two to five months according to location. The climate is also unpredictable, with both precipitation totals and the intensity and duration of the dry season varying appreciably from year to year (Rouse and Watts 1967). In this climatic milieu, the natural vegetation response is a mosaic of different types of forest and scrub. Multi-canopy seasonal rain forests develop within mean precipitation totals of 1250 to 2000 mm, with drier thorn forests or even cactus scrub on coastlands. True rain forest, even cloud forest, is present at higher altitudes. The main danger to vegetation growth lies in the passage of hurricanes, the frequency of which, throughout the region, ranges from one to ten or twelve, occasionally more, per annum. Over individual small islands or particular districts of the larger ones, hurricane frequencies are normally less than might be imagined, occurring perhaps once every 15 or 20 years. Also, Trinidad is too far south to be affected by these violent storms. Animal life within the vegetation systems is naturally numerous and diverse, especially in the two richest faunal habitats, the forest canopies and the sea margins. In contrast, forest-floor fauna is limited. Many of the animal species are

Tab 1 Islands of the West Indies mentioned in the text, their size, present population, and population density 1981

Island	Size (km^2)	Population (millions)	Pop. Density/ (km^2)	Persons/km^2 Arable Land
Cuba	110,922	9.8	88	185
Jamaica	11,424	2.2	192	463
Haiti	27,750	6.0	216	425
Dominican Republic	48,734	5.6	115	...
Puerto Rico	8,897	3.2	360	652
St. Kitts	176	0.037	211	n.a.
Nevis	130	0.015	115	n.a.
Antigua	280	0.055	194	n.a.
Guadeloupe	1,702	0.313	183	425
Martinique	1,090	0.320	293	592
Barbados	440	0.238	540	692
Dominica	790	0.059	76	416
Grenada	345	0.089	257	700
St. Vincent	389	0.080	206	626
Tobago	300	0.035	116	702
Trinidad	4,828	1.0	208	740

Source: Population Reference Bureau

edible. In pre-Columbian times, the sea margins were especially prolific, many shell fish, several species of turtle (Carr 1952; Parsons 1962), the manatee, the West Indian seal, and many fish species finding their home there.

Aboriginal Food Producing Systems

It seems beyond question that the profligacy of wild life which existed in natural habitats in the West Indies and the inherent fertility of most soils meant that there was little danger of food shortages arising under conditions of minimal human disturbance. This appears to have been borne out by all that is known about aboriginal food-producing systems and about dietary patterns in aboriginal times. At the Columbian contact, three groups of aboriginal Indians of different derivations and cultural attainments were present in the West Indies: the unsophisticated hunters and gatherers termed the Ciboney, the Arawak, and the Carib. In 1492, the first of these groups was restricted to the extreme western peninsulas of Cuba and Hispaniola, having been replaced elsewhere in these two islands by the Arawak. They lived in caves or in rough rock shelters by the sea, obtaining a well balanced diet by collecting fruits and herbs from adjacent forest or scrub, and by culling land, fresh-water and salt-water animals, among which were fish, turtles, iguanas and the manatee (Sauer 1966). It is unlikely that they disturbed the food chains which supported them to any great extent.

Originating in northern South America, Island Arawak cultures in 1492 dominated the Greater Antilles and the Bahamas, with the focus of their activities centred in Hispaniola, and important sub-centres in Cuba and Puerto Rico. Throughout the whole of this sub-

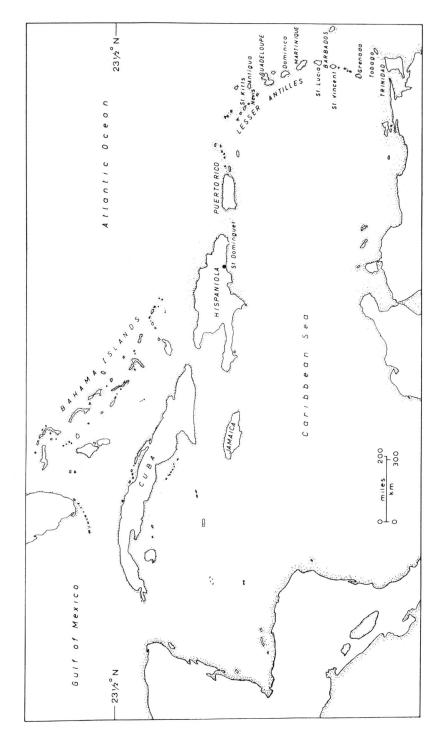

Fig 1 The West Indies

region, Arawak groups presented a marked cultural uniformity in language, patterns of subsistence, organisation, technology and life style. They impressed the Spanish colonisers by their degree of sophistication in agricultural skills, pottery-making, canoe construction, the use of fibres, and the manufacture of gold ornaments. They had evolved comlex social structures, with settlements in villages of 1000 to 2000 people, each with its own chieftain. Their agriculture was essentially conservative in environmental terms, a type of shifting cultivation known as *conuco*, in which crop species which reproduce vegetatively from cuttings were the major element. Seed plants played a very minor role. Tubers were vital components of this agriculture, and since these grow best in well drained situations, the mounding of soil was practised where necessary. Some of the basic features of this type of agriculture are briefly reviewed here as background to later discussion.

The selection of the *conuco* formed the first phase of the shifting cultivation cycle, followed by clearing, cropping and eventual fallowing (Conklin 1957). *Conucos* could be sited on any land, except possibly on the highest and steepest mountain slopes or on grass sod, and were usually close to a village. Clearing was most commonly achieved by ringbarking and then cutting, stumps being left in the ground to rot. Tree trunks and branches were burnt towards the end of the dry season (April-May), thus providing an increase in available phosphorus, exchangeable calcium and magnesium within the surface layers of the soil, as well as increasing its friability, both of which features facilitated planting and increased rates of plant growth (Harris 1971; Scott 1979). No good evidence remains of the size of *conuco* plots in the West Indies. The general rule elsewhere in tropical South America (Carneiro 1956) seems to have been that between 0.2 to 0.5 ha of *conuco* land per person was required to provide adequate subsistence, assuming that the main crop was the calorie-rich manioc, as indeed it mostly was in the West Indies. Once the *conuco* had been cleared, it was then dug over with a digging stick, and often subsequently mounded to heights of 0.7 m (Sturtevant 1961; Sauer 1966). Several different types of cultigen were then set on the same mound, each having a different growth habit so as to make maximum use of it. Some grew tall (manioc), others climbed, still others formed a good ground cover (sweet potato). In this way, mound soil was very well protected from the dangers of soil wash, even on steep slopes and in areas of high precipitation, and the possibilities of soil wash were further reduced by the baulking effect of the mounds themselves. Cap all early reports suggest that soil wash was minimal in areas of West Indian *conuco* agriculture, no matter what the slope angle. Most planting was undertaken at the end of the dry season to take advantage both of the temporary increase in soil nutrients following tree burning, and the impending rains. Crop species used on *conuco* land took relatively few nutrients overall from the soil, although the nutrient store eventually diminished sufficiently to give rise to a cultivation limit in most *conucos* of between 15 to 20 years (Newson 1976). New *conucos* were then cut, and the former *conucos* left fallow for possibly another 30 years to allow for vegetation regrowth and nutrient replenishment.

Most plants grown in *conucos* were well suited to the West Indian environment and the occasional eccentricities of its climate. Most, for example, were drought-tolerant. By far the most useful crop, and the dominant one, was manioc. It is a plant which grows well in both acidic and alkaline soil, is drought resistant, and can be harvested repeatedly. Its caloric yield is phenomenal, being three times that of maize in favourable situations, and it is also unequalled in the region for its starch yield (Davies 1974; Rogers 1965; Hill 1952). Both the poisonous bitter manioc, the tubers of which, after processing to extract the poison, were baked to form a type of flat bread named cassava, and the non-poisonous sweet manioc, which was boiled or baked, were utilised. Almost as important was the sweet potato. Its yield was somewhat lower, but it had the advantage of maturing in only four months. Other important starchy root crops included the yautia (*Xanthosoma* sp.), at least one native yam (*Diascorea* sp.), and a *Canna*. Non-starchy *conuco* food plants were the peanut, the annual pepper *(Capsicum annum)* and the calabash gourd *(Crescentia cujete)*. Small amounts of maize and beans may also have been present on the fringes of *conucos* (Sauer 1966; Newson 1976), the beans seemingly being restricted to Cuba (Sturtevant 1961).

Such *conuco* agriculture provided an exceptional ecologically well-balanced and protective form of land use in which fertility was generally maintained for several years, and soil loss was at a minimum. Little was taken out of the soil which was not subsequently replaced by the regrowth of vegetation. It was well suited to the generally moist Caribbean climate, and to the seasonal and periodic phases of drought which occurred within it. It was also characterised by a flexible harvesting system in which there was typically no one single staple crop, but in which crops were gathered as and when required. Although it was labour-intensive, requiring year-round care (especially to keep the land weed-free) if it was to function maximally, it was also reasonably economical of labour in the long term. At the beginning of the sixteenth century, Las Casas (1520−1561) wrote that "twenty persons working six hours a day for one month will make a planting of such *conucos* that will provide bread for 300 people for two years": and there was no comparable yield, for example, in Europe at that time. But other sources of food, additional to those grown in *conucos*, were also available to the Arawak. Some were raised in household yards, kitchen gardens and 'orchards', among them fruit trees such as the sweet sop and sour sop (*Annona* spp.), the hog plum *(Spondias mombin)*, the mammey apple *(Mammea americana)*, the guava *(Psidium guajava)*, the pineapple *(Ananas comosus)*, and possibly also the pawpaw *(Carica papaya)*. Most fats and proteins, in contrast, were derived from animal sources. Virtually none of these were domesticates, the only animal raised to be eaten being a small type of non-barking dog. Of the available and suitable wild fauna, more were taken from water than from land. Fresh-water fish were caught by hook and line, by poles, and by stupifiers, especially barbasco. But the vast majority of fat and protein requirements were obtained from salt-water animals, or those in salt-water margins. On beaches, shell fish, turtles, crab and manatee were caught and eaten, some of the turtles weighing over 0.75 tonnes. Salt-water fish were especially important, and Newson (1976) has suggested that these accounted for some 20 % of the total diet, providing most of the protein intake of the coastal Arawak. The most common land animals taken were pigeons, doves and parrots from tree canopies, and iguanas and the rabbit-like hutia on the ground (Sauer 1966), but in all cases predation rates were light. Very occasionally, wild fruits, wild tubers or leaves from non-planted species further supplemented the diet.

Taken as a whole, the diet of the Arawak of the West Indies appears to have been extremely well balanced between starches, fats and proteins, with potential for an abundant caloric intake, even during times of drought. Without manioc, the food resource would have been good; with manioc, it was excellent. For similar cultures on the eastern coast of Nicaragua, Nietschmann (1973) has concluded that *conuco* agriculture alone would be sufficient to meet the caloric needs of the population, and there is little doubt that this would also have been the case for the island Arawak. No deficiency diseases were present among them when the Spanish arrived in 1492.

Much less numerous than the Arawak, Carib Indians were confined at the time of Spanish contact to the Lesser Antilles, and possibly the northwestern tip of Trinidad. Their major source of food was also *conuco* agriculture, which in their case was characterised by one additional starchy food plant as well as the others present in Arawak terrain, i.e. arrowroot (Sturtevant 1969). Caribs also resorted widely to hunting, fishing and gathering, and they possessed one semi-domesticated animal, the muscovy duck. Their diet further included human flesh; but how far the practice of cannibalism was the exception rather than the rule is still a matter for debate stet, nor is it known whether human meat was eaten more for reason of ritual than hunger.

All these aboriginal food-producing systems clearly were extremely frugal in the use of solar energy, labour, and nutrients taken from the environment, at the same time conserving soil and vegetative resources. Caloric yields, the nature of the crops grown, and the balance in dietary intake between starches, fats and protein meant that chances of famine were reduced to a minimum. Further, these systems appear to have supported a large population. While the exact size of the population is still in dispute, most current opinion suggests that between 6,000,000 to 8,000,000 Indians must have been present in the West Indies at the time of Spanish contact, about one half of which were in Hispaniola (Sauer 1966; Dobyns 1966; Cook and Borah 1971–1974; Denevan 1976; but for a contrary view, see Rosenblat 1967). Neither the Indians, nor their food-producing sytems, long survived the arrival of the Spanish. The story of their decline has been told elsewhere (Sauer 1966), and is beyond the scope of this paper. A few details should, however, be noted. Even during the 1490's, Columbus had indicated that on Hispaniola "the abundant food of the friendly Indians " was no longer available, because *conucos* were being allowed to fall into disuse, Indian labour being diverted into gold mining. By 1508, an official Spanish census recorded that only 60,000 Hispanolian Arawak were still alive, and from 1515 an almost continuous shortage of food was experienced in that island as *conuco* after *conuco* was abandoned. None of the Arawak survived in Hispaniola after 1522, following which Las Casas commented that "we should remember that we found the island full of people whom we erased from the face of the earth, filling it with dogs and beasts". Within the same decade, Spanish raiding parties had killed off most other Indian groups in the Greater and Lesser Antilles, with the exception of small, resistant bands which remained in the hilly, isolated parts of the volcanic islands of the Lesser Antilles, and in Trinidad. By 1530, through the agency of Spanish intervention, virtually all Indian groups and their complex, intricate food-producing systems had become extinct within the region.

Cycles of Famine in the Seventeenth and Eighteenth Centuries

In a very real sense the Spanish had only a transient interest in the West Indies, apart from their value as a strategic shield which helped to separate their more extensively-settled and lucrative colonies on the mainland of Central and South America from potential European intruders. It was not until the middle years of the seventeenth century that islands in the Caribbean began to be occupied intensively once again, this time by the nations of northwest

Europe, particularly England, France and Holland. Initially, the impetus was towards the Lesser Antilles, and after several not wholly successful attempts at settling plantations of tobacco, cotton, indigo and ginger, colonists turned in 1645 to the raising of sugar cane. This tall, strong and sturdy perennial grass, with its C_4 photosynthetic pathway, is particularly well suited to seasonal Caribbean environments. A reasonably high intake of water (1250 mm per annum as a minimum) is required for its main growth period, followed by a dry, sunny season to encourage the relatively slow natural process of cane sweetening. In West Indian terms, this means that cane is best planted in the rainy season, between August and November, allowed to grow and mature for the next 14 to 18 months, then harvested between January and May/June in the subsequent dry season. Cane succeeds in most soils, as long as they are reasonably deep and fertile. A slight slope, to encourage sub-surface drainage and the removal of excess surface water, has always been favoured for planting. Unlike most other commercial crops in the region, the creole variety of *Saccharum officinarum* which was used throughout the 17th and 18th centuries was remarkably free from pests and diseases. The settling of the crop took place at a time of rapidly-rising demand for it in European markets, a demand which could not be met by the then existing regions of production, notably Brazil, the Canary Islands and Sicily (Deere 1949; Pares 1960). Most of the financial backing for the new crop was directed initially towards Barbados and, to a lesser extent, St. Kitts, and a sugar boom soon developed in both islands. By 1646, Barbados was said to be "full of sugar" (James Parker: Winthrop Papers, V, 434), and most of the larger landholders had planted the crop by 1647 on estates the mean size of which ranged from 50 to 150 ha. In 1650, sugar cane had raised the value of cultivated produce in the island to over L 3 million, an astonishing figure for that period. By 1665, over 80 % of Barbados was under the crop, and it retained that scale of prominence in the island's agricultural landscape for the remainder of the colonial period.

Evidence from Barbados

Much of the detailed documentary evidence for the consequences of the introduction of sugar cane agriculture to West Indian food production comes from Barbados, and it is accordingly this island to which particular attention is paid in this paper. There is no doubt that the local provision of food crops in the 1640's was inadequate for the vast numbers of people who flocked to the island with a view to participating in the sugar boom. Indeed, the acquisition of adequate supplies of food had always been a problem from the first settlement in Barbados in 1627. Almost none of the original colonists had any previous experience of agriculture, or of tropical island conditions (Merrill 1958). It is likely that they brought some basic provisions with them to last for a month or so, but the general plan for colonisation seems to have been to utilise local Indian foodstuffs and local Indian expertise wherever practicable. Yet Barbados had long been an empty island when the English arrived, and no local memory remained of the successful food-growing systems of the former aboriginal inhabitants. To resolve this dilemma, Arawak Indians from the Essequibo district of South America were induced to leave their homeland for Barbados to instruct the English in the correct manner of planting *conuco* crops, "the first that were ever planted there" (Anon 1891). There is, however, no evidence that the English ever followed *conuco* practices widely in Barbados, and the Arawak did not long survive the experience of meeting the English (Watts 1982). In the 1640's, local food production began to lag well behind demand, so much so that an island-wide famine had developed by 1649, the effects of which were accentuated both by a severe drought which followed in the summer of 1650, and by a disease epidemic (Ligon 1657). Together, famine and disease caused the death of some 6,000 to 10,000 whites, together with an unspecified number of black slaves, between 1647 and 1650, or perhaps as many as one-fifth of the island's population. Thereafter, as the economic dependence of the island on sugar cane increased, the provision of adequate amounts of foodstuffs became ever more uncertain.

The reasons for this may be linked to a somewhat complicated set of circumstances, some of them socio-economic, others environmental. Among the former may be included the philosophy which lay behind the establishment and operation of sugar cane estates in tropical environments, and the ways in which this was modified by Barbadian experience. Barbadian sugar cane estates devolved from the Brazilian system of cane production, formulated in the early sixteenth century, and in which an attempt had always been firmly made to maintain a balance between the production of the commercial crop, timber (for fuel, building, and utensils), and foodstuffs. In other words, the estates were designed to be as self-sufficient as possible, and the capital raised by the sale of cane was used only for the purchase of materials which could not be grown or raised on the estate (Boxer 1957; Bridenbaugh and Bridenbaugh 1972; Galloway 1977). At first, in Barbados, a similar pattern of plantation operation was planned and executed. Thus on William Hilliard's relatively large estate of c. 500 acres (223 ha) in 1647, only 200 acres were planted in cane, with 25 under other cash crops (tobacco and cotton), 70 acres (28 ha) in provisions (including maize, sweet potatoes and plantains), 80 acres (32 ha) under pasture, and 120 (50 ha) left in woodland (Ligon 1657). In 1652, more land on the estate owned jointly by Anthony Ashley-Cooper and Gerard Hawtayne was under wood than cane: of 205 acres (82 ha), 95 (38 ha) were in standing wood, 60 (24 ha) in cane, 14 (5.7 ha) under pasture, 12 (4.9 ha) under maize, 6 (2.4 ha) in plantains, 5 (2 ha) under cassava and sweet potatoes, and 5 (2 ha) "runne to ruine", presumably eroded (Hawtayne 1893).

But gradually, towards the end of the 1650's, more and more land was converted into cane production at the expense of wood and provision crops. There were two major economic considerations which encouraged this. First, many of the new estate owners, other than those who were already very rich, quickly found themselves in debt (Harlow 1926). The purchase of an estate was in itself a not inconsiderable item, land values having risen from c £0.50 per acre in 1640 to c. £5 per acre by 1646. Between 1646 and 1648, good quality cane estates in accessible parts of the island were sold, complete with buildings, mill, stock and labour, at from £18 to £45 per acre (Dunn 1972). Estates of the size owned by Hilliard called for a capital outlay of some £14,000 over a three-year period (Ligon 1657). Land price inflation continued throughout the 1650's. Throughout, the preparation of land for cane was expensive, especially where forest had to be cut and removed. Contemporary opinion in Barbados was that the new sugar estates required one labourer for every acre under cultivation, if all stages of production and milling were to be undertaken with reasonable efficiency. After the first years of experimentation with the crop, this was raised to two labourers per acre (Barrett 1965). The labourers could be either indentured servants costing c. £12 per head, or slaves purchased for £25 per head. Their upkeep was extra. In the light of all this, it is not surprising that many estate owners had to borrow money to become established. This was forthcoming from the sophisticated credit system organised for colonial development by the Dutch, who were more than willing to offer "all sorts and necessaries for life and planting, and at very cheap rates" (Scott, c. 1667; see also Thomas 1960). What was more, pressure was put upon the planters to pay off their debts as soon as possible by growing more and more sugar cane, the price of this commodity remaining high throughout the 1650's. Coupled with this pressure of debt was also a social pressure, which became especially strong in the emerging small-island society of planters present in Barbados, to entertain lavishly and prodigally (Ligon 1657). This also could only be achieved by spending large amounts of money, obtained from ever-expanding cane acreages.

A second, more broadly-based economic factor which encouraged cane agriculture at the expense of provision crops derives from the essential concepts of the emerging mercantile trade system of that time. In this, there was a determined attempt by England to develop her North American colonies as food-support bases for the West Indies, thus leaving the latter free to concentrate on the production of tropical commercial crops. Because of this, even by 1650, estate servants in Barbados were eating not only maize, cassava bread, sweet potatoes, peas and plantains grown on estate land but also, for protein, salt turtle, salt cod and mackerel brought in from Nova Scotia and New England on American ships (Ligon 1657). So dependent on fish protein from American sources did many West Indian settlers and their servants and slaves become, that the New Englanders and their small ships quickly came to be regarded as "the key to the Indies, without which they are not able to subsist" (Campbell 1972). Certainly, the official view was not to encourage self-sufficiency in food crops within West Indian plantations.

As sugar cane assumed greater dominance in the landscape at the expense of natural forest and scrub, a further, environmental factor came into play which was to have immense repercussions in subsequent years to both commercial and provision agriculture. This was that the nature of the land resource began to change.

It is now well known that in most tropical environments the main store of nutrients lies within the vegetation rather than the soil (Watts 1974; Scott 1979). In Barbados, accordingly, the removal of forest resulted not only in the permanent destruction of the faunal resource therein, but also in a substantial diminution of the island's nutrient store. The processes by which the latter is achieved operate rapidly. Following felling and burning, ash (which is particularly rich in calcium, magnesium and phosphorus) is added to top soil but on a temporary basis only for, denied the protective forest cover, leaching rates inevitably increase, leading to changes in the structure and the texture of the soil. Freshly-cleared forest soils almost invariably have a good surface layer of litter and an undecomposed fine surface rooting system, beneath which is a loose, well-aerated friable soil structure. But exposure to weathering, in particular to rain-drop impact, quickly leads to soil compaction, the infilling of soil pores, increased surface runoff, and in consequence greater chances of erosion even on slight slopes. Heavy rain encourages nutrient-rich litter to be washed downslope, and then other parts of the A-horizon are removed, representing an additional portion of the longer-term nutrient store. Such losses of soil nutrients, over and above those removed in forest clearance, should not be underestimated: elsewhere in the American tropics, three-year old soils from under a former forest cover have displayed totals of N, P, K, Ca and Mg which are respectively 21 %, 144 %, 43 %, 220 % and 280 % less than when they were first cleared

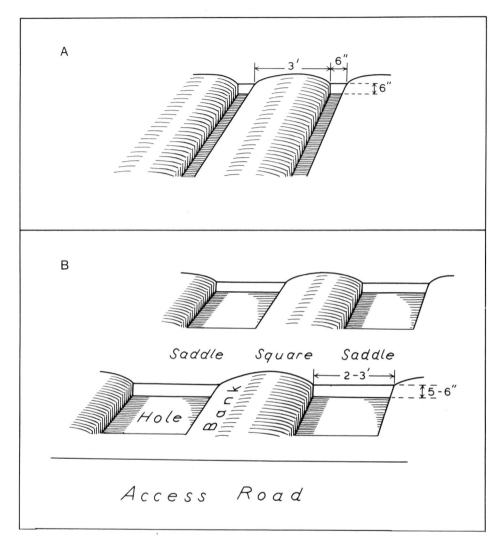

Fig 2 Sugar cane planting techniques
A. Trenches c. 1650 − c. 1700,   B. Ridged cane holes post c. 1700

(Scott 1979). Further, these losses appear to accelerate even more over time, a point very well understood by *conuco* agriculuralists who allowed the forest, with its nutrient store, to regenerate after a relatively short period of cultivation. To the severe loss of nutrients under systems of estate cultivation must be also added specific nutrient removal by crop harvesting which, in the case of cane sugar, was very high.

Tab 2 Population increase in the West Indies, 1660 to 1802

Year	Barbados	Jamaica	Northern Leewards[a]
1660	42,000	3,500	10,000
1670	50,000	14,000	11,000
1680	60,000	27,000	20,000
1690	68,000	40,000	24,000
1700	55,000	47,000	27,000
1713	61,000	62,000	39,000
1768	82,516	184,863	—
1773	87,080	—	—
1778	—	223,681	—
1783	73,601	—	—
1788	—	244,779	—
1802	80,063	—	—

Data from government and other censuses.

[a] The 'Northern Leewards' includes St. Kitts, Nevis and Antigua

Signs of these several processes were present early on land in Barbados which had been planted in cane. By 1661, none but the smallest traces of the natural forest remained (Watts 1966), the first general decrease in soil fertility being noted in the same year, when the President and Council of the island recorded that "the land is much poorer, and makes less sugar than heretofore" (Cal. Col. 1661−68, 45). Soil deterioration and soil loss were accentuated by the custom (adopted from c. 1650 to c. 1700) of planting cane in trenches regardless of slope angle and direction. Any downslope trench served as a channel in which soil particles could move very rapidly in the characteristically severe summer storm conditions, at a time when some land was left bare after cane harvest and prior to the next planting (Fig 2A). Demands for natural animal manure to replenish the soil became stringent towards the end of the seventeenth century, so much so that dung farms, devoted specifically to the commercial sale of animal fertilizer, became a feature of island life for a while (Watts 1972). Soil loss continued on such a scale, however, that by 1700 about one third of cane land had gone temporarily out of cultivation. Shortly thereafter, the custom of trench planting was replaced by a new technique in which canes were set in ridged, cane holes (Fig 2B) (Watts 1968). The baulking effect of the raised edges of the cane holes terminated in large measure the downslope movement of soil, and this in turn eventually resulted in much of the abandoned land being brought back into cultivation. But by then the environmental nutrient store had been greatly depleted, and yields of commercial and food crops alike immeasurably diminished.

These economic and environmental flaws in the estate agriculture of Barbados meant that large numbers of people (Tab 2), both black and white, found themselves dependent on a restricted and uncertain food supply.

From time to time severe food shortages, even outright famine, resulted and these were often initiated by a particular climatic event, such as a hurricane or drought. It was, however, the plantation system of cultivation and its concentration on the commercial crop which was the ultimate cause of them, rather than the physical events in themselves, a sequence of events that may be judged by the ease with which the former *conuco* food producing systems in the same environment had provided more than adequate nutritional supplies even during times of severe climatic stress. This view is further supported by the knowledge that during every instance of severe food shortage during the colonial period, large numbers of people left the island never to return. Even so, their departure did not alleviate the chronic underlying deficiencies in food production, at least until the mercantilist principles which controlled the plantation system were themselves modified towards the end of the eighteenth century.

The periods of food shortage and famine in Barbados are well documented. After the famine of 1649 to 1650, heavy rains destroyed most food crops in 1656 (Cal. Col. 1655−56, 451). Caterpillars and worms between them ate most of the food harvest in 1663, Governor Willoughby noting at the time that "the poorer sort of people, who are very numerous, have been hard put to it, and must have perished if they had not been supplied with victuals from New England ... some thousands have gone from Barbados" (Cal. Col. 1661−68, 167). The next major famine occurred during 1668−1675, initiated by a hurricane of moderate intensity in 1667, followed by severe drought the next year which accelerated the general decline in crop yields (Sheridan 1974), excessive rains in 1669, and a further prolonged drought in 1670. Food shortages continued until 1674, when another moderate hurricane struck the island, and then the most severe hurricane of the century virtually decimated crop production the following year. Within this period, undernourishment, together with an epidemic, had caused the death of many slaves and indentured servants by 1670. In 1672, a reasonably beneficent year in terms of climate, Willoughby recorded that the island "doth not furnish of its own growth one quarter victuals for its inhabitants" (Egerton Ms. 2395, 477). Another batch of white emigrants left for other parts of the New World. Peter Colleton wrote that some 2000 people emigrated in 1670 (Cal. Col. 1669−1674, 141), and the total number between 1668 and 1672 (most of them hitherto established planters) seems to have been between 4000 and 5000, many of them moving to Carolina, New York, New England and Jamaica, where land and food supplies were plentiful. But land was still available in Barbados for those who wanted it. I therefore feel, with Sheridan (1974), that it was more a shortage of food than of land which forced this population movement. Although food scarcity continued after 1672, emigration largely ceased because of the advent of the Third Dutch War (1672−74), which affected shipping movements in the region. However, it picked up again after the two hurricanes of 1674 and 1675, years in which adequate food supplies from New England failed to reach the island (Schomburgk 1848; Starkey 1939) resulting in the departure of another 2000 white planters, mainly for Jamaica, Carolina, New York, Virginia and New England (Chandler 1946).

Except for one difficult year in 1685, when food crops were lost through unspecified bad weather, the years between 1675 and 1697 were not remarkable for any major food shortages. But a further famine cycle commenced in 1697, lasting until 1710. By the former year, problems of soil exhaustion had become so acute that between one-third to one-half of the cultivated land of Barbados had been abandoned as infertile (Cal. Col. 1699, 518; Cal. Col. 1702, 49), and the need for locally-produced food was such that several schemes were mooted to reestablish 'provision plantations' (Cal. Col. 1697−98, 29), although there is no evidence that these were ever put into effect. The shortages were accentuated by a drought which lasted from 1700 to 1702, during which "many of the poor people for want of bread were forced to leave" (Cal. Col. 1702, 507). Food deficiencies continued until 1710, in which year it was stated that "the poor inhabitants have been starving, and forc'd to be relieved by publick contribution" (Walduck 1710−11). In the same year, a large part of the island was described as being "barren rocky gullies, runaway land, waste land, and all the rest worn out and not so fertile as it was" (Tracts on Trade 1710, 267). This period was marked by a major reduction in population (Tab 2). Thereafter, a minor revolution in local food crop production alleviated the problem of food deficiency a little. This was associated with the innovation of the cane hole system of planting (c. 1708), the rudiments of which have already been described (Fig 2). But a further feature of this system was that it allowed for the first time for the planting of food crops on cane land after the cane harvest, a practice which was quickly adopted by planters. Aroids, yams, sweet potatoes, maize and peas were all planted on the ridges between the cane holes from March to June in harvest years. The next crop of cane was often planted in the holes in November while the food crops were still growing, a custom which did not interfere with the growth of either, providing the latter were cropped and lifted by the end of January. These new cultivation methods largely eliminated food shortages in Barbados for the two decades subsequent to 1710, despite occasional bad years, as in 1715 when, following continued drought, the island suffered "a great scarcity of corne and all ground provisions" and unusually large quantities of maize had to be imported from North America to counteract the deficiencies (Cal. Col. 1714−15, 186).

It was a fall in the price of sugar, coupled with a classic economic squeeze and a combination of a hurricane and several years of drought, which initiated the next major period of food shortage in the island, between 1730 and 1735. A glut in European sugar markets produced a fall in the price of sugar of from 24/10 3/4d in 1728 to 16/11 1/4d in 1733 (Sheridan 1974) and this, along with a contemporary major increase in local taxation, meant that profit margins on estates were vastly reduced or entirely eliminated. At the same time, debts were called in by money-lenders and traders. The result was that many estates were abandoned (Cal. Col. 1735−36, 29), or their food-crop component decimated. The severe food shortages which began in 1731 owed their immediate inception, however, to the passage of another hurricane, which destroyed many crops and thus reduced the island's locally-produced food store still further. This situation was subsequently exacerbated by a prolonged drought which, particularly severe in 1732 and 1733, continued into the following year, when the Governor wrote of the "terrible prospect of having no crops this year by the excessive drought, the number of people running off, and the miserable condition and poverty of the island" (Cal. Col. 1734, 34). In a charity sermon, preached in Bridgetown in May of the same year, the clergyman stated that he beheld all the signs of an approaching major famine: "the face of the earth appeared, as it were, a dry crust, burnt up and gaping". In Christchurch parish, some people died through want of food, and from 1734−35, outmigration of families to the Dutch and Danish islands, Pennsylvania and Virginia (Schomburgk 1848) again increased.

Following this, agricultural production of cane and provision crops recovered, especially during the 1740's and 1750's and, although there were occasional bad years in which the sugar crop was reduced through bad weather, as in 1749 and 1750, no major shortages of food were reported until 1763—70, when there was a further period of famine. This appears to have been particularly severe in the northern parish of St. Philip, from which many white planters emigrated (Poyer 1808). Also during this time, a good deal of land which, over the years had proved to be marginal for good cane production, was taken out of the commercial crop and replanted with provisions, so adding substantially to the island's food crop resource (Bennett 1958). That the island was still largely dependent on imported food from the American colonies however, may be seen from the effect of the War of Independence on Barbadian food supplies from 1776 to 1778, when planters made representation to the British Government that provision stocks were running dangerously low and, in 1777, that famine was looming (Ragatz 1963). As a result of these pleas, six ships were sent with cargoes of flour, beans and peas from England, and a further two laden with fish, all arriving early in 1778. The War of Independence seems, however, to have brought home to Barbadian planters just how vulnerable were their food supplies to outside interference, and from that time additional efforts were made to increase the amount of local produce. The planting of yams, sweet potatoes, plantains and cassava was increased throughout the island (Pinckard 1806). More Guinea corn was grown, especially close to Bridgetown and in the dry southeast (Lucas 1819). Several new varieties were utilised in the extension of maize cultivation, and during the 1780's it was even grown in sufficient quantities for part of the crop to be exported to adjacent islands. Resulting from Bligh's expedition to the Pacific, a few exotic tree foods were introduced, including the breadfruit which, although it reached Barbados in the 1790's, was not widely taken up as a foodstuff until after emancipation. All in all, the island's food resource structure was better ensured after 1778 than during previous colonial times, and thereafter the occasional severe drought (1785) or hurricane (1781) (Addit. Ms. 35655, 228—9) seems merely to have given rise to a temporary minor shortage in supply rather than to any major famine (Haynes 1820; Waller 1820). In this at least, the planters had learnt from experience. Although they continued to remain dependent on some imports from North America (e.g. bread, flour, corn grain, meal, rice, salted meat, and eventually fish and fresh meat packed in ice: Allen 1784) — and indeed still do to some extent (Blume 1974) — they had begun to endow the plantation system with a degree of flexibility in management and operation which enabled it to produce sufficient provisions to tide them over during years of climate difficulty.

It is likely that these changes to the system had been initiated more by the efforts of individuals rather than by any government policy, a point delicately referred to by Governor Leith in 1814, when, speaking to planters, he stated: "The increased cultivation of provisions I also congratulate you upon, as a measure that is of great advantage; for it seems evident that whatever is produced under a well-regulated system of agriculture must generally be cheaper to the cultivator than to the purchaser: and the serious risk of disappointment in supplying your wants by importation, and the drain of specie from the colony, will thereby be diminished. I am aware that this is principally depending on individual industry, but it is a subject that can never be considered but as closely interwoven with the policy of the colony" (Schomburgk 1848).

Tab 3 Periods of food shortage and famine in Barbados, 1627 to 1830

Date	Food Shortage and Famine	Food Adequate	Comments
1647–1650	+		Few provision lands: beginning of sugar boom, large population
1651–1667		+	Destruction of forest, spread of cane agriculture, beginnings of soil depletion and erosion
1668–1675	+		Undernourishment: white emigration
1676–1696		+	Good weather conditions, adequate yields, but further decline in soil fertility
1697–1710	+		Soil erosion severe, with very poor yields, abandonment of estates. White emigration
1711–1729		+	Cane-hole system introduced and adopted
1730–1735	+		Severe weather, economic squeeze, abandonment of estates: white emigration
1736–1762		+	Steady agricultural production
1763–1770	+		Severe drought
1771–1774		+	More provision lands
1776–1780	+		War of Independence: interruption of North American food supplies
1781–1830		+	More provision lands: more provision crops

A general summary of the major periods of famine in Barbados throughout this period is given in Tab 3 along with the major innovations which sought to alleviate the problem.

Evidence from elsewhere in the West Indies

The full development of plantation agriculture in other English-speaking islands of the West Indies took place later than in Barbados, initially in the northern Leeward Islands (especially St. Kitts, Nevis and Antigua) and subsequently in Jamaica.

Towards the early years of the 18th century (Tab 4) the northern Leewards began to rival the worn-out lands of Barbados as a major sugar producing region, and these in turn were replaced after 1750 by Jamaica. Towards the end of the 18th century, the Ceded Islands of the Lesser Antilles – Tobago, Grenada, St. Vincent and Dominica, ceded to British control after the Treaty of Paris in 1763 – also became important producers of sugar. But after the 1740's until 1789 when revolution decimated estates, all sugar production from islands in the Caribbean region was dwarfed by that coming out of the French colony of Santo Domingo in the western part of Hispaniola (Haiti). Cane production in the other French islands (mainly Martinique and Guadeloupe) was always on a much smaller scale, reaching its peak in the 1750's.

Tab 4   Sugar imports into England and Wales, '000 cwts 1650—54 to 1770—74

Years	Barbados	Jamaica	Leeward Is.	Ceded Is.	St. Domingue [a]
1650—54	c. 75.0	—	—	—	
1655—59	c. 155.0	—	—	—	
1660—64	c. 143.5	—	c. 20.0	—	
1665—69	c. 190.5	c. 10.0	c. 33.6	—	
1670—74	?	c. 10.4	?	—	
1675—79	?	c. 34.1	c. 51.1	—	
1680—84	c. 200.0	c. 79.1	c. 66.1	—	
1685—89	?	c. 129.0	?	—	
1690—94	c. 183.8	c. 119.1	?	—	
1695—99	c. 187.5	c. 112.1	?	—	
1700—04	160.4	78.3	135.1	—	
1705—09	165.6	103.4	89.1	—	
1710—14	152.0	120.5	172.2	—	
1715—19	213.1	172.1	240.4	—	
1720—24	159.1	199.1	272.5	—	
1725—29	196.1	256.7	370.0	—	
1730—34	146.6	311.3	408.0	—	
1735—39	122.6	319.7	379.7	—	848.0
1740—44	139.5	326.6	320.1	—	
1745—49	125.2	307.0	347.1	—	
1750—54	132.7	411.8	341.0	—	
1755—59	142.7	511.9	450.4	—	
1760—64	172.2	633.1	414.3	104.9	
1765—69	159.8	669.0	455.0	112.4	1224.9
1770—74	133.0	832.7	439.8	272.5	

Data from Government reports

[a] St. Domingue figures are for production of cane

Although much of the evidence for periodic food shortages in the cane-planting economies of these other islands has not yet been worked over in detail, there is at least a *prima facie* case for supposing that they did occur from time to time, along with famine conditions. There also seems little doubt that the frequency and intensity of these occurrences varied considerably from island to island. All the islands did, however, have one major advantage over Barbados in respect of their food production potential. Many of the mistakes made in provision crop agriculture experienced in the latter island had already been largely corrected by the time that the other islands began to develop their own estate systems, so they were accordingly able to benefit from this. Also, the cane-hole system of planting was already widespread by the second decade of the eighteenth century, thus avoiding the worst excesses of soil loss derived from the earlier trench pattern of planting in the new sugar lands.

To begin with, the situation in the northern Leewards was akin to that in Barbados in that there was relatively little land available for food production, and in consequence food provision was largely dependent on imports from North America. Early on, the legislature of Nevis passed a law requiring that a certain amount of land on every estate be planted to provisions, but it is unlikely that this was ever enforced. Most of the provision plots that did exist were located in the mountains and tended by slaves, with yams, sweet potatoes, cassava and dasheen being the most common crops to be raised. No doubt, as in Barbados, the diet of both servants and slaves was deficient in protein, the major sources of which, apart from imported salt fish, were turtle eggs. As well, ship's rats which had escaped to become naturalised in cane fields, were eaten in Nevis by means of wrapping them in banana leaves, then baking them (Sloane 1707; Smith 1745). In contrast, the fish-rich waters of coasts and estuaries were not utilised.

In general, the quantity of provisions present in the northern Leewards was minimal, particularly in St. Kitts and Nevis, and food supplies were to a major extent always at risk. The worst time for food shortages was in the 1720's and 1730's. Between 1719 and 1723, four years of drought, followed by a hurricane late in the latter year, decimated food crops and cane fields alike. This was followed by nearly a decade of drought in the 1730's interspersed by a short period of heavy rains in 1732 and a crop blast in 1733 (Sheridan 1974). Crop yields were further reduced by dry weather in 1749 and 1750, with a hurricane the following year. Throughout these periods, provisions were maintained largely by imports from North America. In Antigua, by mid-century, some moves were already under way to try to increase the island's self-sufficiency in foodstuffs and, as in Barbados, these were again set in motion by individuals rather than by government. Thus the attorney of an estate at Winthorpe's Bay in 1745 planted ten or twelve acres (4 to 5 ha) of guinea corn on good land along with yams and sweet potatoes, thereby hoping "to have little expense for provisions this ensuing year" (Harris 1965). Samuel Martin, probably the most progressive and enterprising planter on the island at the time, allowed his slaves to cultivate some of the most fertile land on his estate for food crops, advising other planters to do likewise (Sheridan 1974). As much as one-third of his 600-acre (242 ha) estate was devoted to provision grounds and pasture, the rest to cane, but elsewhere in the island planters were less inclined to allot that much of their land to the raising of provisions.

The northern Leewards were particularly severely hit by the restrictions on trade associated with the American War of Independence, and subsequently Merrill (1958) notes that on many occasions at this time the islands pleaded an empty cupboard, the distress being most acute from 1787 to 1791. At one stage in the former year there was but a month's supply of food left in Nevis, and in July 1789 less than one week's supply in both St. Kitts and Nevis. At the same time, Antigua underwent a particularly severe drought which destroyed most food crops (Edwards 1801). Under the circumstances, normal trade restrictions were relaxed, emergency food being brought in from adjacent French, Spanish and Danish islands (Ragatz 1963).

Although still low in absolute terms, dietary standards were probably better in Jamaica than in any of the other English-speaking sugar islands prior to emancipation. There was more land available, and slaves were given land to plant their own corn and yams as a means of supplementing the food doled out by plantation owners (Dunn 1972; Mintz and Hall 1960). From the very beginning of cane development, provision plantations in the island were established alongside cane estates, of which there were many. Long (1744) indicates that there were 72,000 provision plantations in Jamaica in 1751, while in St. Andrew or Liguanea parish in the vicinity of present-day Kingston in 1753, 154 estates were listed, 128 of which produced no sugar at all (Pitman 1931). Of these, 8 had no land devoted to provisions or pasture but, on the remainder, all had provision plots ranging from 10 to 250 acres (4 to 100 ha) in size. However, estates which concentrated on the raising of cane did so, as in other islands, virtually to the exclusion of any other crop, and the prevailing philosophy of cane planters in Jamaica to the end of the century was expressed in a comment by Edwards (1793): "it is true economy to the planter, rather to buy provisions from others, than to raise them by his own labour. The product of a single acre of his cane fields will purchase more Indian corn than can be raised in five times that extent of land, and pay besides the freight". But in the event, despite the number of provision plantations, some major food shortages did occur from time to time. Food deficiencies developed in 1734 and 1751 as hurricanes crossed the island, but the worst decade was that of the 1780's when a combination of trade restrictions with North America, and extreme weather, created immense distress. In 1781 a tropical storm ravaged much of the island, and despite surplus military stores being placed at the planters' disposal, together with imported rice and corn from Georgia and South Carolina, famine soon developed and some thousands of slaves died of starvation. Even worse was to come in the middle years of the decade, marked as they were by severe hurricanes in 1784, 1785 and 1786. Though Jamaican ports were opened for the free importation of provisions during this period, famine again became rife and the number of slaves estimated to have died, either from actual starvation or from diseases caused by a scanty or unwholesome diet, has been calculated at 15,000 (Edwards 1793).

Little is known in detail about the situation in the French islands. Food crops were cultivated extensively in Martinique from the very beginning of European settlement; and French officials, attempting to enforce minimum dietary standards required planters to devote a percentage of their estates to provisions (Lasserre 1961). Moreover, certain food crop statistics were recorded as, for example, in 1736, when it was noted there were 4,806,142 banana trees, 34,583,000 trenches of cassava, with 247 plots of potatoes and yams listed for the island. However, Debien (1964) has suggested that most French planters underfed their slaves and that this population group was particularly vulnerable to famine situations. Indeed, there is little doubt (Sheridan 1970) that provisioning was always a problem in Martinique whenever shipping was interrupted, as occurred in the 1730's, when a combination of drought years and restrictions in food imports gave rise to a short period of famine.

Summary and Conclusions

The contrast between the stable aboriginal food-producing systems present in the West Indies prior to European colonisation, and the uncertainty of food availability under the plantation system of the same region in the seventeeth, eighteenth and early nineteenth centuries, is a striking one.

Ignorance of the delicate nature and nutrient balance of the tropical environment, poor land-management techniques, and severe socio-economic pressures within the colonial period all helped to exaggerate the adverse effects on cultivation of a sometimes less-than-beneficent climate instead of minimising them, as had been the case in the agricultural and cultural milieu of Indian times. The consequence was that the islands of plenty, characterised as such in terms of their food supplies by Colombus and many of the early Spanish settlers, quickly became islands associated with periodic famine, from which many settlers from time to time felt constrained to emigrate, and in which many others died from an inadequate nutritional intake. After emancipation, food shortages continued, although they were to some extent less prevalent, as freed slaves established many more provision grounds than were formerly present. All colonies, however, continued to depend in large measure on food imports, supplies of which were never entirely sure. On a more contemporary note, some of the problems of food production under the plantation system in the West Indies during colonial times, which have been described herein, clearly have important ramifications for present-day situations, especially for those seeking to impose simplistic ideas of intensive food or commercial crop-raising in similar, physically-complex, tropical habitats. The evidence suggests that these habitats yield food most successfully when they are treated gently, and utilised in the short term with long fallow periods interspersing those of cultivation, rather than when they are subjected to frontal, prolonged technologically intensive assaults.

Acknowledgements

The library research for this paper was undertaken with the assistance of grants from the Canada Council and McGill University, which are gratefully acknowledged. The diagrams were drawn by K. Scurr, of the Department of Geography, University of Hull.

References

Allen, J.: Considerations of the present state of the intercourse between His Majesty's sugar colonies and the Dominions of the United States of America. London 1784.

Anon.: Statement by Henry Powell to the Masters of Chancery, 20th February 1656. Papers relating to the history of Barbados. Georgetown, Guyana 1891.

Barrett, W.: Caribbean sugar production standards in the seventeenth and eighteenth centuries. In: J. Parker (ed.), Merchants and scholars, pp. 169–177, University of Minnesota Press, Minneapolis 1965.

Bennett, J.H.: Bondsmen and bishops: slavery and apprenticeship on the Codrington plantations of Barbados 1710–1838. University of California Press, Berkeley and Los Angeles 1958.

Biet, A.: Voyage de la France equinoxiale et l'Isle de Cayenne, enterpris par les français en l'année MDCLII. Paris 1664.

Blume, H.: The Caribbean islands. Longman, London 1974.

Boxer, C.R.: The Dutch in Brazil. Oxford University Press, Oxford 1957.

Bridenbaugh, C. and Bridenbaugh, R.: No peace beyond the line: the English in the Caribbean, 1624 to 1690. Oxford University Press, London 1972.

Campbell, P.F.: Merchants and traders of Barbados. Barbados Museum and Historical Society Journal, 34, 85–98 (1972)

Carneiro, R.L.: Slash and burn agriculture: a closer look at its implication for settlement patterns. In: E.K. Fisk (ed.), Men and cultures, pp. 229–234. 5th Congress of Anthropological and Ethnological Sciences 1956.

Carr, A.F.: Handbook of turtles: the turtles of the United States, Canada and Baja California. Ithaca, New York 1952.

Chandler, A.D.: The expansion of Barbados. Barbados Museum and Historical Society Journal, 13, 106–136 (1946)

Conklin, H.C.: Hanunoo agriculture: a report of an integral system of shifting cultivation in the Philippines. FAO, Rome 1957.

Cook, S.F. and Borah, W.: Essays in population history: Mexico and the Caribbean. 2 vols. University of California Press, Berkeley and Los Angeles 1971 and 1974.

Currey, B.: Famine in the Pacific: losing the chances for change. GeoJournal 4.5, 447−466 (1980)

Davis, D.D.: The strategy of early Spanish ecosystem management in Cuba. Journal of Anthropological Research 30, 294−314 (1974)

Debien, G.: La nourriture des esclaves sur les plantations des Antilles françaises aux XVIIe et XVIIIe siècles. Caribbean Studies 4, 3−27 (1964)

Deere, N.: The history of sugar. 2 vols. Chapman and Hall, London 1949 and 1950.

Denevan, W.M.: The native population of the Americas in 1492. University of Wisconsin Press, Madison 1976.

Dobyns, H.F.: Estimating aboriginal American populations: an appraisal of techniques, with a New Hemispheric estimate. Current Anthropology 7, 395−450 (1966)

Dunn, R.S.: Sugar and slaves: the rise of the planter class in the English West Indies, 1624 to 1713. Johnathan Cape, London 1972.

Edwards, B.: The history, civil and commercial, of the British colonies in the West Indies, 2 vols. London 1793.

Edwards, B.: An historical survey of the island of St. Domingo. London 1801.

Franke, R.W. and Chasin, B.H.: Seeds of famine: ecological destruction and the development dilemma in the West African Sahel. Oxford University Press, London 1980.

Galloway, J.H.: The Mediterranean sugar industry. Geographical Review 67, 177−194 (1977)

Handy, E.S.C. and Handy, E.G.: Native planters in old Hawaii: their life, lore and environment. Bernice P. Bishop Museum Bulletin, 233. Bishop Museum Press, Honolulu, Hawaii 1972.

Harlow, V.T.: A history of Barbados, 1625 to 1685. Oxford University Press, Oxford 1926.

Harris, D.R.: Plants, animals and man in the outer Leeward Islands, West Indies. University of California Publications in Geography, 18 (1965)

Harris, D.R.: The ecology of swidden vegetation in the upper Orinoco rain forest, Venezuela. Geographical Review, 61, 475−495 (1971)

Hawtayne, G.H.: A cavalier planter in Barbados. Timehri 7, 21 (1893)

Haynes, R.: Notes by General Robert Haynes of Newcastle, Clifton Hall and the Bath plantations in the island of Barbados. London 1820.

Hill, A.F.: Economic botany. McGraw-Hill, New York 1952.

Labat, P.: Nouveau voyage aux isles de l'Amérique. 6 vols. P. Husson, La Haye 1724.

Las Casas, B. de.: Historia de las Indias. Madrid 1520−61.

Lasserre, G.: La Guadeloupe. Bordeaux 1961.

Ligon, R.: A true and exact history of the island of Barbados. London 1657.

Long, E.: The history of Jamaica. 3 vols. London 1774.

Lucas, W.: Guinea corn, false corn, flag corn. Lucas Ms., 29, 37−41. Bridgetown Library, Barbados 1819.

Merrill, G.C.: The historical geography of St. Kitts and Nevis, the West Indies. Instituto pan Americano de Geografia e Historia, Mexico DF 1958.

Mintz, S. and Hall, D.: The origins of the Jamaican internal marketing system. Yale University Publications in Anthropology 57, 3−26 (1960)

Newson, L.: Aboriginal and Spanish colonial Trinidad. Academic Press, London, New York and San Francisco 1976.

Nietschmann, B.: Between land and water: the subsistence economy of the Miskito indians, eastern Nicaragua. Seminar Press, New York and London 1973.

Pares, R.: Merchants and planters. Economic History Review, Supplement 4, 1−91 (1960)

Parsons, J.J.: The green turtle and man. University of Florida Press, Gainesville, Florida 1962.

Pinckard, G.: Notes on the West Indies. London 1806.

Pitman, F.W.: The settlement and financing of British West India plantations in the eighteenth century. New Haven, Connecticut 1931.

Poyer, J.: The history of Barbados. London 1808.

Ragatz, L.J.: The fall of the planter class in the British Caribbean, 1763 to 1833. Octagon Books, New York 1963.

Raynal, Abbé: A philosophical and political history of the east and west Indies. tr. J.O. Justamond. 8 vols. London 1788.

Rogers, D.J.: Some botanical and ethnological considerations of *Manihot esculenta*. Economic Botany 19, 367–377 (1965)

Rosenblatt, A.: La población de América en 1492: viejos y nuevos calculos. El Colégio de México 1967.

Rouse, W.R. and Watts, D.: Two studies in Barbadian climatology. Climatological Research Series No. 1, McGill University 1966.

Sauer, C.O.: The early Spanish Main. University of California Press, Berkeley and Los Angeles 1966.

Schmitt, R.C.: Famine mortality in Hawaii. Journal of Pacific History 5, 109–115 (1970)

Schomburgk, R.H.: The history of Barbados. London 1848.

Scott, G.A.J.: Grassland development in the Gran Pajonal of eastern Peru: a study of soil-vegetation nutrient systems. Hawaii Monographs in Geography No. 1. University of Hawaii at Manoa, Honolulu 1979.

Scott, J.: The description of Barbados. Sloane Manuscripts 3662, 56–62. British Museum c. 1667.

Sheridan, R.B.: The development of the plantations to 1750. Caribbean Universities Press, Kingston, Jamaica 1970.

Sheridan, R.B.: Sugar and slavery: an economic history of the British West Indies. Caribbean Universities Press, Barbados 1974.

Sloane, Sir H.: A voyage to the islands of Madera, Barbados, Nieves, S. Christopers and Jamaica. 2 vols. London 1707.

Smith, W.: A natural history of Nevis and the rest of the English Leeward Charibbee islands in America. Cambridge 1745.

Spitz, P. (ed.): Famine risk in the modern world. UNRISD, Geneva 1976.

Starkey, O.T.: The economic geography of Barbados. New York 1939.

Sturtevant, W.C.: Taino agriculture. The evolution of horticultural systems in native South America: causes and consequences, pp. 69–82, J. Wilbert (ed.). Anthropologica, Supplement 3 (1961)

Sturtevant, W.C.: The ethnography of some West Indian starches. The domestication and exploitation of plants and animals, pp. 177–199, P.J. Ucko and G.W. Dimbleby (eds.). Duckworth, London 1969.

Thomas, D.: An historical account of the rise and growth of the West Indian colonies. London 1960.

Walduck, J.: Letters respecting Barbados, 1710 to 1711. Sloane Mss. 2302. British Museum, London 1710 to 1711.

Waller, J.A.: A voyage in the West Indies. London 1820.

Watts, D.: Man's influence on the vegetation of Barbados, 1627 to 1800. Occasional Papers in Geography No. 4. University of Hull 1966.

Watts, D.: Origins of Barbados cane-hole agriculture. Barbados Museum and Historical Society Journal 32, 143–151 (1968)

Watts, D.: Dung-farming: a seventeenth-century experiment in Barbadian agricultural improvisation. Barbados Museum and Historical Society Journal 34, 58–63 (1972)

Watts, D.: Biogeochemical cycles and energy flows in environmental systems. In: I.R. Manners and M.W. Mikesell (eds.), Perspectives on environment, pp. 24–56. Association of American Geographers, Washington DC 1974.

Groups of manuscripts used in the preparation of this paper have been abbreviated as follows:

Addit. Ms.: Additional Manuscripts, British Museum, London.
Cal. Col.: Catalogue of State Papers, Colonial Series, British Museum, London.
Egerton Ms.: Egerton Manuscripts, British Museum, London.

Spatial and Temporal Patterns of Famine in Southern India before the Famine Codes

Murton, B., Professor, Department of Geography, The University of Hawaii, Honolulu, HI 96822, USA

Abstract: Differences in scale and origin of source materials allow varying levels of historical analysis. Spatial and temporal patterns of famine in Madras Presidency before 1880, in particular those recorded in the *Jamabandi* or Annual Settlement Reports in Salem District, are examined. Improved understanding of contemporary famine vulnerability, the operation of famine warning systems, together with relief and rehabilitation strategies, may be possible from this archival data at the local level.

Introduction

Famine in India has been the subject of a large number of studies from a variety of perspectives. In most histories, even economic ones, all but the most catastrophic famines are relegated to a few lines at the end of a chapter, or to a short chapter which in one way or another gives the impression that famine was an interruption of "normal" processes (for example, Raghavaiyangar 1893; Digby 1901; Raju 1941; Kumar 1965), rather than being a normal event. Those historical surveys of famine which do exist (for example, Bhatia 1963, 1967; Mukherjee 1965; Srivastava 1966, 1968; Ambirajan 1971, 1976, 1978; McAlpin 1974, 1979; Morris 1974, 1979) place special emphasis upon the events that "triggered" famine, most often a natural disaster such as drought or flood.

The dimensions of famine which have been ignored in these accounts are the relationship between the nature of the source materials and the scale of enquiry, and the variation of famine over area and through time. Chronological lists of famines and scarcities in southern India after 1780 certainly exist in legion and the various Famine Commissions produced maps, many of which have been reproduced by historians working on famines. But there are serious limitations inherent in these lists and maps because they are based upon particular types of materials gathered at a certain scale of enquiry. This paper deals with these limitations in relationship to the spatial and temporal patterns of famine in the Madras Presidency before the publication of the *Report* of the first Famine Commission in 1880 (Great Britain, *Report of the Indian Famine Commission*, 1880).

The Importance of Scale and Nature of Sources

Any complete study of famine must entail a consideration of various process operating on different scales. Scales of utmost importance, because the size of the observed area and community affects not only the intensity of perception, but also the kinds of generalisations

Tab 1 Famine in inscriptions: Eleventh to sixteenth centuries

Date	Locality	Some Details
1054	Alangudi, Tanjore	Failure of rain, temple helps
1116–1119	Deccan	
1124	Tiruvathur, Tanjore	Severe inundation
1160	Tirrukkadayur, Tanjore	Drought, failure of crops
1201	Tiruppamburam, Tanjore	Price of padi rises, temple helps
1241	Tirumangalakkudi, Tanjore	Migration
	Nandalur, Cuddapah	
1387–1395	Deccan	State helps
1390–1391	Tirukkalar, North Arcot	Drought, price of padi rises
1509	Kankanhalli, Bangalore	

Source: Appadorai 1936, p. 748.

that can be made. In fact, the level of general conclusions will differ with scale and there would not be so many disputes about the validity of generalisations if people took careful note of the scale of investigation on which the findings were based (Webb 1976). Certainly, the factors predisposing a community to famine vary depending upon the scale of enquiry. For example, factors that affect famine vulnerability at a national scale, such as inflation or the lack of agricultural statistics for famine forecasting, may not operate at the regional scale, where drought or flood may be more directly important. At any given scale of enquiry, of course, famine vulnerability may be affected by factors operating at other scales: a village dependent upon an export crop is vulnerable to famine because of factors at the global scale such as changes in consumer tastes or preference.

Unfortunately, the nature of the sources prejudice the details in which we can view famines in the past. The evidence for the occurence of famine in pre-British southern India is obviously incomplete and locationally biased.

There are five basic sources of information about famines. First, there are "legendary" famines, fundamentally ones of which the memory was kept alive by oral tradition. For example, according to stories from Ganjam District, the *Dvadasavarsha Panjam*, which is undated, is supposed to have lasted twelve years. The *Durga Deves* famine which began in 1396 in the Deccan also lived on in oral tradition. A second category of source materials are Indian writings, including the Vedas, the Jataka stories, and the Arthashastra. While these deal with the northern part of the country, they indicate that famine has an ancient history in India. For southern India, a seventh century famine in Tanjore District due to absence of rain and floods in the Kaveri is mentioned in the *Periya Puranam (Hemingway* 1906). On this occasion the Tamil saints, Sambandhar and Appar, were helped by Siva to relieve distress.

For famine before the sixteenth century, stone and metal inscriptions are the primary source of information, as indeed they are for all aspects of society and economy in southern India (Stein 1980). Thousands of these inscriptions have been noted in the annual reports of the Epigraphical Department of the Government of Madras (Tamil Nadu) and India, and those of several princely states. As well, the texts of many inscriptions have been published. Our knowledge of famines in southern India in the eleventh, twelfth, and thirteenth centuries comes mostly from these inscriptions which are also important, albeit not the only, sources for the fourteenth, fifteenth, and sixteenth centuries. For example an inscription records the famine which occurred at Alangudi in Tanjore District in 1054, and notes that at Koviladi nearby, "times became bad, the village was ruined, and the cultivation flood" (Hemingway 1906). Most of the inscriptions describe the cause of the famine, its location, and the details of any response on the part of the affected population (Tab 1).

The writings of Muslim historians provide information on famines in the Deccan portion of southern India during the fifteenth century. Firishtah (II, 1908–1910), for example, records two of these famines, 1423–1424 and 1472. From the sixteenth century onwards, the primary sources of information are European trading company records, travellers' accounts, and the records of the Madurai Jesuit Mission. From the late sixteenth century onwards, the extent and degree of coverage of famine in the records is much more extensive than previously (Tab 2).

Tab 2   Some famines mentioned in European sources

Date	Locality	Source
1570	Tinnevelly Coast	Portuguese Mission
1614	Chingleput and South Arcot Districts	Madurai Jesuit Mission
1618–1619	Chingleput, South Arcot, North Arcot, Cuddapah, Anantapur, Bellary, Kurnool Districts	Madurai Jesuit Mission
1648	Coimbatore District	Madurai Jesuit Mission
1659–1661	Trichinopoly, Tanjore, Madurai Districts	Madurai Jesuit Mission
1677	Madurai	Madurai Jesuit Mission
1687	Kurnool, Bellary, Cuddapah, Anantapur Districts	Dutch East India Company Records
1709–1721	Madurai District	Madurai Jesuit Mission
1733	Chingleput District	British East India Company Records
1780–1782	Chingleput, South Arcot, North Arcot	British East India Company Records
1790–1793	Ganjam, Vizagapatam Godavari Districts	British East India Company Records

In the century before the establishment of the first Famine Commission in 1880, it becomes possible to document the occurrence and severity of famine and scarcity in Madras Presidency in some detail. In the first place, each of the administrative districts has both a *Manual*, compiled between the 1870s and the early 1890s and a *Gazetteer*, compiled in the first two decades of the twentieth century (Scholberg 1970). While these sources list only the major scarcities and famines, they nevertheless give us an overview of the entire Presidency, although not without some inconsistency and bias. For example, the Gazetteer record for Salem states that:

> Four times during the nineteenth century scarcity deepened into famine with all its terrible concommitants, namely in 1833, in 1866, 1877−78 and 1891−92. There was acute distress also in 1845 and 1857, dates which suggest a cyclic recurrency of famine once in eleven years (Richards, 1918).

Another source of information about famine at the regional scale are Statistical Atlases of the Madras Province. The first of these was published in 1895 (Benson 1895) and subsequent volumes appeared in 1913, 1949, and 1965 (Government Press, Madras 1913, 1949, 1965). They contained times-series statistics and descriptive information, including material on scarcities and famine for each of the Districts of the Presidency.

These sources, which are selective syntheses of correspondence and reports from District Collectors to the Board of Revenue, permit us to obtain a general picture of the occurrence of famine and of scarcity, and some comprehension of the "triggers", the precipitating events. But they do not give us much understanding of the causes of famine, other than at the most facile level, neither do they tell us much about famine warning systems, or responses to them both at official or administrative levels, nor at the scale of local populations. They do permit us, however, to gain some insight into areas of famine vulnerability, and of increasing vulnerability.

However, if we begin to utilize archival materials we can further refine our scale of analysis. In Madras Presidency, the Government was directly involved in settling and collecting land revenue, apart from a few areas where previous chieftains became *zamindars*, and others where a permanent revenue settlement with newly created *zamindars* was established. This system, administered by a Board of Revenue down through a hierarchy of administrative units (Districts and taluks), generated an enormous amount of material (Murton 1970). The *Proceedings* of the Board of Revenue (henceforth P.B.R. in citations) contain correspondence between both the Board and the Governor-in-Council, and the Board and District Collectors. The latter contain the *jamabandi* or annual settlement reports for each district, together with special *ad hoc* reports by local officers. It is these two kinds of materials that contain data of great value for analysis of land and people. Revenue was naturally the prime concern of the authorities, but the collection of revenue necessarily involved an occasional examination of the economic condition of the country, since the annual settlement reports were expected to deal with every subject of economic interest. Detailed instructions were issued by the Board of Revenue to obtain "every information which may tend to promote the prosperity and improvement of the country and ease the happiness of the people" (P.B.R. 31 July 1794). Although Collectors usually confined themselves to details of revenue settlement and collection, statistical data are available in these reports for every *taluk* of every district in the Presidency. For example, there are statistics on cultivated area, waste land, assessment rates, the weather, state of the season, estimated crop production, grain prices, number and condition of different irrigation sources population, migration, number of cultivators, number of shops, number of looms, number of livestock, and number of ploughs. Frequently detailed information relating to special questions raised by the Board of Revenue is also in the annual settlement reports.

It is these records that provide us with District scale data on the state of the season, on scarcity, and on famine. In the District considered in this paper, Salem, all of the *jamabandi* after 1822 contain this kind of information. Between 1800 and 1820, the *jamabandi* are more perfunctory, because between 1800 and 1805 the District was placed under the *Zamindari* system of revenue management. However, many of the estates gradually reverted to direct government control, and the *ryotwari* system of revenue management was reinstated. Information about the state of the season between 1800 and 1820 is thus scattered and less precise. For Salem, we also have information for the 1790s in the *Proceedings* of the Board of Revenue and in the series of volumes called the *Records of Salem and the Baramahal*. These records also contain an assessment of the seasons and harvests from 1774 to 1792.

While it is difficult to assess the general reliability of the data in these materials, it should nevertheless be remembered that the details were compiled by persons working in the field. Admittedly, the materials do reflect the view of a handful of Englishmen. In this sense the data contain certain cultural biases, especially about the causes of famine. We suggest, however, that the sources give us a reasonably accurate account of what was actually happening in regard to the weather and the crops in relationship to scarcity and, ultimately, famine.

Famines before the British

Famine had long been part of life in that part of southern India which became the Madras Presidency in the nineteenth century. The area has always been prey to natural disaster – drought, flood, tropical cyclone, insect infestations – and warfare between major kingdoms and empires was relatively common, particularly after 1400 AD. Although a complete account of the pre-European period of Indian history is nonexistent, the evidence suggests that a major famine took place every forty years (Dando 1980). What evidence we have from Madras Presidency suggests that from the twelfth century onwards, the incidence of famine may have been more frequent than this, but certainly nowhere near as often as in the eighteenth and nineteenth centuries.

Until the sixteenth century, the knowledge of the patterns of famine occurrence is incomplete, and reflects the relative distribution of the evidence, as well as the natural and human factors which cause famine (Tab 3). From the twelfth century to the sixteenth century, the study area averaged two to three major famines each century. All of these can be attributed to natural causes, either drought or flood. We should note that the prevalence of famine in the Deccan in the late fourteenth century, and none of the Deccan famines (1412–1413, 1423, and 1472) of the fifteenth century are included in this counting. We suspect that they would have ravaged Bellary, Cuddapah, Anantapur, and Kurnool Districts (Fig 1), but there is no published record of them in these Districts.

This reflects one of the biases in the sources: the data is best in areas that were relatively heavily populated, and which were the centres of kingdoms with important temples. This is certainly the case in Tanjore District, which suffered from at least twelve years of famine over the centuries before 1799 (Fig 2). We also note some evidence for famines in the drier interior of the peninsular in the thirteenth and fourteenth centuries (Cuddapah and North Arcot) and, as noted, it is speculated that much of this part of the study area was also affected by famine in the fourteenth and fifteenth centuries.

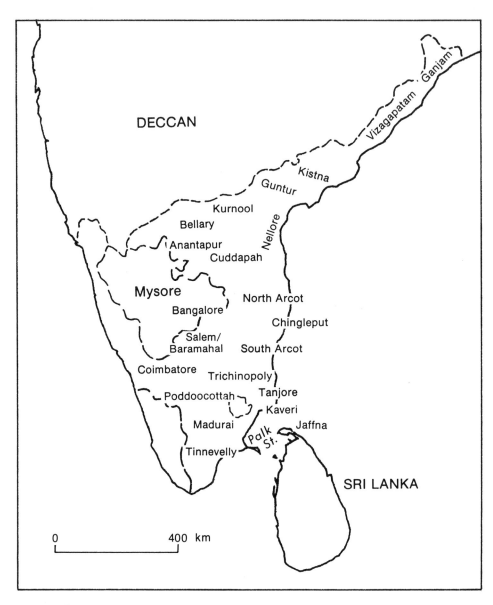

Fig 1 Reference map

Between 1500 and 1599, known famines, located in the coastal tracts of the southern and central coasts, most certainly reflect the type of source material. Once again, comprehensive coverage by European accounts become available after 1600 and not only does the number of famine years per century greatly increase (eighteen in the seventeenth, and

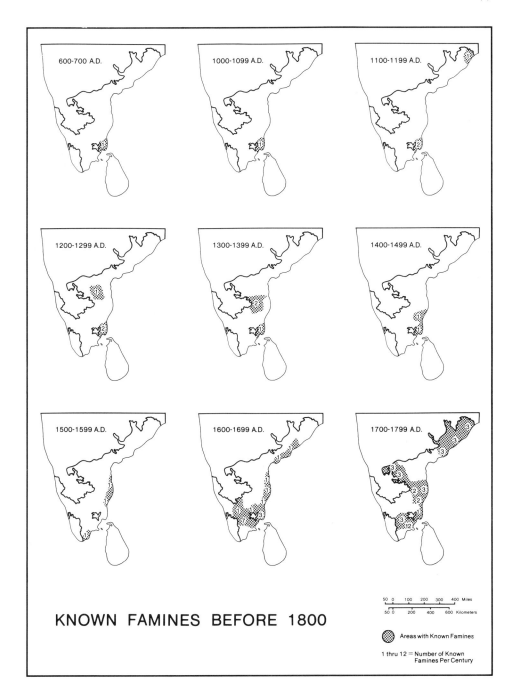

Fig 2 Spatial patterns of famines in Madras Presidency before the British period

Tab 3 Causes of major pre-British-famines

Date	Cause
1054	Drought
1124	Flood
1390—1391	Drought
1396	Drought
1472	Drought
1540	Drought
1614	Civil war
1648	Drought
1659—1662	Warfare, drought
1677	Flood
1709—1721	Drought
1733	Neglect of irrigation facilities
1780—1782	Warfare
1790—1793	Drought

thirty-eight in the eighteenth century), but the distribution is also more widespread. The causes of famine also began to change because, in addition to drought and flood, warfare and neglect of irrigation facilities became siginificant (Tab 3). Indeed, the more devasting famines during the seventeenth and eighteenth centuries were the outcome of the break-down of order, accompanied by drought or flood. In southern India from the late sixteenth century onwards, Muslim invasions, warfare between various Hindu warrior states, and in the eighteenth century between the British, the French, and the so-called "country-powers", meant that the countryside was in constant economic, social, and political turmoil. Under these conditions, any slight variation in factors which contributed to food production or distribution resulted in famine.

Famines 1780—1880

The Presidency Scale

(a) The Temporal Dimension

From the beginning of British territorial control in Madras in the late eighteenth century, gazetteers and statistical accounts documented cases of natural calamities, famines, and scarcities (Fig 3). Cycles of famine, initially apparent from these sources must, however, be treated with scepticism since the cycles probably reflect the history of this type of record, rather than the actual history of the occurrences of famine. The greatly increased number of famine years during the period 1780—1880 may simply reflect more detailed reporting of famines although we suggest, along with other scholars (Dutt 1900; Bhatia 1963; Srivastava 1968), that the introduction of new social, economic, and administrative

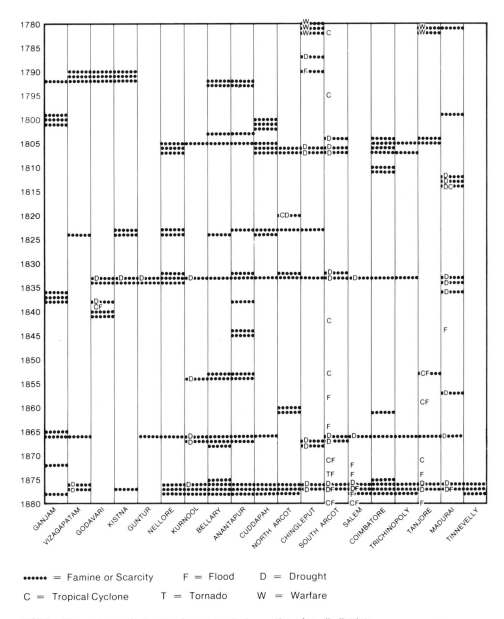

●●●●● = Famine or Scarcity   F = Flood   D = Drought

C = Tropical Cyclone   T = Tornado   W = Warfare

NOTE : The pattern of disaster frequency is incomplete for all districts

Fig 3 The temporal patterns of natural calamities, famins and scarcities by district in Madras Presidency from 1780–1880 derived from gazetteers and statistical accounts.

structures plus the influence of economic ideas on famine policy, created a syndrome in which a disruption, be it natural or man-made, could have been seen as famine "triggers".

Certainly, widespread famines occurred in 1790−1792, 1799−1801, 1806−1807, 1823−24, 1832−33, 1866−1867, and 1876−1878, with more localized ones in 1780−1782, 1812−1813, 1836−1838, 1844−1845, 1854 and 1860. The juxtaposition of calamities and famines throughout this period strengthens the evidence of an association of famine with natural hazard. The latter appears to trigger the former, a large proportion of the recorded famines and scarcities occurring in the same year, or in the year immediately following the recording of a calamity. However, famines certainly did occur without any natural calamity being recorded. Natural hazards also occurred without "triggering" famines, especially if the natural event was localized. Certain disasters appeared to have triggered famines more than others. Droughts, floods, and tropical cyclones were strongly associated with famines. Of course, flooding was limited to riverine and deltaic tracts, while tropical cyclones severely affected only low-lying coastal areas. Drought was much more pervasive and was the primary "trigger" for famines of great areal extent. Often, several events in combination either "triggered" or deepened a famine. This occurred in Godavari in 1838−1841, and in Salem and Madurai in 1876−1878.

(b) The Spatial Dimension

As already noted, some famines were quite localized whereas others covered much of the Presidency (Fig 4). That of 1780−1782, caused by warfare, was confined to Chingleput and parts of adjoining districts. Droughts and floods affected the same area in 1790−92, but during these years the areas worst hit were Bellary and Anantapur Districts in the interior, together with Ganjam, Vizagapatam, Godavari, and Kistna Districts on the northern coast. In 1805−1807 scarcities occurred in Tanjore and Salem, while true famine conditions wracked Bellary, Kurnool, Anantapur, Cuddapah, Nellore, North Arcot, Chingleput, South Arcot, Trichinopoly, and Coimbatore. Severe scarcity was experienced in Coimbatore and Madurai in 1812−1813 (Fig 1). In 1823−1824 famine conditions existed over a wide swathe of the northern interior and coastal district, except for Ganjam, Godavari, and Guntur. The famine of 1832−33 was particularly widespread, and was especially severe in Guntur (it is known als the "Guntur Famine'). Famine conditions, including intense conditions, were restricted to the northern interior districts in 1854. In 1866−1867 extreme famine occurred in Ganjam and Bellary, famine in the remainder of the northern districts, except for Godavari and Kistna, slight scarcities in the central parts of the Presidency, while normal conditions prevailed in the south. The worst famine of the century was that of 1876−1878. The northern coastal districts escaped famine entirely, but elsewhere in the northern and central areas of the Presidency, famine of exceptional severity took its toll. The southern districts were touched by "normal" famine conditions.

From this general summary, despite incomplete information from this scale of record, certain areas emerged as being more vulnerable to famine than others as the nineteenth century proceeded. We can eliminate the famine of 1780−1782 from consideration. It was caused by warfare, a condition which did not occur on a large scale in southern India after 1800. Every district experienced famine and scarcity throughout the period. However, the southern districts clearly appear to have been the least vulnerable in terms of famine,

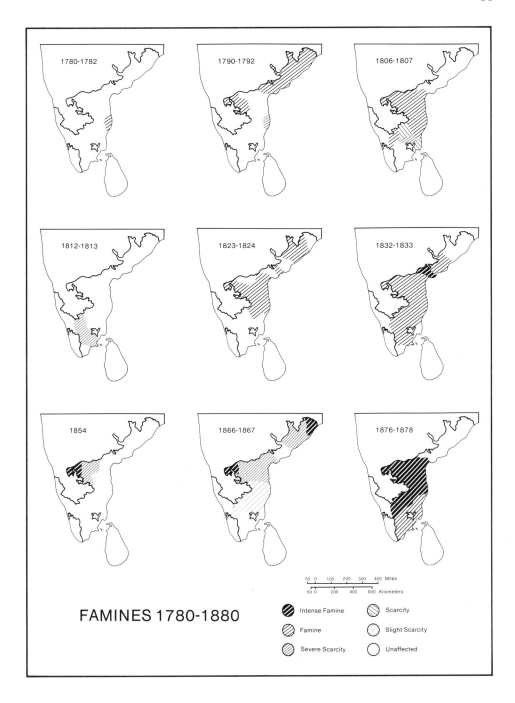

Fig 4 The spatial patterns of famines and scarcities in Madras Presidency 1780–1880.

although numerous scarcities are recorded. Tanjore and Tinnevelly, for example, were only stricken in the 1876–1878 famine. During the nineteenth century, the irrigation facilities in Tanjore were greatly expanded. Similarly, in Kistna and Godavari, irrigation facilities were greatly developed. Here, the creation of over a half million acres of rice land was the work of Sir Arthur Cotton in the 1840s and 1850s. After this period, agriculture in these districts was relatively secure.

Basically, then it was the rain, river-fed, tank-irrigated areas or the dry interior tracts that were most vulnerable to famine. For example, Bellary recorded no fewer than fifteen famines or scarcities, three of which were especially severe. The other northern and central coastal and interior Districts also recorded large numbers of famines or scarcities, although Guntur with but three (one particularly severe) does not appear to have been as vulnerable. Salem and Coimbatore both had one severe episode, as well as many lesser famines and scarcities.

The District Scale

The use of more detailed records, especially the *Jamabandi* or Annual Settlement Reports and special Season Reports, give us insight into scarcity and famine at the District Scale. To demonstrate how this type of source at this scale can change our perspective on famine, information from one District, Salem (Fig 1), is used.

(a) State of the Season, 1773–1822.

In the twenty years before the British took control of Salem District, "full" dry crops were harvested in only five years *(Land Rent,* The Baramahal Records 1918). In seven years, three-quarter crops were produced; in five years, half crops; in two years, three-eighth crops; and in one year, a quarter crop. The worst years were 1778–79, 1785–86, and 1790–91. In these years the "crops were thin" *(Land Rent,* The Baramahal Records 1918), and during the period 1790 to 1793 only one crop of dry grain was cultivated in the Talaghat (MacLeod to Read, 29 June 1793, The Records of Salem and the Baramahal, 1791–1800, MSS). The drought of 1792–93 was acknowledged as the "worst for many years" (Read to Haliburton, 29 January 1793, *Miscellany,* The Baramahal Records 1925). Further comments, by British officers in the 1790s, indicate that drought hazard at that time was no less than it is today. It was well-known

That the rains are extremely precarious and that when they do fall, they are either partial and scanty, or if plentiful, that the season has passed and the only purpose they serve as at present is from their violence to destroy half the tanks in the country. How often has the farmer, deceived by a passing shower, imprudently committed his seed to the ground, and how often have his hopes of a return been blasted by a succeeding drought, equally fatal to his crops, as to his cattle. (Graham to Read, 24 August 1797, *Review,* The Baramahal Record 1933).

In addition, there is a three year statistical record of daily temperatures, together with a descriptive record of precipitation in the 1790s for Krishnagiri *(Geography,* The Records of Salem and the Baramahal, 1791–1800, MSS). The modern mean monthly temperatures correspond closely with the means for the 1790s, and the precipitation also followed much the same pattern as it does today. Between 1793 and 1798, the first

Tab 4 Partial assessment of state of the seasons, Salem District, 1800–1822

State of Season	Number of Years	Dates
Very Favourable	1	1800–1801
Favourable	1	1811–1812
Somewhat Less Favourable	1	1814–1815
Unfavourable	9	1802–1803, 1803–1804, 1806–1807, 1810–1811, 1812–1813, 1816–1817, 1817–1818
Very Unfavourable	4	1807–1808, 1813–1814, 1818–1819, 1819–1820.
Famine	0	

rains usually fell between April 15 and 28 " and continued with intervals of frequently a week till June, when they became heavy and often lasted several days" (Geography, The Records of Salem and the Baramahal, 1791–1800, MSS). This was followed by dry weather, with more and more cloud until mid-September, when the Northeast Monsoon set "and continues with intervals of fair weather through all of October and November, when fair weather begins and lasts to April" (Geography, The Records of Salem and the Baramahal, 1791–1800, MSS).

Between 1800 and 1822 we have information on the state of the season for only fourteen of the years (Tab 4). Essentially, this information represents an official assessment of how climatic and other natural conditions affected harvest outcome and yields. There were no famines in Salem during this period, but there were four very unfavourable and seven unfavourable seasons, that is 50 % of the seasons falling into these catagories. Elsewhere in the Presidency, 1806–1807 was a famine year. In Salem it was merely unfavourable, although it did cause hardship. The Collector reported that in Attur Taluk "the present calamitous year has been so highly injurious to the ryots that I very much doubt if it will be even in their power to fulfill their arrangements" (P.B.R., 23 March, 1807). However, in Salem, there was enough grain on hand so that although the crops failed in places, there was not an immediate want of grain (Salem District Records, 19 May, 1807). In the season of 1810–1811, the rains came late, and this was again the case in 1814. The season of 1817 was thought to be "calamitous", although the part of the District lying on the Mysore tableland had a very favourable year (P.B.R., 21 September, 1818). But in 1818–1819 the season was "bad" everywhere (P.B.R., 20 September, 1819; P.B.R., 25 October, 1819).

(b) State of the Season, 1822–1880

The record of assessment of the state of the season for this period is complete (Fig 5). It confirms the fragmentary pattern of 1773–1822, the one constant feature being the variability from one year to the next. Good years were followed by bad, bad by average, and in four years very unfavourable conditions deepened into famine (1832–1833, 1866–1867, 1876–1878).

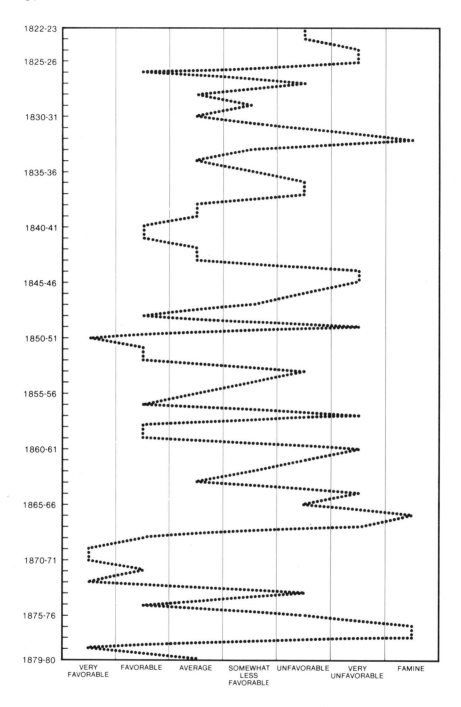

Fig 5 Official assessment of the state of the season: Salem District.

Tab 5 Assessment of the state of the season, Salem District, 1822–1880

State of the Season	Number of Years	Dates
Famine	4	1832–33, 1866–67, 1876–78.
Very Unfavourable	9	1824–25, 1825–26, 1845–46, 1846–47, 1849–50, 1857–58, 1860–61, 1864–65, 1867–68.
Unfavourable	10	1822–23, 1823–24, 1827–28, 1831–32, 1836–37, 1837–38, 1853–54, 1861–62, 1873–74, 1875–76.
Somewhat Less Favourable	6	1829–30, 1833–34, 1835–36, 1847–48, 1854–55, 1862–63.
Average	9	1828–29, 1830–31, 1834–35, 1838–39, 1839–40, 1842–43, 1843–44, 1863–64, 1879–80.
Favourable	11	1826–27, 1840–41, 1841–42, 1848–49, 1851–52, 1852–53, 1856–57, 1858–59, 1859–60, 1868–69, 1871–72, 1874–75.
Very Favourable	5	1850–51, 1869–70, 1870–71, 1872–73, 1878–79.

Tab 5 shows that unfavourable or worse seasons were balanced out by those which were average or better, but this must be seen as small consolation when twenty-three of the fifty-eight years had much less than desirable outcomes. Particularly bad times were experienced between 1824 and 1826 when there were two very unfavourable seasons, again between 1845 and 1847, and between 1864 and 1868, when conditions ranged from unfavourable to famine. As previously noted, 1876–1878 were the years of the worst famine to strike southern India. There were favourable seasons in 1826–1827, 1841–1842, 1842–1843, and 1848–1849, but there were no really superb harvests until after 1850. The late 1860s and early 1870s in particular, were times of plenty in Salem, a condition which unfortunately came to an end with the famine of 1876–1878.

What were conditions like in years representative of different assessment of the state of the season? The year 1832–1833 was one of famine in Salem. According to the *Jamabandi* for that year, "The season commenced favourably, but the rains subsequently failed entirely" (P.B.R., 16 March, 1835). Cultivators lost their crops, and prices rose by 71 %. This was good for the "big farmers", but catastrophic for the small who had no surplus to market after they fed their families. Any surplus was sold to obtain cash to pay the land revenue. Under the conditions of 1832–1833, they did not even have enough to feed their families, let alone to pay the required revenue. The poorer cultivators could not even sell their cattle since most had died from want of water and pasture. Many survived by gathering roots and herbs in the jungle, though these apparently led to the deaths of many. Cholera was also prevalent. The *Jamabandi* for 1866–1867 reported that when the year opened, the District was on the verge of a famine following an unfavourable year (P.B.R., 10 July, 1868). The early rains of April and May failed, as did those of the Southwest Monsoon. No rain fell until October, when cultivation began. Until the harvests of January-February 1867, people lived on roots and herbs, and 150,000 cattle died.

The season of 1845−1846 was considered to be "very unfavourable" (P.B.R., 10 December, 1846). It started with "partial showers" in places in April which permitted the fields to be ploughed. Further showers in May led to the sowing of dry grains, such as sorghum, pearl millet, and oil seed. But in June there was no rain in the southern part of the District. Although some rain fell in July, most of the crops perished. Lack of rain also meant that the tanks remained empty, so that irrigated cultivation was not possible. September finally brought general rainfall, and new crops were again sown, but lack of rain in October and November in many parts of the District reduced their yield. Overall, it was estimated that the dry crops gave from one eighth to one half their normal yield, with considerable variation from place to place.

An "unfavourable season" occurred in 1837−1838 (P.B.R., 8 November, 1838). In that year there was no rain until July. After August, rains failed until October so that the crops were heavily damaged. However, despite the late rains, the dry crops managed to yield one half of normal. A "somewhat less favourable" season was that of 1854−55 (P.B.R., 2 January, 1856). During the twelve month period output was below average, but sufficient for local consumption. Prices rose, mainly because of "a large export to North Arcot, Coimbatore, and other Districts". The "average" season of 1842−1843 started poorly, but there were showers from July through to September, and rainfall in October and November. The scantiness of the rain in July and August led to dry crop yields of between five-eighths and three-quarters.

1840−1841 was a "favourable" year (P.B.R., 28 October, 1841). Although there was no rain in July, the season began well, and the "October and November rains were plentiful and enabled the remainder of the cultivation to be carried on favourably". The "very favourable" season of 1850−1851 produced a three-quarters dry crop and a seven-eighths wet crop overall, although there was considerable areal variation. Rainfall was "slightly deficient" in some places in June and July, although the latter part of the year was excellent everywhere.

These descriptions illustrate a number of features relating to famine vulnerability. First, the official in the District had a clear idea of the difference between a favourable, an average, or an unfavourable season. Famines, once they occurred, were very obvious. Both the 1832−1833 and 1866−1867 famines occurred because of drought, not only in Salem, but in neighbouring Districts as well. This meant that grain was not available from outside the District. "Very unfavourable" seasons seem to have involved yields of from one-quarter to one-half of normal, whereas "unfavourable" ones yielded about one-half of normal. A "somewhat less favourable" season was one in which the "outturn of both descriptions of crops was below the average yield" (P.B.R., 2 January, 1856). An "average" season seems to have involved yields in the region of one-half to three-quarters, a "favourable" season yielded about three-quarters, and a "very favourable" season yielded three-quarters or more of normal.

A reading of the description of the seasons in Salem reveals just how uncertain rainfall was (and still is). Good early rains could be followed by none. If the early rains did not come, all was not lost because adequate falls later in the season could still ensure a favourable season. Perhaps more important than the total amount of rain, was its timeliness. Too much, as well as too little, at the wrong times could be disastrous. Above all, the *Jamabandi* seasonal reports demonstrate how the use of one indicator, rainfall, was insufficient to predict the outcome of a season, even as late as August or September. Many other factors were involved.

Furthermore, the *Jamabandi* reveal what was going on in different parts of the District. Each year in Salem, rainfall varied from place to place, and yields ranged widely in a given year. It is also fairly obvious that there was a considerable grain trade throughout the District, and from Salem to other areas. Salem, it appears, although a "dry" district, normally had a grain surplus. In fact, in the "unusually bad" season of 1857−1858 it was commented that

> It is a very unusual thing for grain to be imported from other districts ... in the year that has just closed other Districts supplied large quantities of grain both wet and dry. (P.B.R., 18 May 1860).

Another matter of frequent comment in the *Jamabandi* was the price of grain. In years of deficient rainfall and lower output, prices normally rose. However, while imports could lower prices, in a good year in Salem prices could still rise if large quantities of grain were dispatched to other Districts. Price was of great concern to the revenue officials, as cultivators had to sell grain for cash to pay the land revenue. If prices were low, cultivators very often could not obtain sufficient cash to do this, even though the season was favourable. High rates of assessment in some parts of Salem had much to do with the cultivators' inability to pay revenue, particularly before rates were legally lowered in the 1820s, and again in the 1870s. The relationships between grain prices, the state of the season, the rates of assessment, and the cultivators' ability to pay the land revenue, color official correspondence throughout the period.

After the disastrous famines in Bellary, Anantapur, and Kurnool in 1853−54, the Board of Revenue instituted a system of season reports. Certainly, for Salem, the first appeared during the "unfavourable" season of 1853−54, and continued on into the 1854−1855 season. At this time of crisis, the reports were dated at ten day intervals in Salem, and were considered by the Board of Revenue seven to ten days later. During the 1860s, "Season Reports" came to be filed once a month by the Collector, even during the famine of 1866−1867. Monthly reports also remained the norm through the 1870s, except during the famine of 1876−1878 when the reporting interval was once again reduced. Following the opening of the rail link between Salem and Madras, on 1st February 1861, communication times to and from the Board of Revenue improved. The railway was accompanied by the telegraph which further speeded up official communication, although a public telegraph office was not opened until 1884 (Richards, I, 1918).

The season reports, submitted monthly or weekly during crises, constituted part of the informal famine warning system in Madras which preceeded the Famine Code of the 1880s. They contained information on rainfall, the amount of water in irrigation tanks, the condition of crops in the ground, and grain prices. For example, on September 11, 1854, the Collector advised

> Since the last report there has been no material fall of rain and the tanks have not received any further supplies of water. But previous falls have led to crops in the ground thriving. People were also sowing both punja and nunja lands. Market prices of grain remained unaltered. (P.B.R., 14 September, 1854).

The Collector processed and synthesized the information coming in from his subordinates throughout the District, and transmitted the information to a central clearing house, the Board of Revenue in Madras.

Conclusions and Suggestions

There is little question that the nature of source materials used to study historical famines may prejudice the types of meaningfull conclusions which can be drawn. For the period before 1650 to 1700, the information from all sources is fragmentary, and while it is often locationally specific, is of a very general nature, permitting only the grossest possible generalisations to be made. Even for the nineteenth century, when certain types of records and sources were used, only the most general outline can be gained of the problems of increasing famine impacts, of famine relief, and rehabilitation. To analyse these topics, it is necessary to use more detailed types of material available only after intensive archival research.

Different types of source materials permit different levels of generalisation to be made. It is, however, only at the District scale and below that the variability of the "state-of-the-season" and the thin line that existed between plenty and scarcity, even by 1800, becomes readily apparent. Only too often this level of information has been ignored by those writing about historical famines. At best, middle-range, partially synthesized source materials have been used to document the impact of British famine policy, the causes of famine, and increasing famine vulnerability under colonial rule.

While I would not go as far to claim that alternative lines of modern famine policy can be drawn from historical records, it is nevertheless suggested that the past has lessons for the present, particularly when the scale factor in relationship to level of generalisation is considered. As policy-makers and planners always operate consciously or unconsciously under certain historical assumptions, if it turns out that the historical record has been misread and the historical parameters are different than the policy-makers assumed when they laid their plans, then significantly different policy judgements could well be called for. In the case of famine in India, since most of the interpretation has been at the macro-scale, the assumptions concerning vulnerability, warning systems operation, relief, and rehabilitation are at this level. To improve our understanding of these subjects, it is suggested that more research is required at the micro-scale level, if historical knowledge is to be incorporated into contemporary consciousness.

References

Ambirajan, S.: Political economy and Indian famines. South Asia, 1, 20–28 (1971)
Ambirajan, S.: Malthusian population theory and Indian famine policy in the nineteenth century. Population Studies, 30, 5–14 (1976)
Ambirajan, S.: Classical Political Economy and British Policy in India. Cambridge University Press, Cambridge, 1978.
Appadorai, A.: Economic Conditions in Southern India, 1000–1500 A.D. Madras University Press, Madras, 1936.
Benson, C.: A Statistical Atlas of the Madras Presidency, Government Press, Madras, 1895.
Bhatia, B.M.: Famines in India. A Study in Some Aspects of the Economic History of India, 1860–1945. Asia Publishing House, Bombay, 1963.

Bhatia, B.M.: Famines in India. A Study in Some Aspects of the Economic History of India (1860–1965). Asia Publishing House, Bombay, 1967.
Dando, W.A.: The Geography of Famine. John Wiley and Sons, New York, 1980.
Digby, W.: "Prosperous" British India. A Revelation From Official Records, originally published 1901, republished Sagar Publications, New Dehli, 1969.
Dutt, R.C.: Open Letters to Lord Curzon on Famines and Land Assessment in India. K. Paul, Trench, and Trubner, London, 1900.
Firishtah, M.K.: History of the Rise of the Mahomedan Power in India Till the Year AD 1612, in 4 volumes, translated by Briggs, J., R. Cambray, Calcutta, 1908–1910.
Great Britain. Parliament. Report of the Indian Famine Commission. For Her Majesty's Stationery Office by Eyre and Spottiswoode, London, 1880.
Hemingway, F.R.: Tanjore. Madras District Gazetteers, Government Press, Madras, 1906.
Kumar, D.: Land and Caste in South India, Agricultural Labour in the Madras Presidency During the Nineteenth Century. Cambridge University Press, Cambridge, 1965.
Madras. Government of Madras. A Statistical Atlas of the Madras Presidency. Revised and Brought Up to the End of Fasli 1320. Government Press, Madras, 1913.
Madras. Government of Madras. A Statistical Atlas of the Madras Presidency. Revised and Brought Up to the End of Fasli 1350. (1940–41). Government Press, Madras, 1949.
Madras. Government of Madras. A Statistical Atlas of the Madras Presidency. Revised and Brought Up to the End of Fasli 1360. (1950–1951). Stationery and Printing Office, Madras, 1965.
Madras. Government of Madras. Board of Revenue Records. Section XIV. Miscellaneous Records, Salem. The Records of Salem and the Baramahal, Section II, Geography, Tamilnadu Archives.
Madras. Government of Madras. Guide to the Records of Salem District, 1791–1835. Government Press, Madras, 1934.
Madras. Government of Madras. Revenue Department. Proceedings of the Board of Revenue (P.B.R.) 31 July, 1794; 23 March, 1807; 21 September, 1818; 20 October, 1819; 25 October, 1819; 16 March, 1835; 8 November, 1838; 28 October, 1841; 10 December, 1846; 14 September, 1854; 2 January, 1856; 18 May, 1869; 10 July, 1868.
Madras. Government of Madras. The Baramahal Records, Section VI, Land Rent. Government Press, Madras, 1918; Section XXI, Miscellany. Government Press, Madras, 1925; Section XXII, Review. Government Press, Madras, 1933.
McAlpin, M.B.: Railroads, prices, and peasant rationality, India 1860–1900. Journal of Economic History, 662–684 (1974)
McAlpin, M.B.: Impact of trade on agricultural development, Bombay Presidency. Explorations in Economic History, 17, 26–47 (1980)
Morris, M.D.: What is a famine? Economic and Political Weekly, 9, 1855–1864 (1974)
Morris, M.D.: Weather instability, food scarcity and famine policy. Zeitschrift für Ausländische Landwirtschaft, 317–330 (1979)
Mukerjee, R.K.: Agriculture, Famine and Rehabilitaion in South Asia. Ranajit Ray, Santinikatan, 1965.

Murton, B.J.: Some sources for the geography of South India, 1763−1843. Pacific View Point, 11, 181−187 (1970)

Raghavaiyangar, S.S.: Memorandum on the Progress of the Madras Presidency During the Last Forty Years of British Administration. Government Press, Madras, 1893.

Raju, A.S.: Economic Conditions in the Madras Presidency, 1800−1850. Madras University Press, Madras, 1941.

Richards, F.J.: Salem, Volume I, Part I., Volume I, Part II, Madras District Gazetteers, Government Press, Madras, 1918.

Scholberg, H. The District Gazetteers of British India. A Bibliography. Inter Documentation Company, Zug, Switzerland, 1970.

Srivastava, H.S.: The Indian famine of 1876−79. Journal of Indian History, 44, 853−886 (1966)

Srivastava, H.S.: The History of Indian Famines and Development of Famine Policy (1858−1918). Ram Mehra & Co., Agra, 1968.

Stein, B.: Peasant State and Society in Medieval South India Oxford University Press, Dehli, 1980.

Webb, J.W.: Geographers and Scales. In: Kosinski, L.A. and Webb, J.W. (eds.), Population at the Microscale: Special Publication No. 8, Hamilton, New Zealand, New Zealand Geographical Society pp. 13−20, 1976.

The Development of the Indian Famine Codes[1)]
Personalities, Politics, and Policies

Brennan, L., Senior Lecturer, History Discipline, The Flinders University of South Australia, Bedford Park, South Australia 5042, Australia.

Abstract: A sequence of famines in India from 1860−1877 caused loss of life, great expense and political controversy. To establish policy the Indian Famine Commission was formed, its composition, determined by the dominant personalities of the India Office and central and provincial governments, reflecting the interests involved. Conflict continued within the Commission, and though much common ground was reached, a minority report was submitted on two crucial issues. In 1880 from the majority report, the Secretary to the Commission drew up a Draft Indian Famine Code. This, subjected to the internal political processes of the Raj, emerged transformed as the provincial Famines Codes. These, amended, would be the basic doctrines of famine relief until the 1970s.

In his discussions of the lessons to be learnt from the Bihar famine of 1966−67, Alan Berg points to the advantage that the existence of a famine code − an existing set of instructions − provided for those engaged in relief work (Berg 1973). The Bihar famine code used in 1966−67, along with those of the other Indian states, was the result of the experience of government officials involved in famine relief over the previous hundred or so years. These provincial famine codes were developed after the Indian Famine Commission of 1878−80 had set down a number of principles for administrative action. These codes were not, of course, the first sets of administrative instructions for famine relief. Outhwaite discusses the Book of Orders issued during sixteenth century famines in England (Outhwaite 1978), and there were codes issued during the 1876−79 period in some provinces as their governments grappled with widespread and prolonged food crises. But the codes produced in the 1880s do seem to have been the first serious attempts to systematize the prediction of famine, and to set down steps to ameliorate its impact before its onset.

The Famine Commission did not produce a code itself, but its secretary, Charles Elliott, wrote a 'draft' code which was not only in line with the findings of the majority of the Commission, but also stemmed from his own experiences in the North Western Provinces (NWP) and Mysore (Government of India, PWD, 1882). This was circulated to the provinces in 1880 as a model for provincial codes, though at the time neither the Government of India nor the India Office in London had approved of it or of the principles of relief espoused by the Commission. Criticism of the code by the provinces prompted the Revenue and Agriculture Department of the Government of India to issue its own 'provisional' code. This was to be a model code for provisional use until codes, based on principles agreed to by the Government of India and India Office and adapted to their

[1)] The research for this paper was carried out with grants from the Flinders University Research Committee and the Australian Research Grants Committee. Figures 1, 2, 4, 5 and 7 are reproduced with the kind permission of the Illustrated London News Picture Library. The author gratefully acknowledges that assistance.

own particular circumstances, had been developed by the provinces. The codes which eventually emerged were the product of a complex process beginning with the experience of the famines of 1876−9, continuing through the investigations of the Famine Commission, and ending with the discussions of the 'draft', 'provisional', and final provincial codes. This exercise produced answers to the major questions of famine relief which, though not immutable, were to influence famine policy for the following ninety years. As such, it is useful to examine the processes which led to the enshrinement of these principles in administrative thinking since it seems likely that they remained influential in subsequent utilization, analysis and amendment of the codes.

Influences on Famine Policy

Two major explanations of British policy at this time have been advanced. The first demonstrates the influence of the classical economists on British thinking in India on the question of famine policy (Ambirajan 1978). It is clear that many officials at the time were convinced by the arguments of Adam Smith et al. about the inadvisability of interfering with the grain trade: their minutes and letters give ample evidence. Moreover, there does seem to have been a shift of policy during the first sixty years of the nineteenth century in the direction such views would indicate. Nevertheless, famine policy from that time started to swing back against laissez-faire towards greater intervention. The very fact that famine codes were constructed bespoke intervention, even though 'political economy' was still a potent weapon in arguments about the extent of government responsibility for food supplies.

The second explanation concludes that a major concern of the British was to keep famine relief as cheap as possible, so that new taxes did not have to be raised. Behind the smokescreen of laissez-faire lay the fear that new taxes would undermine the British hold on the landowning and mercantile classes whose support was required to hold India (Bhatia 1967). This is an attractive argument since there is ample evidence of the administration's concern for economy. Moreover, it has also been pointed out that in order to raise the resources necessary for the development of urban and rural infrastructure, the British were prepared to concede local self-governing institutions; perhaps the other side of Bhatia's argument (Seal 1973). Yet the British did raise new taxes, specifically on the merchants and landlords, directed towards providing famine insurance. But even given the concern for economy and the difficulties of raising new taxation, there remained ample space for manoeuvre in other aspects of the final shape of the standing instructions for dealing with famine. What other possible factors are there?

A significant possibility was the influence of developments in Britain not concerned with famine, which had vanished as a threat, but in relation to the operation of the New Poor Law of 1834. Relief of the poor was a hotly debated matter in Victorian England, and the issues debated there included a number of the same issues that were involved in famine relief in India, viz. should people needing support have to work for it in workhouses or on special public works; how could administrators, identify those who needed relief using self-administered and deterrent tests of labour for basic subsistence, separation (in England), and distance (India); and whose responsibility was it to fund and control provisions for the poor or the famished? Those responsible for policy, both in England and in India, also shared a concern about the possible 'demoralizing' effect of reliance upon relief. Endemic pauperism was perceived as of a different order from poverty. In both systems, administrators were faced with the problem that the poor lived such deprived lives that too often they were better off on relief than they were in normal times. But there lay the crucial difference: while the British were committed to the maintenance of the eligible poor in England, they refused to consider this as a possibility in normal times in India, preferring to rely upon the private charitable institutions and practices of the people over whom they ruled. They were prepared to interfere only when whole populations were endangered by widespread famine. The last thing they wished to consider was an Indian equivalent of the New Poor Law. And yet they seem to have been influenced by the same, albeit contradictory, currents of opinion which flowed in England. In the 1870s, which is the crucial period for this paper, the attack in England on outdoor (gratuitous) relief coincided with the improvement of medical care for paupers and the education of their children. The first of these is of particular interest, not only in the concern to limit the extent to which people called upon gratuitous relief (depauperization), but also in the importance attached by the poor law inspectorate to codes of rules for outdoor relief voluntarily drawn up by local administrators of the poor laws (Williams 1981). The concern for specific sets of rules of administrative practice was a response to the laxity with which, in many cases, the New Poor Laws had been implemented by local organizations (Rose 1971). Senior administrators in India shared this anxiety to secure the adherence of local officers to fixed rules. But though there was also a concern to tap local resources for famine relief, there was no sense in which the Indian officers were prepared to place the control of famine relief in the hands of Indians. The logic of imperialism intruded here too: the district officer was to remain the key executive in famine relief. As well as attempting to avoid the continuing commitments of the New Poor Law, the rulers in India believed that any large-scale famine relief had to be kept under their control.

There remains another possible source of influence on policy related to a colonial rather than a metropolitan situation and concerned with famine rather than endemic poverty, viz. British experience with the Irish famine of 1846−9. This is a question which would almost certainly repay closer inquiry, but while on the surface there are a number of points of similarity, sich as the absence of any impediments to the export of food from either country during the famines, and the common concern to secure labour for relief, the Irish situation was not drawn upon as an example in the Indian correspondence on policy making during the later 1870s. The influences would seem to be deeper and related to the general views on free trade and the relief of the poor.

Later, in the 1870s, policy makers and administrators worked in India in a climate of opinion in which metropolitan views on pauperism, free trade, and administrative efficiency had been brought into contact with a growing sense of government responsibility for the victims of famine (Bhatia 1967). It is clear that Indian famine policy had been influenced by these ideas in the past, but just as the administration of the New Poor Law was marked by differences over time and in local approach, so in the provinces of India a wide variety of famine policies had been used between 1860 and 1878. This had caused political conflict at the highest level as Secretaries of State, Viceroys, Governors and their subordinates struggled to come to grips with the famines that struck India in

94

those years, and then fought the political battles necessary to justify their actions or attack those of their rivals. During these conflicts, policy and personality became intertwined to such an extent that the outcomes were not infrequently determined as much by the manipulations of patronage and power within the Imperial system, as they were by the cogency of the argumentation. Thus, to the influences on British famine policy in India already mentioned, should also be added the nature of the political system within the British bureaucracy in India and its relationship with the India Office in London.

Famine Problems 1860—1877

The establishment of the Famine Commission of 1878—80 arose out of a number of circumstances embarrassing to the Conservative government of Benjamin Disraeli. Some of these were short-term, others of a more permanent nature. The most crucial of the latter was the confusion surrounding famine policy which had accompanied the sequence of famines which struck the sub-continent (Fig 8) between 1860 and 1877 (Tab 1). Policies had swung from relying substantially on the private grain trade in the Orissa famine of 1865—6 (which resulted in a death toll of 1.3 million), to wholesale government intervention in the procurement and distribution of food in the Bengal and Bihar famine of 1873—4 (which contributed to a total cost to the government of about £6.5 million but saved almost everyone threatened by the famine). The specific circumstances of 1877, when the British government decided to establish an enquiry, included difficulties caused by famines in Madras and Bombay, triggered by two years of drought and deepened by the export of grain to Europe. Wheat was usually much cheaper in India than in England (Matsui 1977), but during the late 1870s this was compounded by a decline in the value of the rupee from 2/- to 1/8 due to the devaluation of silver, and reduced costs of shipment (Rothermund 1970).

The response of the administrative systems to the famine was confounded by confusion and bitter hostility. One aspect of this was antipathy between the Government of India and the governments of the provinces. At first, for example, the Government of India favoured use of small local works for the employment of those on relief and chided the Government of Bombay for using large scale public works. When it came to believe that the latter were less expensive, it changed its mind and complained of the Government of Madras' extravagant use of small relief works. There was even more conflict over the purchase of grain by the Government of Madras, against the injunctions of the central government. These conflicts over policy led to acrimonious political controversy between the Viceroy, Lord Lytton (Fig 1), and the Governor of Madras, the Duke of Buckingham and Chandos (Fig 2). The Government of India's policy was actually devised by Sir John Strachey, Finance Member of Lytton's Executive Council and an experienced officer who had had a brilliant career in the NWP Lytton wholeheartedly accepted John Strachey's advice about famine policy as he did about most questions. In an attempt to enforce his will on Madras, Lytton travelled to the south in late 1877. After discussing the situation with Buckingham, he believed they had come to an agreement which would produce the necessary economy in famine management. While in the south, he also visited the headquarters of the relief organization in Mysore where he found such confusion that

Tab 1 Famines in British India 1860–1880

Provinces (Fig 8) (Cause)	Years (Months)	% Land uncultivated or crop affected	Government Action			Cost in millions	
			Interference with grain trade	Average Number daily on work relief (1000's)	Number daily on gratuitous relief (1000's)	Rupees	Deaths
NWP and Punjab (drought)	1860–1 (10)	35	no	34	84	4.5	NA
Orissa (drought)	1865–6 (21)	30–40	not until too late	6.6	55	NA	1.3
Bengal & Bihar (drought)	1866 (21)	NA	no	belated and inadequate	NA (private)	0.1	0.135
Madras (imports nearly halved & delay in rains)	1866 (11)	5	no	highest 17 belated	45	0.89	0.45
NWP (drought)	1868–9 (12)	33	freed of taxes and freight lowered	66	19	2.9	0.9
Bengal & Bihar (drought)	1873–4 (10)	78	exports allowed govt. imported grain (Rs. 39m)	662	452	22.0	0.0 (23 died)
Madras (drought)	1876–8 (22)	40	yes	460	327	68.2	3.5
Bombay (drought)	1876–7 (13)	30	no	285	33	12.8	0.8
NWP (drought and grain drain to the south)	1877–8 (12)	30	no	belated	14	2.0	1.25

Note: The cost does not include loss of land revenue.

Source: Report of the Indian Famine Commission, P.P., 1880, vol. LII, p. 432.

Fig 1 Lord Lytton, The Viceroy of India. Source: Ext. Supplement. Illustrated London News, 26 Feb., 1876

Fig 2 The Duke of Buckingham and Chandos, The Governor of Madras Province. Source: Illustrated London News, 6 April 1889, p. 443.

Fig 3 Sir Charles A. Elliott. Source: Frontispiece to Laborious Days. Calcutta, 1892.

Fig 4 The Marquis of Salisbury, Secretary of State for India. Source: Illustrated London News, L. 1, 22nd June, 1878.

Colonel Sankey, the PWD officer in charger of relief, was relieved of his post and replaced by Charles Elliott (Fig 3), a senior civil servant from the NWP. When a viceroy had to interfere at this level of administration, it was clear that there were severe problems in the management of famine – at all levels.

There were problems in England, too. Lord Salisbury (Fig 4), Secretary of State for India, was coming under pressure from 'old India hands' and others, as stories of the famine became known. These people, referred to as 'crotchets'[1], complained about policy, and urged the development of canal irrigation to prevent famine. Salisbury was himself worried about Lytton's relief policies, fearing that the latter was tyring to overcome the financial problems caused by the devaluation of silver and the loss of revenue caused by the famine, by "bearing too hard on the people"[2].

Salisbury, then, was anxious to have an enquiry for a mixture of reasons. First, to head off complaints in Parliament and to settle conflict in the India Council[3]. Secondly, he wanted to overcom the confusion of policy which had cost lives and money. Thirdly, he wanted to heal the divisions between Lytton and Buckingham. He therefore wrote to Lytton in November 1877 telling him that he wanted an enquiry. Lytton could not disagree but, as the following quotation indicates, he was anxious not to have a Parliamentary enquiry in England, and pressed for an investigation over which he would have some influence:

And now I am anxious to submit to you at once my own view of the important question touched on in your letter viz, the necessity you anticipate for an enquiry to gather up the experience collected in the recent famine, "and record it in an authoritative form for future guidance". I think such an enquiry would be a very proper one, and might have most beneficial results if fairly conducted. It seems to me that it would be impolitic to discourage or oppose it. But I am quite convinced that anything in the shape of an ordinary Parliamentary Committee for this purpose would be worse than useless (Lytton to Salisbury, 21 Dec. 1877).

The alternative was a commission appointed in India. This was what Sir John Strachey had been angling for since February 1877, when he had written to his brother General Richard Strachey (Fig 5) (a member of the India Council) asking him to

"reflect on the course which ought to be followed for utilizing and placing on permanent record in an authoritative shape the lessons taught us by this and former famines." (Strachey to Strachey, 23 Feb. 1877)

He repeated these sentiments later in the year, confident that they would

"be able to lay down those principles in a manner which ought to go far to render impossible the gross mismanagement and extravagance of the past." (Strachey to Strachey, 19 Sept. 1877)

His concern to lay down a set of rules to guide future famine administration stemmed not only from his supreme confidence in the rectitude of his own policies and the error of his opponents, but also from his plan to make the provinces responsible for their own famine expenditure – or at least a good part of it – and therefore anxious to exercise economy. In this objective, to produce a set of administrative instructions, lies one of the sources of the famine codes.

Shaping the Famine Commission

The manoeuvres surrounding the creation of the Famine Commission were mainly controlled by the Strachey brothers. It is clear from a letter from Salisbury to Lytton

Fig 5 Lt. General Sir Richard Strachey, a member of the India Council in London.
Source: Illustrated London News, 22 Feb. 1908, p. 262.

(written one week after the correspondence had been received intimating that an enquiry would be established) that General Strachey and Salisbury had been discussing a Famine Commission for some time, and that since General Strachey was on his way to India in connection with certain railway matters, he could explain Salisbury's views to Lytton. As he wrote,

"Strachey will also explain to you what I have talked a good deal to him about – the necessity of some commission on Famine measures in the future, in order to save ourselves from the Irrigation quacks. They will undoubtedly make a strong fight: for I observe that under the Presidency of Cotton, they have been beginning a sort of League ... for the Parliamentary campaign."

(Salisbury to Lytton, 15 Nov. 1877)

When it became clear that an enquiry was going to be held, John Strachey persuaded Lytton that he should take the wind out of his opponents' sails by promoting, in a manifesto to the Legislative Council, the expansion of railways and irrigation as a means of providing a programme of famine protection for India, while leaving it to Strachey, as Finance Member, to administer the bitter pill of announcing the taxes which would pay for the development schemes. These taxes were to be an additional rural cess and a licence tax on merchants which, though unwelcome, were less so than the income tax feared by the Indians. The taxes were, ostensibly, to be raised as famine insurance (Strachey to Lytton, 15 Dec. 1877). The speed with which the Government of India could work, when its interests were threatened, is indicated by the fact that these measures of taxation and expenditure were brought before the Legislative Council some twelve days after John Strachey had raised the matter with Lytton. In his speech, Lytton stressed that in his view there were only three ways in which the government could assist practically in ameliorating the impact of those "disturbances of the natural forces which produced famine", viz. railways, irrigation (provided it could pay its way), and "the intelligent application of sound principles" (Lytton, Viceregal Speech, 27 Dec. 1877). These sound principles were to emerge from investigation of the way the recent famine had been handled in the different provinces, and were to be recorded for future guidance. He thus signalled his agreement to an enquiry, the shape of which the India Office was in the process of delineating [4].

With the establishment of an enquiry agreed, the next step was to decide upon the composition of the Commission (Fig 6). Salisbury, having failed to find a President for the Famine Commission in England, passed the task to Lytton, not without relief, as his vomment to Lytton suggests:

"So I gave it up and I am consoled with the reflection that so long as we can avoid a false and superficial enquiry *here*, the less splash there is about the Indian Inquiry the better."

(Salisbury to Lytton, 18. Jan. 1878)

Lytton's task was to find in India an appropriate leader for the Commission. Earlier he had felt that General Strachey's relationship with his brother made him ineligible for the task (Lytton to Salisbury, 21 Dec. 1877), but in January 1878 he changed his mind, following the prompting of Sir Richard Temple, Governor of Bombay, then visiting Calcutta (Temple to Lytton, 23 Jan. 1878). Sir John Strachey, also in Calcutta, added his own pressure, urging that his brother be kept in India to manage the Public Works Department, and that the "famine inquiry appears to afford a complete justification of the request that this may be allowed by Lord Salisbury" (Strachey to Lytton, 25 Jan. 1878). Strachey went on to suggest the text of a telegram to the Secretary of State which, besides putting forward General Strachey as President of the Famine Commission, continued by requesting that should John Strachey have to go to England on sick leave, General Strachey should temporarily replace him as Finance Member. The extent of John Strachey's influence on the Viceroy can be measured from the fact that the telegram sent by Lytton to Salisbury agreed word for word with the suggested text (Lytton to Salisbury, c. Jan. 1878). Salisbury replied that the choice of the Commission was entirely up to Lytton, and that he would ensure that General Strachey's seat on the India Council would be kept for him. But he also extracted a price in suggesting that James Caird (Fig 7), an agricultural authority and Copyhold Commissioner, should be appointed as the English member of the commission. His name had been put forward by Sir Louis Mallet, the permanent head of the India Office (Salisbury to Lytton, Jan. 1878).

By early February, General Strachey and James Caird had been appointed to the Commission and it remained for Lytton to find the remaining members, a task over which he agonized for some time, since officers involved in the relief of the famine were barred from membership. He was especially concerned to have " a good, and in any case a *safe*, man to represent Madras ..." (Lytton to Kennedy, 3 March, 1878). But it is clear that Buckingham was equally concerned to have a *safe* man representing Madras interests, and appointed G.A. Ballard, a member of the Madras Board of Revenue, the body largely responsible for famine relief in Madras prior to Lytton's visit in 1877. Lytton, ostensibly taking to heart Salisbury's injunction to give Madras a strong representation on the Commission, also appointed H.S. Cunningham, a judge of the High Court at Calcutta whose initial connection in India was with Madras. He was, however, the brother-

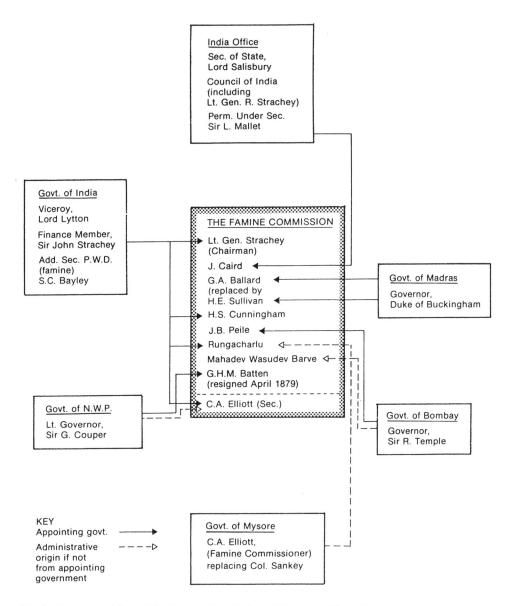

Fig 6 The composition of The Famine Commission which reported in 1880.

in-law of Fitzjames Stephen, Lytton's close friend, and had been promoted to the High Court at his request – he had also gone to school with Lytton (Strachey to Lytton, March, 1878). To these were added J.B. Peile from Bombay, who had been the Political Agent to the Kathiawar States during the famine (and therefore not involved in famine relief), and two Indians, Mahadev Wasudev Barve, the chief minister of the princely state of

Fig 7 Sir James Caird, an economist who had written on agrarian relations and Copyhold Commissioner from England.
Source: Illustrated London News, 20th February, 1892, p. 30.

Kolhapur, and Rungacharlu, controller of the household of the Maharaja of Mysore. Charles Elliott, who had been appointed Chief Secretary in the N W P , became Secretary of the Commission.

Of the members of the Commission, General Strachey and James Caird stand out as men firm in their views and pungent in their defence. To a certain extent this was a function of their comparative independence, but in General Strachey's case it was also a deeply ingrained aspect of his personality. When Lytton needed to re-assure the new Secretary of State for India, Lord Cranbrook, that General Strachey would not be influenced by Elliott (who had been involved in the relief of the Mysore famine) he pointed out that Strachey

"is certainly no respecter of persons, but maketh his criticisms to rain upon the just and unjust, with celestial disregard of human blessing or cursing." (Lytton to Cranbrook, 2 June 1878)

He would have been an ideal President of the Famine Commission − if he had not been so closely involved with his brother. Caird, an economist who had written on English agrarian relations and had an important position in Britain, brought to the question a mind free of Indian Civil Service thought patterns, but equally unfamiliar with India (Caird, 1968). The other members needed to be more careful in what they said, since though each held a senior position, the plums of higher office were rare and competition fierce (Spangenberg 1976).

Report and Dissent

The Famine Commission, nominated in early 1878, did not present their report to the Secretary of State until June 1880 − and even then it was not unanimous. Elliott and Cunningham were employed virtually all the time on the project, first in Simla from May to November 1878 framing a questionnaire sent to all administrations, then on tour (Fig 8) with the other members of the Commission, until early March 1879, when

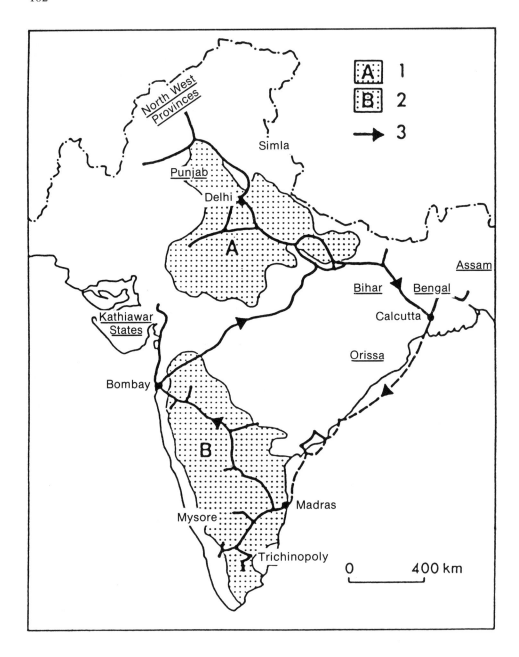

Fig 8 The context of the 1880 Indian Famine Commission. 1. Area affected by famine in the North West Provinces 1877–78. 2. Area affected by famine in Madras 1876–1878 and Bombay 1876–77. 3. Route followed by the Famine Commission beginning and ending at Bombay.

they repaired again to Simla while their colleagues dispersed to their normal duties (Elliott to officiating Secretary to Government, March, 1879). During the tour Ballard fell ill and was replaced by another Madras civil servant, H.E. Sullivan, Collector of Trichinopoly. Apart from the Indian members, who declined the opportunity (Temple to Lytton, 29 Aug. 1879 and Gordon to Lytton, 30 Aug. 1879), the Commission met again in London from mid-November 1879 to June 1880. Despite the extent of time involved and some compromise, the Commission could not agree on two major issues of policy and Caird and Sullivan at the last moment wrote a minute of dissent. That Caird would not accept the views of the Government of India, which were espoused by General Strachey and Elliott, was not surprising (Lytton to Caird, 1 March 1879). He and Lytton had already disagreed over a number of points of policy and Elliott had been very critical of his ideas about India. Indeed, Elliott had been critical of most of his colleagues – apart from the general (Elliott to Strachey, 3 April 1879; Strachey to Strachey, 26 May 1879; Gordon to Strachey, 1 May 1978) 5).

The first point of dissent was the proposal for the experimental storage of grain by the government in comparatively inaccessible districts where it would be difficult, with the existing communications, to make good a famine deficit (Caird and Sullivan, 11 June 1880). This challenge to economic orthodoxy was justified in terms of the practical problems of supplying inaccessible famine tracts, and of Caird and Sullivan's doubts both about their colleague's estimate of an average surplus yield of five million tons of grain, and whether, in any season of drought, India produced sufficient food for its population. It also, in a way, supported the actions of the Madras Government in 1876 in purchasing Rs 300,000 worth of grain at the onset of the famine – an action severely criticized by Lytton 6). The majority of the Commission attacked the scheme on the grounds of cost and on the basis of the teaching of classical economics. No merchant would import grain into districts where the government could feed the people – even though Caird was planning to feed only some 5 % of the population 7). This position was supported by both the Secretary of State and the Government of India, so that the 'provisional' Famine Code envisaged no interference with the grain trade, and payment in grain to relief workers was allowed only when food could not be obtained in the local market (Revenue and Agriculture Dept., Oct. 1883).

The second and more important point of conflict, however, was over the organisation of relief works. Caird and Sullivan argued that only capable workers should be employed on public work, and that they should be paid in the normal manner, i.e. at piece rates. The weak and infirm should be maintained in their villages without "extracting other labour than such sanitary or other light work as could be advantageously done near their homes" (Caird and Sullivan, 11 June 1880). They pointed out that this was the more economical approach since, where people forced to work for their subsistence, they would need more food. Moreover, it would preserve the fabric of village society by removing the need for the poor to leave the village to live in relief camps, and save life by providing subsistence without forcing people to travel to relief works when they were in a weakened condition. The agent deciding who would receive assistance was to be the village headman (under supervision) who would know each individual's circumstances. In order to restrain the headman from being too free with gratuitous relief, the village would have to pay something towards the feeding of its own poor (Caird and Sullivan,

11 June 1880) [8]. The majority of the European members of the Commission were strongly opposed to this plan. For Elliott, the first part must have seemed remarkably similar to what had been happening in Mysore in 1877 before Lytton appointed him to take Sankey's place. It was clearly different from John Strachey's policy, and diametrically opposed to the system in Bombay where there had been no relief in the villages, and all those not working on large relief works had been sent to live in poor-houses. It was not surprising, therefore, that General Strachey and his colleagues attacked the minority view on a number of counts. They argued that the proposals would destroy the use of labour as a test of need, and would therefore "bring the great mass of the population" on the heads of government, i.e. the proposals would be too expensive. The other argument was that the plan to disburse gratuitous relief through the village authorities betrayed ignorance about the extent of the village system and its nature, since it did not exist in many parts of India, and if the local landlords had to pay for half the gratuitous relief where it did, they "would be exercised to refuse gratuitous relief even to those who need it most" [9]. On these counts, the proposals were deemed impracticable. What was deemed both practical and economical was the system that had developed during the recent famine under Lytton (Lytton, 5 Sep. 1877).

The crucial instrument of famine relief was seen as the large public works programme under P.W.D. supervision, to which all those requiring relief, and able to work, were to be sent. This provided three checks on waste: first, the famine victims would have to prove that they were in need by leaving their homes to go to the relief work − the *distance test;* secondly, they would have to fulfil a task not less than 75 % of that performed by labourers in ordinary times, and for a sum gauged to provide only enough to sustain life − *the task and wage tests;* thirdly, they would be under PWD (i.e. European) supervisors who would prevent slack discipline and be personally honest (Indian Famine Commission Report, 1880b). For those without support and unable to work there was to be gratuitous relief, in their villages, or in poor houses, "if the case so require", working through the village officers and making use of local superintendents (India Famine Commission Report, 1880a). That the majority of the Commissioners agreed to village relief was the result of Caird's insistence. It marks a considerable shift from Elliott's position in Mysore in 1877, when he insisted that all those receiving gratuitous relief should *life* in the relief camps rather than using them just for dining, and everyone should workat something, however slight. Elliott propably had a point in his comment that "For the sake of their own health and spirits and self respect, it is better that they should do this than they should sit idle all day" (Mysore Famine Code, 1877).

The Direction of Famine Policy

By mid-1880, when the first part of the Famine Commission's report had been published, and largely accepted, trends in the government's action to reduce the impact of famine were beginning to become clear.

First the non-controversial points:

1. The need to gather information which would point to possible failure of cropa. This all members of the Famine Commission agreed, should be centred in the same depart-

ment that would control famine relief. The Government of India did not agree. It kept the control of famine within the regular district administrative structure, though it did re-establish the Revenue and Agriculture Department — under the Home Member.

2. The organization of village-inspection during famines to ensure that people knew of the relief measures, and the administration was aware of the condition of the people.

3. The granting of aid to landowners and tenants through the suspension of revenue demand, and through loans to landlords.

4. Provincial governments to have precise limits placed on their responsibility for expenditure on relief, local bodies being required to cooperate in this exercise.

As we have seen, there was disagreement over:

5. Who was to participate in relief work, under what conditions, and under whose control, and

6. Wheter there was to be any substantial interference with the grain trade (Indian Famine Commission Report, 1880 c).

The nature of gratuitous relief was left an open question in the Report, since where there was a strong village organization it would be left in its hands — and where not, relief camps or poor-houses would be established.

As we have seen, it was the recommendations of the majority on the Commission that were accepted by the India Office and the Government of India (Governor-General in Council to Secretary of State, 14 March, 1881). These recommendations informed famine policy in the future, even though they were based on assumptions that would be sorely tested:

1. The essential problem was shortage of work rather than food. People should therefore be given work.

2. The Indian poor would go to relief works to save their lives but, if you did not make the work hard enough and the pay poor enough, *everyone* would come whether they needed to or not, and the poor would stay longer than was necessary.

3. Because the food required for relief was in India, another major problem was in getting it to the famine area through private trade. The growth of the railway system would see to that, rater than interference with private trade.

4. Indian officials could not be trusted with the management of relief works: so

(a) wherever possible, relief works should be made large enough to need European supervision;

(b) some sort of hold (either financial (a bond!) or career-wise) should be maintained over any Indian it was necessary to employ.

Each of the assumptions brought problems with it. One final element of their approach, however, did make sense. There was general agreement that the time for *ad hoc* responses to individual famines was past. Indeed, some provinces had set up codes of instructions during the famines of 1876−9. It was, however, generally agreed that using principles drafted by the Government of India as a basis, the provincial governments should each "draw up a famine code, containing detailed instructions suitable to the varying wants and administrative systems of (their) provinces and embracing, as far as human foresight can go, all matters falling within the scope of relief administration" (Indian Famine Commission Report, 1880e). During the period 1880−1884, and starting with Charles Elliott, the Government of India *and* the provincial governments each produced famine codes, with the result that many of the battles were rejoined.

The Drafting of the Famine Codes

Towards the end of 1880, at the same time as the draft code prepared by Elliott was received by the Government of India, there was renewed fear of famine in several parts of India. Although neither the India Office nor the Government of India had pronounced upon the Commission's findings, the Home, Agriculture and Revenue Department forwarded to the provincial governments copies of Part I of the Report of the Commission drawing attention to paragraph 112 which spelt out some general rules. They followed this with Elliott's code, asking for comments (Governor General in Council to Secretary of State, 14 March, 1881). This set in train a long bureaucratic bungle. The Commission had suggested that the Government of India should "issue a set of rules embodying the main principles that should govern the administration of famine relief and ... these broad principles being ... fixed, it would be the duty of the several local governments to apply them by drawing up a famine code ... suitable to the varying wants and administrative systems of the different provinces" (Indian Famine Commission Report, 1880d). But, by sending out Elliott's 'draft' code as a model before compiling their own set of instructions, the central government had muddied the water. Indeed, it appears that the Secretaries in the Home, Revenue and Agriculture department may have been playing for time to see which way Lord Ripon, the new Viceroy would move on the matter. Hopefully, he would leave it to the new department, as the Famine Commission had suggested, to draw up the rules [10].

The Government of the North-West Provinces was the first major province to reply. With Sir George Couper as Lieutenant Governor, still hostile about criticisms of his famine policy during 1878−79 and the part he believed Elliott had played in his troubles (Couper to Strachey, 25 July, 1878), it was clear that the Draft Code would receive a critical reception. The NWP reply ranged widely over all aspects of the code, including attacks on the emphasis on large relief works, and on the *distance test* with its concommitant relief camps. It was pointed out that

"there are very grave objections to hutting ... In the first place, labourers get comfortably settled, and do not willingly go back to their ruined homes; (moreover) away from their villages they are completely released from the restraints of the only public opinion they care for. They become grossly immoral, and contract *liaisons* which may make it next to impossible for them to go back to their old life. No worse blow could be dealt on the constitution of village society. From a merely sanitary point of view, the objections are many and obvious. (Bennett, 13 April, 1881)

Similar criticisms, usually based on recent experience of district level officials during a famine, were made of village relief, the role of famine commissioners, and the scale of wages paid.

After he had read these remarks, the Home Member of the Viceroy's Council, A. Rivers-Thomson, remarked that they would have to modify their rules before they could "satisfy the officers in the NWP ... (and) before ... we can issue any general outline code of our own, we must hear what other administrations have to say" (Rivers-Thomson, 23 April 1881). The central authorities had clearly lost the initiative in making policy, almost, it seemed, deliberately.

At this stage (mid-1881) the Agriculture and Revenue Department was re-established with E.C. Buck as its secretary, though still responsible to the Home Member. Buck, a scholarly, "genial and conciliatory" (Spangenburg) officer from the NWP, had developed ties with Caird who had procured his election to the Royal Agricultural Society (Buck to Caird, 4 Nov. 1879). By September 1881, Buck had developed a code of his own which he called 'the Provisional Code'. It is clear that he had in mind provincial criticisms of Elliott's code. He therefore strengthened the role of Commissioners and District Officers, and separated able-bodied labourers from unprofessional labour, the former to be supervised by PWD officers, the latter by Civil officers. The Code also attempted to keep agricultural labour on agricultural work, by making it possible for them to be employed hoeing land instead of building roads. He hoped thereby to keep them, as he explained to Caird, from wandering from their villages. The other major point of difference between his own and Elliott's code was his belief that with Ripon's Local Self-Government legislation, there would be local agencies to assist the District Officer, thus providing the local resources to which Caird had looked (Buck, 27 Sept. 1881; Buck to Caird, 12 Feb. 1882). All told, it moved much closer to the Caird view of famine relief. This was consolidated when he travelled to Madras in the following year. Both Sankey and Sullivan were on the committee set up by the Madras Government to construct a famine code, an initiative spurred by the arrival of Elliott's code. They were delighted with Buck's plans. As he reported to Caird:

So we have taken the weaker (illegible) from Col. Sankey's huge and distant works (which pleases him) and brought them on smaller diet and light work to agricultural operations, close to their homes, which pleases Sullivan. This is the next thing to feeding them on the minimum scale in their own houses — and removes the charge of "demoralization" brought by those who object to our feeding the idle. (Buck to Caird, 12 Feb. 1882)

One imagines that Caird also was pleased.

Buck's success, however, was short-lived. Although his plans for agricultural "famine employment" were popular in Madras, back in Calcutta his new superior as Home Member, S.C. Bayley, overruled him, and they were relegated to the position of possibilities to be investigated by the Agriculture Department. Bayley had been appointed by Sir John Strachey and Lytton to the crucial post of Additional Secretary responsible for famine administration in the P.W.D. during 1877—78. It was unlikely that he would overturn the basic policies of Strachey and Lytton.

By the mid-1880s, some four to five years after the Famine Commission Report was published, most of the provinces had famine codes but, apart from a reliance on public works for famine relief and injunctions about interfering with the grain trade, they were not uniform. The opportunity for the Government of India to fix a relatively uniform policy in the early 1880s had been lost, and neither Bayley nor Buck were men likely to force the provinces to come into line.

This points again to the importance of people — their ambitions and connections as well as their ideas — in the formulation of famine policy.

Personalities, Politics and Policies

At all stages of the process by which the codes came into beingm the internal politics of the I.C.S. (Indian Civil Service) were at least as important, and in some aspects more so.

than the ideas on famine relief of the protagonists or the wider concerns of Empire. The establishment of the Famine Commission was carried out as a political exercise to produce a favourable report, rather than as a measured response to one of the most significant problems of the Government of India. General Strachey protected his brother's policies, while the I.C.S. members carefully followed those paths best suited to their own advancement, most of them doing well out of their association with the Commission. Elliott went furthest, becoming Lt. Governor of Bengal, after postings as Census Commissioner and Chief Commissioner of Assam. Peile also made rapid progress after the Famine Commission, rising through membership of the Council of the Governor of Bombay, for which job he sought the support of both General Strachey and Caird on the grounds of his work on the Commission (Peile to Ferguson, 20 Oct. 1881), through the Viceroy's Council, to the Council of India. Sullivan, who had upheld the honour of Madras, quickly became a member of the Madras Board of Revenue, and moved on to the Council of the Governor of Madras. Cunningham moved back to his position as Judge on the bench of the High Court, but was never made Chief Justice. Caird returned to his work in Britain, and was eventually knighted. But even though the investigation was not carried out by the Commissioners (apart from Caird) in a completely open minded manner, the political nature of the exercise was not entirely without its benefits. Because of the desire — especially of General Strachey — to submit a unanimous report, and Caird's insistence on such points as using local knowledge of distress, the final report was much less supportive of the Government of India's policies than the majority of its members would have liked (Strachey to Caird, 22 May 1880). As such, it made respectable more liberal views of famine relief.

The major outcome of the Commission was the famine codes developed during the 1880s. Here again, political influences were important, as the Government of India lost control of the codes — again, perhaps deliberately — and the provinces produced their own codes within the very broad parameters set by the weak Revenue and Agriculture Department [11].

Conclusion

This paper has traced the early development of the famine codes during which proccess provincial and personal loyalty, along with career considerations, were important elements in the protection of policies developed in the famine years. The process was to be repeated nearly twenty years later when, between 1896 and 1901, famine again ravaged much of India, and the government responded with massive relief schemes, two famine commissions, and a revision of the famine codes [12]. From the interplay of the problems and bureaucratic conflict associated with these famines emerged the famine codes that were to remain the basic guide to the British response to famine in India over the next forty years.

As we have seen, that the codes emerged at all owed as much to Sir John Strachey's resolve to force provincial governments to toe his policy line, as it did to the ideological shifts and humanitarianism that encouraged state intervention in food crises. Subsequently, they were shaped by the complex interests of contending camps within the Famine Commission of 1878—80, the Government of India, and the provincial governments.

In the terms dictated by the drought-triggered famines of the last quarter of the nineteenth century, the codes were workable — if somewhat over-elaborate. This is not to say that all the assumptions on which they were based were correct. Some, such as the non-interference in the grain trade, could have been dangerous; others, such as the belief that the main problem was the shortage of work, were limited in their application. But the codes were practicable enough, in most provinces, to enable a district officer to manage the complex task of providing either work or gratuitous relief to those who needed it in his district. And since, in the highly competitive world of the I.C.S., personal advancement could be influenced by the administration of famine situations, officers at various levels worked — or adapted — the codes to suit the local situation. Where lives could be saved economically, there was considerable kudos for the officer responsible. There were also perhaps greater opportunities, for the secretariat officers who oversaw the famine campaign, and for those who participated in the commissions which analysed the errors and successes of their colleagues in the anticipation of learning lessons for future guidance. It was not, however, just the ideas or energy of the later counterparts of men such as Elliott, Sullivan, Buck and Bayley which counted in the decisions that were made: their allegiances, connections and influence were equally significant in the formation of the policies with which the British in India confronted their major internal problems in the late nineteenth and early twentieth century. It would be naive not to expect that today the same processes continue to operate, even where highly-educated technocrats occupy important policy-making positions in national bureaucracies.

Notes

1) The 'crotchets' included Sir Arthur Cotton and John Bright. Florence Nightingale was also interested but there is no evidence of pressure from her at this stage of affairs. Later her estimates of mortality were more accurate than those published by the Government of India.

2) Salisbury to Disraeli, 6 September 1877, Disraeli Papers, Bodleian Library, Oxford. The devaluation of silver meant that it cost a greater proportion of government revenue (paid to it in silver) to meet the 'Home Charges' in gold in London.

3) The Council of India had considerable informal influence if little direct power. A Secretary of State for India hesitated to override its views.

4) The draft of Despatch 2 of 1878 was written on Salisbury's instruction of 6 December 1877, considered by the Council of India on 8 January 1878, and the resulting despatch signed by Salisbury on 10 January 1878. L/E/3/498, India Office Records (hereafter I.O.R.), London.

5) In the letter Gordon thanks Strachey for protecting Rungacharlu from Elliott.

6) For details of the purchase and subsequent conflict see Govt. of India, Revenue and Agriculture Dept., Famine branch, January 1881, B proc., 1—4, N.A.I. It was claimed in this document that the grain purchases actually cost £500,000, though there is no evidence to support this asserthion.

7) Rejoinder to Mr Caird's Protest (unsigned, but written by the majority group of members), n.d. , (c. June 1880), Caird Papers, Home Miscellaneous 796.

8) This plan had been in Caird's mind for some time. See Caird to Elliott, 1 August 1879, Home Miscellaneous, 796.

9) Rejoinder to Mr Caird's Protest (c. June 1880), Caird Papers, Home Miscellaneous, 796

10) See the minutes by C.L. Tupper (Under Secretary, Home, Revenue and Agriculture Department) and Charles Grant (Secretary, Home Revenue and Agriculture Department), 20 April 1881 and 22 April 1881, in Revenue and Agriculture, Famine Branch, June 1883, A proc., 31–52, K.W.

11) See Bayley's memo. on the financial weakness of the Revenue and Agriculture Department, 27 October 1882, Ripon Papers, Add. MS. 43579, British Library.

12) Between 1880 and 1885 when droughts were few and localized many of the codes were re-examined and modified.

References

Ambirajan, S.: Classical Political Economy and British Policy in India, Cambridge, 59–100 (1978)

Bennet, W.C. (1881) Assistant Commissioner, Gonda quoted in R. Smeaton Officiating Secretary to Government, N.W.P.), to Secretary to Government of India, Home Revenue and Agriculture Department, 13 April 1881, Home, Revenue and Agriculture, Famine Branch, June 1883, A Proc., 38.

Berg, A.: The Nutrition Factor. Brookings Institution, New York 1973, p. 219.

Bhatia, B.M.: Famines in India, Asian Publishing House, Bombay 1967, pp. 10–27 and p. 113.

Buck, E.C. (Director of Agriculture, N.W.P.), to Caird, 4 November 1879, Home Miscellaneous, 796.

Buck, E.C. (1881) Minute 27th September 1881, Revenue and Agriculture, Famine Branch, June 1883, A. Proc., 31–52, K.W.

Buck, E.C. (1882) to Caird, 12th February 1882, Home Miscellaneous, 796.

James Caird (1880) and H.E. Sullivan, answer to the Explanatory Paper of General Strachey, Mr. Cunningham and Mr. Peile, London, 11 June 1880. Caird Papers, Home Miscellaneous 796.

Caird, H.: English Agriculture in 1850:51, 2nd Edition, Cass 1968.

Couper (1878) to R. Strachey, 25 July 1878, R. Strachey papers, MSS. Eur. F. 127/10.

Elliott, C.A. (1879) to Officiating Secretary to Government Home Dept., 3rd March 1879 P.W.D., March 1879, A proc., 11.

Elliott, C.A. (1879) to R. Strachey, 3rd April 1879, R. Strachey Papers, MSS Eur. F.127/12.

Fraser, D. (ed.): The New Poor Law in the Nineteenth Century. Macmillan London 1976, p. 17.

Gordon, J.D. (1879) Resident of Mysore to R. Strachey, Ist May 1879, R. Strachey Papers MSS Eur. F. 127/11. In the letter Gordon thanks Strachey for protecting Rungacharlu from Elliott.

Government of India, Public Works Department (1882) C-W Misc., May 1882, B Proc. 15–17, National Archives of India (hereafter N.A.I.), New Delhi.

Governor General in Council to Secretary of State, 14 March 1881, Home, Revenue and Agriculture, Famine Branch, March 1881, A Proc., 27; Revenue and Agriculture, Famine Branch, June 1883, A Proc., I, 31–52, K.W.

Indian Famine Commission (1880a) Report Part 1, P.P., LII, para 112

Indian Famine Commission (1880b) Report Part 1, P.P., LII, para 131.

Indian Famine Commission (1880c) Report Part 1, P.P., LII, pp. 444–45.

Indian Famine Commission (1880d) Report Part 1, P.P., LII, para 445.

Indian Famine Commission (1880e) Report Part 1, P.P., LII, para 446.

Lytton's (1977) Despatch 34, 5 September 1877, in L/E/3/86, I.O.R., where he outlines the agreement on policy he made with Buckingham during his tour of Madras.

Lytton (1877) to Salisbury, 21 December 1877, Lytton Papers, MSS. Eur. F. 218/516/2B. India Office Library (hereafter I.O.L.), London.

Lytton (1877) Speech by H.E. the Viceroy in the Legislative Council of the Government of India, Calcutta, 27 December 1877, Lytton Papers, MSS. Eur. E. 218/521/8(b).

Lytton (1878) to Salisbury, (c. January 1878), in R. Strachey Papers, MSS. Eur. F. 127/9, IOR.

Lytton (1878) to General Sir Michael Kennedy, 3 March 1878, Lytton Papers, MSS. Eur. E. 218/518/3. Kennedy, a P.W.D. official from Bombay, had been sent in 1877 to 'assist' Buckingham in Madras.

Lytton (1878) to Cranbrook, 2 June 1878, Lytton Papers, MSS. Eur. 218/518/3.

Lytton (1879) to Caird, 1 March 1879, Caird Papers, Home Miscellaneous, 796. I.O.R.

Matsui, T.: Agricultural Prices in Northern India, 1861–1921. vol. II, Daigaku Shuppankai, Tokyo 1977, figs. N–19, N–14.

Mysore Famine Code, 1877, p. viii, (2) 1936, I.O.R.

Outhwaite, R.B.: Food Crises in Early Modern England: patterns of public response. Proceedings of the Seventh International Economic History Congress, Edinburgh 1878.

Peile, J.B. to Sir James Ferguson, 26 October (1882), Ferguson Papers, MSS. Eur. E. 214/13, I.O.L.

Rivers Thomson, A. (1881) Minute, 23 April 1881, Revenue and Agriculture, Famine Braanch, June 1883, A Proc., 31–52, K.W.

Rose, M.: The English Poor Law, 1780–1930. David & Charles, Newton Abbott 1971, pp. 22–30.

Rothermund, D.: The monetary policy of British Imperialism. Indian Economic and Social History Review, 7, 91–107 (1970)

Salisbury (1877) to Lytton, 15 November 1877, Lytton Papers, MSS. Eur. E. 218/516/2B.

Salisbury (1878) to Lytton, 18 January 1878, Lytton Papers, MSS. Eur. E. 218/516/3.

Salibury (1878) to Lytton (January 1878), (copy) in MSS. Eur. F. 127/9. R. Strachey Papers. Salisbury realised that Madras would 'raise a great cry of partiality, and counselled General Strachey on the advisability of having Madras strongly represented on the Committee. Salisbury to R. Strachey, 1 February 1878, MSS. Eur. F. 127/9.

Seal, A.: Imperialism and Nationalism in India. Modern Asian Studies, 7, 12–3 (1973)

Spangenburg, B.: British Bureaucracy in India: Status, Policy and the I.C.S. South Asia Books, Colombia, MO 1976.

Strachey, J. (1877) to R. Strachey, 23 February 1877, R Strachey Papers, MSS. Eur. F. 127/6, I.O.L.

Strachey, J. (1877) to R. Strachey, 19 September 1877, R. Strachey Papers, MSS. Eur. F. 127/6.

Strachey, J. (1877) to Lytton, 15 December 1877, Lytton Papers, MMS. Eur. E. 218/519/6. Strachey had been planning the taxation manoeuvre for some time. John to Richard Strachey, 11 June 1877, R. Strachey Papers, MSS. Eur. E.F. 127/6.

Strachey, J. (1878) to Lytton, 25 January 1878, Lytton Papers, MSS. Eur. E. 218/519/7.

Strachey, R. (n.d.) to Lytton (c. late March 1878), Lytton Papers, MSS. Eur. E. 218/519/7. B. Spangenburg, British Bureaucracy in India, New Delhi, 1976, p. 150. He was a barrister, and had been appointed Advocate-General in Madras before rising to the judicial positions in Calcutta. His wife was a daughter of Lord John Lawrence.

Strachey, J. (1879) to R. Strachey, 26th May 1879, R. Strachey Papers, MSS. Eur. F. 127/8.

Strachey, R. (1880) to Caird, 22 May 1880, R. Strachey Papers, MSS. Eur. F. 127/12.

Temple (1878) to Lytton, 23 January 1878, Lytton Papers, MSS. Eur. E. 218/519/7. In early 1877 Temple had been sent by Lytton to enforce economics on the Madras government. He had spent some time in Calcutta prior to writing this letter to the Viceroy.

Temple (1879) to Lytton, 29 August 1879, and J.D. Gordon (Chief Commissioner, Mysore) to Lytton, 30 August, 1879, both Lytton Papers, MSS. Eur. E. 218/5/1.

Williams, K.: From Pauperism to Poverty. Routledge & Kegan Paul, London 1981, pp. 96–101.

Woman in Famine: The Paradox of Status in India

Ali, Mehtabunisa, Research Officer, Morphett Vale Community Health Centre, Department of Primary Care and Community Medicine, Flinders Medical Centre, Bedford Park, SA 5042, Australia.
Present adress: International Center for Diarrhoeal Disease Research, Bangladesh

Abstract: Offical criteria for assessing the status of women in development throughout different areas of India and particularly in Bengal (Fig 1) are evaluated against the value of women during historical and recent famines. Their traditional roles as food preparers are extended during food crises to include increased decision-making and food procurement, particularly with regard to wild food gathering, gainful employment, the selling of personal assets and the final decision for the family to migrate. The paradox of women apparently improving their "status" at times of famine indicates the need to re-examine the existing criteria for assessing "status" and women's roles in the development process.

Introduction

"Famine is a charred spot in a dried-up river bed where a woman's corpse was burnt today; she fed her husband first, then she gave her children what was left, and then she died".

(Wallston, N., 1967)

The Report of the Committee on the Status of women in India (1975), after examining the implications of recent trends in demographic data relating to women claimed that there had been an "intensifying devaluation" in the status of women. The Committee were particularly concerned about:
- the declining ratio of women to men between the 1951 and 1971 censuses,
- the declining numbers of women employed in agricultural and non-agricultural labour;
- declining participation of women in paid employment;
- increasing migration of women to rural areas;
- lower literacy and life expectancy rates and higher mortality rates among women compared to men.

This paper disagrees with the Report's conclusion concerning the devaluation of women, because it uses only broadly based demographic indicators which do not adequately represent the concept of "the status of Indian women"[1].

A study of women in Indian famines or food crises provides examples of socio-demographic trends *opposite* in some respects to those indicated by census data. Women's participation in paid employment actually increases during famine, as does their migration to

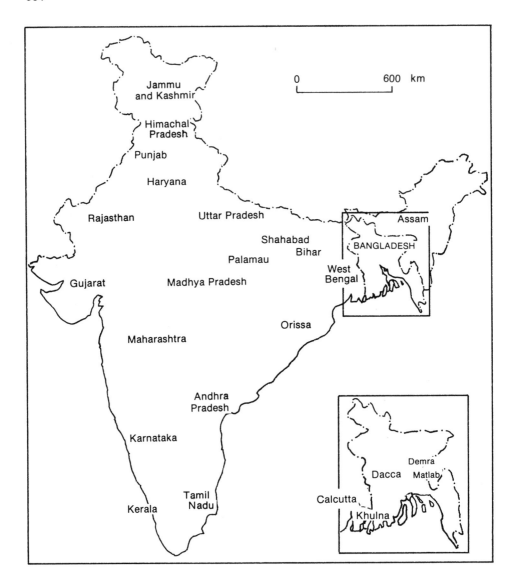

Fig 1 Reference map.

urban areas. Mortality statistics show lower famine-related deaths among women than among men. Do these opposite trends then indicate a process of change towards development? Do famines and other food-related crises represent a socio-economic climate conducive to greater participation of women in development projects? How does this greater participation reflect on their status? Are we in fact studying the right variables in examining women's status?

In attempting to answer the above questions, this paper summarises some literature on the roles and status of women in India. It examines departures during famine from women's traditional roles and highlights the ability of women to expand their traditional roles as food processors and food preparers to fulfill traditionally male roles as income earners and food procurers.

Famine: A First Bibliography (Currey et al. 1981) indicates that the famine syndrome has been well researched, documented and recorded, but the specific responses of women to famine have rarely been studied as an independent topic. Some information on women in famines can be found in general reports, notably those of the Indian Famine Commission 1898 and 1948. Mahalanobis et al. (1974) and Singh (1975) surveyed more recent post-famine reactions in rural Bengal and Bihar respectively, but they did not analyse data specific to women. Torry (1979) and Dirks (1980) omit mention of any differentiation between male and female responses to famine in their anthropological and sociological reviews.

Comparisons of the 1941 and 1951 Indian censuses should also provide demographic changes indicating alterations in the role of women following the 1943 famine, e.g. higher female participation in non-agricultural or paid labour due to increased landlessness or migration from rural to urban areas in 1951. Variations in the classification of women's occupations between the two censuses, however, make direct comparisons impossible.

On the other hand, the work of Das (1949) includes age-sex analysis of destitutes who had migrated to Calcutta in response to the 1943–44 Bengal famine. The study focussed on some of the specific responses of women, who outnumbered men among the destitutes. More recently, Chen and Guznavi (1977) specifically studied the role and status of women in Bangladesh in food-for-work programmes. Notable among other sources of information on the responses of women during famines are the literary works of the renowned Bengali novelist Bankim Chandra Chatterjee in *Anandamath* and of Bibhuti Bhusan in *Ashani Shanket*. While subjective in content, such sources nevertheless highlight the value of women as the principal household food-procurers and decision makers during famines.

This paper concentrates on the famine-responses of poor women, that sub-group of the female population most vulnerable to food-crises. It largely focuses on studies of women in famines in Bihar and Bengal, including studies of Bengali women in present day Bangladesh.

The Role and Status of Women in India: A Review of Current Research

Comments on the role and status of women in India are made difficult by the many combinations of religion, caste and culture that exist within and between regions and that have their individual interpretations of status. Further difficulties are introduced by differences between belief in principle, and practical reality, a phenomenon observed by Jain (1976) who remarked that "status (often) lies in the eye of the beholder".

Certain generalisations can be made about the role of women in India, for example, the role of women in agriculture is different in the rice producing areas in the south and east of India from their role in wheat producing areas in the north and west, but such generalisations give no indication of status. Also among sub-groups influenced by Islamic culture, sex segregation occurs and women practise some form of *purdah*. The indigenous interpretation

Tab 1 Primary occupations of Indian women (Census 1971). Figures represent proportions of total female population.

Workers (12 %)		Non-Workers (88 %)	
Cultivator	4.0 %	Full time Student	7.0 %
Agricultural Labourer	6.0 %	Household Duties	45.0 %
Other	2.0 %	Dependent	35.0 %
		Other	1.0 %

Source: Census of India 1974

of *purdah* is status related, i.e., women of high status practice *purdah*. Yet today, when westernized women's consciousness about status is aroused, *purdah* is interpreted as discrimination. If as the Committee on the Status of Women in India concluded, the decreasing rate of participation in the labour force denotes devaluation of women's status, then in south India, in some of the most fertile rice growing districts the reverse must also be true as women outnumber men among agricultural labourers (Beteille 1976). Yet women are paid lower wages than men, which again colours "status " in a different hue. These examples highlight some of the difficulties of commenting on the status of women although a great deal of empirical and theoretical work has been done in explaining variations in status, particularly variations as reflected by women's participation in the labour force.

Women in rural India are traditionally home-makers, largely occupied in household duties and classified as dependents (Tab 1). As described by Srinivas (1976), "the wife cooks and serves food at least twice a day to all members of the household, and cooking in rural India often involves the processing of grain grown or bought. This work the women must do and extra-mural chores are always additional. The feeding, disciplining and socialisation of young children is also her task unless she has a grown daughter who then plays the role of mother to her young brothers and sisters." (Abdullah 1974; Jahan 1974; Kalakdina 1976; See also Rudra 1976; Sattar 1975;).

While men are traditionally income-earners and food procurers, religion and culture bind women to their principal role of home-maker (Rudra 1976; Beteille 1976; Kalakdina 1976). However, religion and culture vary within India, and different regions of the country also have their own interpretation of women's roles. Even "in the same region and within the same religious group one might find a variety of social customs" affecting the status of women, while the "most conspicuous variations in the position of women are the ones we find within the different strata". (Beteille 1976). Their observations include:
● the variation in women's freedom of movement between north and south India;
● the segregation of women *(purdah)* in some north Indian States;
● the differences in age at marriage and the corresponding differences in domestic roles between different religious and caste groups;
● the higher status enjoyed by women in matrilineal societies, e.g. the Nairs in Kerala;
● "the lack of restraint" enjoyed by tribal women in Andhra Pradesh and Madhya Pradesh; and
the status imposed on women by caste or class (Nanda 1976).

Such examples provide a clear indication of the spatial variation in the status of women.

Significant spatial variation also occurs in the level of women's participation in the labour force (Tab 2 − see also Note 1). The hill State of Himachal Pradesh has the highest female working population, while West Bengal, Haryana and Punjab have the least. However, it should also be noted that the central States of Andhra Pradesh, Maharashtra, and Madhya Pradesh have high proportions of female workers as do most of the States in the south and west. Despite efforts to explain this variation (Gulati 1975, a, b, c; Nath 1970; Reddy 1975; Sinha 1975), there is no clear consensus on the factors responsible. Reddy's simple economic explantion is that where agricultural productivity, income and wage rates are low, female participation in the work force tends to be high mainly because women of the poorest families are forced to work. This agrees with Srinivas' (1976) contention that "at the bottom level of the rural hierarchy women do both intramural and extramural work, the latter being paid for".

Overriding these variations is the tacit understanding within agrarian societies that work is a hardship rather than a privilege, and "ability to keep away from manual work has been an important distinguishing sign of socio-economic status . . . Therefore non-participation of women in any work, and particularly manual work outdoors, is everywhere considered as value" (Gadgil 1965). Working for a wage is a mark of low status, and caste status varies inversely with participation in manual labour (Srinivas 1976). Among 'scheduled' caste women (formerly classified as untouchables), participation in agricultural labour is much greater than among higher caste women. Omvedt (1978) notes that while women of poor and middle peasant families of non-Brahman castes have worked in the fields, among *Dalitis* (untouchables or 'scheduled' castes) and *Adivasis* (tribals or 'scheduled' tribes) women's participation is high, with some 52 % of *Adivasi* women employed as labourers compared to 28 % for the general female population.

Caste alone, however, does not explain the high proportion of women in Bihar engaged in the construction industry. Indeed, their expertise as 'carriers' of bricks, mortar and other building materials at construction sites is utilised in neighbouring Bengal where Bengali women do not lend themselves to such labour. Status among Bengali women is preserved through the combination of *purdah* with an understanding that 'respectable' women do not undertake paid labour. Despite poverty, rural women in Bangladesh do not usually work for pay even in such acceptable home-based industries as paddy-husking. To the question, "Why don't you work?", the poor Bengal village woman's reply is "It isn't possible. We might starve to death but we have to maintain our status. Otherwise the neighbours will speak of us." And when they do work, it is secretly, thus avoiding the criticism of neighbours. "One may know how to work, but not be able to get any use out of it." (Abdullah and Zeidenstein 1979).

The above reference to "work" presumably refers to work for pay, for as Cain et al. (1979) shows in one of the most detailed studies of women's work in rural Bangladesh, women process food, cultivate vines and other crops, look after household animals, and in general specialise in tasks that keep them close to the house. Classifying households as rich or poor by ownership of land (those with more than 2 hectares are considered rich), the authors record that poor women are often engaged in wage-labour outside the home, usually in traditionally 'female' jobs such as rice-processing or employment as servants in more wealthy households. However, with rising economic status, women's work hours increase in contrast to those of men which decrease. As they earn more, men reduce their own labour by hiring

Tab 2 Spatial variations in women's participation in the labour force

State	Proportion of Female Workers (of total female population)
Himachal Pradesh	40.56
Andhra Pradesh	33.12
Maharashtra	27.98
Madhya Pradesh	25.36
Karnataka	21.98
Tamilnadu	21.10
Jammu and Kashmir	20.34
Gujarat	20.27
Rajasthan	19.67
Kerala	16.65
Uttar Pradesh	15.70
Assam	14.23
Bihar	13.84
Orissa	11.37
Haryana	8.45
West Bengal	3.72
Punjab	2.25

Source: Census of India 1974

field hands. Conversely the authors explain, as poverty increases women deviate more from their 'normal' or accepted roles. Women's low participation in income-earning activities is perpetuated by limited opportunities. Furthermore, while men do not lend themselves to traditionally female home-production activities, women often lend themselves to male income earning activities, particularly when male earnings are lowest. Although Cain et al. feel there is insufficient evidence in their study to conclude that wives' income-earning activity is responsive to the husband's income activity level, it is nevertheless a crucial point for determining the value of women.

Women in Famines and other Food Crises

This section documents evidence that during famines or food crises when poverty levels worsen and income earning opportunities for men decrease, the resourcefulness of women enables them to assume a non-traditional roles. They suddenly assume the role of primary decision makers and food procucers for their households. Food crises occur often in India, and depending on their degree of severity, they challenge the traditional roles of women. A common example is the extension of their roles as food processors and preparers to include food procurement. As shown in the following sections, when there is little or no food to process or prepare, it is women who accept the responsibility for producing food to feed their families. They thus complement or replace the traditional roles in the household of men who may have lost the opportunity to earn or who may have migrated in search of paid work. Women procure food either directly by gathering wild foods or famine foods or indirectly by working for food or money.

In view of the spatial variation in the status of women and in their participation in the workforce, it might be expected that women of high status who did not usually participate in income-earning activities would prefer to gather wild foods. In contrast, women who prior to the food crises had worked for wages (or whose caste allowed them to earn money or food), would retain a preference for indirect food) procurement methods. The severity of a food crisis also would determine the degree and extent of change in a woman's traditional role. If, for example, the food crisis was mild, it would be unlikely to have much effect on the women of higher socio-economic status, whereas poor women might be obliged to gather wild foods to feed their families. Alternatively in a severe food crisis or widespread famine, socio economically higher status women might have to sell their assets of jewellery or land to purchase food, thereby indirectly becoming food procurers. If the famine of food crisis continued, it might then become necessary for these women to move in with relatives who were less severely affected and, through performing household chores for them, become procurers of food in more subtle ways. Poorer women would doubtless be driven from wage-labour to destitution and perhaps migration to urban areas, with little choice between begging or prostitution as a means of survival. The range of possible options available for women to procure food during famines or food crises (as determined by the severity and length of the famine and the pre-famine status of the women) may be seen either specifically as a single choice or as a series of choices through which they regress as the famine continues. Very broadly classified these choices, as already discussed, are:

1. Wild food gathering
2. Employment to earn money
3. Selling personal assets
4. Migration to better opportunity areas.

Wild Food Gathering

As the famine sets in and the pots in the kitchen continue to remain empty, inability to serve food to the family compels women to break traditional barriers of status and role, and join other women in search of food (Fig 2). The *Reports of the Famine Commission (1898)* refer to women at the beginning of the famine moving through the country in groups in search of food, sometimes travelling up to 25 km (16 miles) to hunt for *sag* in the jungles. Singh, in his study of the 1967 Bihar famine, noted the substantial measure of dependence on forest produce such as flowers, fruits, leaves and roots in the early days of the scarcity. Government owned forests were thrown open to enable people to collect the *mahua* flower to supplement their diet but, as the famine continued, there were also "knots of women beating dried grass and preparing a lean diet of tubers and roots" (Singh 1975). More recently Currey (1979) observed a similar change-over to famine foods among villagers in Rangpur during the 1974–75 famine in Bangladesh. Satyajit Ray's film adaption of Bibhuti Bhusan's powerful novel *Ashani Shanket* portrayed the tremendous adaptive capacities and resourcefulness of women in procuring food. At the onset of the famine they gathered *susni sag* (clover) and

120

Fig 2 Perception of famine by the Bengali artist Zainul Abedin. The simple sketch portrays the women's vital role in sustaining her family. (Courtesy: the Abedin family. Dacca, Bangladesh.)

bon kochu (wild arum), and when these were depleted, they searched in waist-deep water for snails and cockles. Their resourcefulness was their weapon against hunger. In both documented studies and local literature the gathering of famine foods is depicted as a woman's task.

Men did not show similar resourcefulness or adaptive capacities during famines. When they failed to earn their income or food through their usual channels, they initially became helpless while their women gathered wild foods to sustain the family. For men the alternatives then were either to register for food-for-work programmes, or to migrate in search of work to urban or non-famine rural areas, or, if they were incapable of work, to seek food from gruel kitchens set up by the government whenever a famine was declared. In *Ashani Shanket* Ray highlighted the different ways men and women handled the formidable barrier of caste. At the onset of famine, the Brahman exercised his caste rights to gain free food or priority to food from other villagers. As the famine intensified caste itself became a barrier to him[2], for he could neither undertake the work usually performed by non-Brahmans nor did he possess many work skills. The Brahman's wife on the other hand, found it eastier to cross caste barriers to earn food by husking paddy for others, or by gathering wild foods with other village women. When the Brahman returned empty handed from the bazaar because no rice was available in the shops, his wife was able to offer him the symbolic handful of rice which she had procured through her own labour. According to Singh (1975), in rural areas of India the phenomenon of groups of women gathering wild foods, or a greater than usual number of women seeking grain or food in exchange for rice husking or other household work, is symbolic of the onset of famine and should serve as a "warning signal" for administrators to mobilise famine relief.

Employment to Earn Money

When administrators acknowledge the existence of famines or food crises, relief measures are mobilised including such food-for-work programmes as earthworks and road-building projects. These create employment for famine victims who are then paid in money or food. The policy as outlined in the Famine Code is to employ able men, women and children, with the objective according to Singh (1975) of securing "human survival by preventing death from starvation and maintaining the integrity of village and family institutions which could be undermined by destitution and migration." Famine wage is a minimum daily wage kept purposely lower than standard daily wages in government departmental works (to forestall diversion of labour). One half of the famine wage is paid in grain from "fair-price" shops.

While Singh mentions that no distinction was made between the sexes in payment of adult famine wages during the 1966−67 Bihar famine, in practice these were often higher for males as the tasks performed by them were different. Men were mainly employed as diggers or earthcutters. These jobs were scaled as heavier or more difficult and therefore a higher wage was paid. Women were usually employed as carriers, scaled as a less difficult task and therefore paid less. This has been true through the history of famines in India (Tab 3 and 4).

Despite the lower wages for women, a significant feature of relief works in the 1868−69 and 1898 famines was the extraordinary proportions of women and children employed (Fig 3A). Between January and March 1897, after the winter rice harvest, males numbered more among relief workers, but from March to September consistently more women were employed in the relief works than men. This was largely because the men were periodically called away for cultivation and crop harvest. The notable feature is not so much the higher ratio of females in the relief works, rather the large number of them who participated despite the social setting where wage for work is considered status-reducing. The Famine Commission Reports of 1898 recorded that women, not usually employed as labourers, were actually employed as diggers and carriers during food crises. In Shahabad district the sex ratio of participants in relief works was 216 women for every 100 men, due again to the exodus of able-bodied males to the tea estates of North Bengal. Singh did not differentiate the relief workers for the 1966−67 Bihar famine by sex. He noted, however, that women from backward communities assumed new roles as "carriers" for men employed as diggers, and middle class women sought paid relief through light manual tasks such as spinning. These examples provide indications of the extent to which the traditional division of labour between the sexes had broken down.

The Famine Commission Reports also noted that all kinds of manual labour were looked down upon in Bengal (Khulna Division). Even at the height of the famine local labour for relief earthworks was difficult to find. Among the few who laboured in roadworks the participation rate of women was 20 for every 100 men, a substantial figure when considering

PERSONS ON RELIEF
DARBHANGA DISTRICT 1897

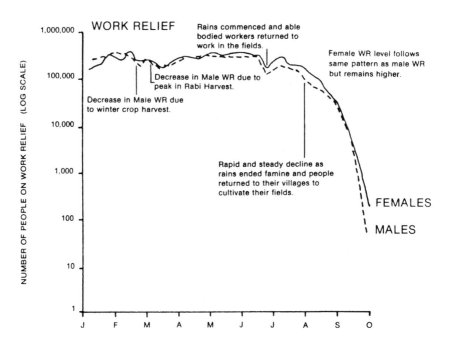

Fig 3 A   Work Relief

Female participation in work relief was slightly higher than male participation almost throughout the famine period. The overall lower level of male participation during the famine period may have been caused by lower numbers of males in the famine area, as many had left in search of work elsewhere. There were some seasonal fluctuations in male participation usually caused by the demand for male labour during crop harvesting. Fluctuations in female participation also occurred, usually following the fall in male participation during crop harvests. The return of the males to the relief works perhaps temporarily allowed the females to attend to their families before taking up relief work again. It could also be that the return of the males led to a decrease in the demand for female labour in the relief works.

the degree of contempt by Bengali women for paid public work. A more recent account of Bengali women's attitudes to paid labour during famines is the study of women in Bangladesh food-for-work programmes (Chen and Guznavi 1977). Although the food-for-work schemes commenced in the immediate post-famine period of 1975–76, their success ensured their continuation through to 1977. Among the millions of seasonal labourers attracted to the programme were a significant number of women who had come to take advantage of the opportunity to earn food despite the requirement of hard manual labour. This was a new phenomenon since Bengali women traditionally had a lower participation rate in the labour force during non-famine times (Tab 2), and een in periods of severe food crisis, ratios of female to male labourers had generally been very low. However, as poverty increased and

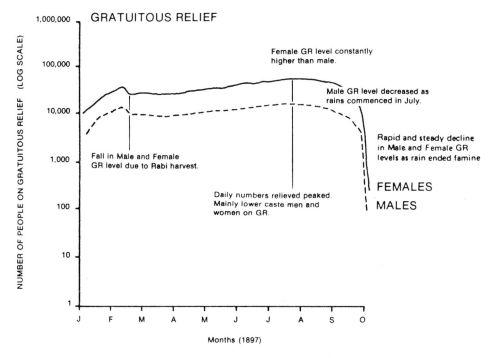

Fig 3 B Gratuitous Relief
The number of females receiving gratuitous relief was considerably higher during the famine period. There were slight seasonal fluctuations in both males and females on gratuitous relief, usually during crop harvest time. As the famine climaxed the numbers on gratuitous relief increased, but the end of the famine saw a sharp fall in numbers.

they could no longer depend upon their male family members to provide sustenance, destitution forced them to break tradition by seeking work for wages. Because of their novelty in Bangladesh, these working women were often referred to locally as "vagrant", "vulnerable" or "wretched strugglers for survival". Rather than beg or prostitute themselves these progressive women had chosen to work and earn food despite the non-liberal social structure. According to Chen and Guznavi the women's break with tradition was not a consequence of one famine, but rather the result of a continuing process. As the subsistence economy of Bangladesh continues to deteriorate and landlessness increases more destitute women are seeking permanent labour. While the food for work programmes provide some opportunities for women, they are only temporary. Chen and Guznavi recommend more permanent and on-going options in the rural wage sector.

Reports on early Indian famines record that women also undertook paid labour outside public works. In Bihar, for example, those unable to participate in earthwork programmes

124

Tab 3   Daily Food-for-Work Programme wages[a] in Patna 1897

	Male		Female		Big Children		Small Children	
	Wage	Task	Wage	Task	Wage	Task	Wage	Task
Maximum Wage[b]	2a 0p	200cft	1a 0p	150cft	0a 9p	200cft	0a 6p	None
Minimum Wage	1a 3p	100cft	1a 0p	80cft	0a 9p	100cft	0a 6p	None

[a] In the poor houses where gruel was doled out in the form of gratuitous relief to those incapable of work, the average meal was worth about 1a 7p. The monetary system then was 4p to 1 anna and 16 annas to 1 Rupee.

[b] Maximum and the minimum wages were determined by a number of factors such as the physical fitness of the worker, and the conditions of the soil, e.g. hard, sandy or gravelly etc. For small children (determined by age) the payment was as a dependent and the rate was therefore set and no task expected.

Source: Report of the Indian Famine Commission (1898). Vol. 8.

were employed at home twisting jute or spinning cotton. Bengali women also were recorded as seeking this form of home-based labour, although they preferred husking and cleaning paddy. For every 27 seers of cleaned rice, three seers were earned by the women for about two days of intensive labour plus the cost of pots and fuel for steeping and boiling the paddy. This form of famine relief appealed both to the people and to the administrators. Moreover, in view of the great aversion to earthworks and wage labour by men in Bengal, paddy husking as a form of relief work was considered for both men and women. In the extensive survey of the after-effects of the 1943 Bengal famine Mahalanobis (1946) documented that the "greatest economic deterioration" occurred among agricultural labourers. These labourers also had the greatest changes in occupations following the famine leading to a 26 % increase in those employed in paddy husking − a common alternative for women in their new role as food procurers. Women were also known to collect reeds growing in the *bils* for making mats as a source of income.

Because of these alternative income earning and food procuring capabilities of women, not many able women claimed gratuitous relief either as "dependents" of men or as "incapable of work". In defining those "incapable of work" who qualified for gratuitous relief the famine code specifically listed "women of respectable birth who by custom do not appear in public". Yet in some of the poor houses in Bihar where gratuitous relief was given, in 1898 there were fewer adult women than adult men. The proportion of adult men, adult women and children in the poor houses were roughly 50−35−15 *(Report of the Indian Famine Commission 1898)*. It is probable that the majority of these men were either too old or too malnourished to be able to work. In the gruel kitchens, however, the number of women on gratuitous relief were always more than men (Fig 3B), perhaps because women with babies in arms or with young children were served in these kitchens. Also like halfway houses, the kitchens served only those capable of regaining health and returning to work.

Tab 4   Revised Famine wage[a] 1967

State	Digger (male)	Carrier (female)	Helper (children 14+ years)
Gujarat	Rs. 2.00	Rs. 1.50	Rs. 1.00
Madhya Pradesh	Rs. 2.25	Rs. 0.90	Rs. 0.50
Bihar	Rs. 2.95	–	–
Rajasthan	Rs. 1.50	Rs. 1.25	Rs. 1.00
Uttar Pradesh	Rs. 1.00	Rs. 0.85	Rs. 0.60
West Bengal	Rs. 2.00	–	–

[a] The monetary system in 1967 as at present in India is 100 naya paise to 1 Rupee.

Source: Singh (1975) Appendix

Selling Personal Assets

The transition in individual responses as the famine spreads and intensifies is well depicted in *Ashani Shanket* (Bhusan, undated). The first major role change for the respected and *purdah*-observing Brahman's wife was to labour, along with other women, husking rice in return for food. When rice husking was no longer available she offered her gold bangles to her husband to raise money for food, retaining her new role as the family's food procurer. Bose (1961) quoting from *The Arthasastra* and *The Dharmasastra* mentions that the legal injunction on the inviolability of women's property *(stridhana)* is relaxed in case of famine when the husband may consume it without obligation to refund.

The high incidence of selling and mortgaging of land and livestock during famines has been noted in the *Reports of The Famine Commission* (1898); by Mahalanobis (1946) who remarked that such transactions were efforts to generate income to procure food; by Singh (1965) who noticed it was prevalent particularly among the middle class and small group farmers and by Currey (1976) in his study of the 1974–75 famine in Bangladesh. Both Singh and Currey recorded the loss of other property through sale as well, particularly jewellery, household goods, utensils, cooking pots and sometimes doors from village homes. It should be mentioned that women often control a large part of the family wealth in the form of jewellery or household goods and at times of food-crises they are bound to play a vital role in procuring food for the family.

Migrating to Areas with more Opportunity

When famines threaten the sustenance of a rural community and breakdown its mechanism of interdependence, the population migrates in search of food (Fig 4) or work. The survey of the 1943 Bengal Famine victims (Mahalanobis 1946) showed a startling increase in the number of destitutes, (of whom men formed the greatest proportion), migrating to urban areas as rural poverty increased. Chatterjee (undated), in his novel *Anandamath* emphasized the central role of women in making that final important decision for the family to leave

Fig 4 Zainul Abedin's sketch of the image of famine in the city – women and children living on the pavements after having migrated from the rural areas. Again the woman is portrayed as the food provider for her children. (Courtesy: Abedin family. Dacca, Bangladesh.)

home in search of food in the city. Kalyani at first resisted her husband's suggestion to leave the village arguing that as long as she survived she would fend for her husband and child and only after her death should the family move. But as the famine continued she decided to move the family to the city with the counter argument that even if she were to die, at least she would have seen her family on their way to survival in the city. Migration is therefore the last remaining strategy for women in their effort to fight the famine, but only when their capabilities are heavily taxed by their own malnourished condition and by their anxiety to save their families.

The most thought provoking narrative is perhaps Das' (1949) study of the destitutes arriving in Calcutta during the 1943 famine. Through skillful use of descriptive and analytic techniques he vividly sketched the plight of the famine victims. According to his survey, about 45 % of the destitutes were children aged 0–10 years, and about 39 % were men and women aged 20–60 years. Females accounted for 53 % of those between the ages of 15 and 60, a ratio of 111 females for every 100 males. In the 15–20 year age group, however, the proportion was far greater: 204 females for every 100 males. the higher ratio of females in general was, according to Das, due to:

the determination of young mothers not to remain in the villages where children would die from starvation, but to move to the city where was food available;

the large proportion of widows (71 %) among women aged 50–60 years, and

the decision by many adult males to remain in the villages either to care for property or prospective crops or because they had become too malnourished to move. Das also mentioned that the males may have decided to stay back because they felt that gruel kitchens in the city discriminated in favour of females and children who did not have as many options to earn food as did the males. (Fig 5).

Das observed in detail the background of the women destitutes and their self-sacrificing roles in securing food for their children.

Other studies highlighted the extent of famine-enforced migration from rural to urban areas. Singh (1975) found that some 5 % of households in Palamau district migrated during the 1966 famine in Bihar. Currey (1979) graphically portrayed the numbers of migrants and their destinations from a village in Matlab Thana, south of Dacca, during the Bangladesh famine of 1974–75. More detailed analysis of the data concluded that contrary to prevalent thinking on sex selective migration during famines, the outmigration from that Matlab village was equally distributed among the sexes (Currey 1983). Ruzicka and Chowdhury (1978) computed that in contrast with 'normal' (i.e. non-famine) times, when the proportion of male migrants from Matlab was greater there was in fact no sex differentiation during the 1974–75 famine when outmigration trebled in response to the shortage of food. In a study of the *Bastuhara* camp of landless rural migrants in Demra on the outskirts of Dacca, Islam et al. (1977) drew attention to:

the higher sex ratio of women to men in the camp (106 females per 100 males against the national averae of 92 females per 100 males;

the significantly greater proportion of female headed households;

the small number of women in the camp earning wages, and

the much lower wages earned by women, compared to that earned by men (*Taka* 106, forfemales and *Taka* 278 for males being the average monthly income).

In suggesting strategies to improve conditions within such camps, the authors stressed the need for governments to create special employment programmes for families whose household heads were female because such women not only found it more difficult to obtain paid work but were also underpaid when they did.

Pearson (1982) noted that women invariably outnumbered men among the influx of famine refugees into Indian urban areas and drew attentiono the influence of women's groups in the initiation of relief measures, the administration of gruel kitchens and the agitations for food Supplies. The aims of these women's groups included the provision of paid work for female destitutes enabling them to buy food. Cottage industries, largely established by and for women, included the making of hand-made paper; spinning; weaving of bamboo baskets; production of brooms, rope, oilseed, soap and paper-packets. Making glass bangles, traditionalla male occupation, was carried out by women of high caste during famines.

In *Ashani Shanket* Ray realistically depicted the breakdown of traditional attitudes, customary sex roles and social attitudes in response to famine. He portrayed the desperation induced by hunger which finally drove women to prostitution. Pearson (1982) referred to efforts of the *Mahila Atma Raksha Samity* in 1944 to open homes for destitute women to curb the rise in famine-related prostitution and to organise 'rescue' operations to rehabilitate women forced into prostitution by men posing as labour contractors. Das (1949) attributes

Fig 5 Famine-striken woman and child queuing for food at a gruel kitchen in Dacca city during the 1974—75 Bangladesh famine, just as Das describes in Calcutta during the 1943 famine.

the much lower proportion of females in the population of destitutes in Calcutta aged between 10—15 years to "their absorption in large numbers in the brothels" of that city. This particular phenomenon of the increase in the number of women in brothels or the increase in the actual number of brothels during or just after the famine has, understandably, not been studied in India. Such a study would provide additionally useful indicators of the geographical extent and severity of food crises. Like the aetiology of disease, studying the aetiology of famine-related prostitution could isolate information on the true 'value' of women as income earners in time of acute food shortage. Currey hypothesized[3] from his famine research in Bangladesh in 1974—76 that venereal disease (possibly related to the increase in prostitution) should be included as a famine-related disease, as opposed to only the starvation related diseases listed by Bang (1978) in his landmark article on the role of disease in the ecology of famine.

The role of food procurer acquired by Indian women during famines and food crises started with the gathering of wild foods, changed as the famine continued, to income-earning activities, and culminated with migration and prostitution. Yet woman may survive famine better than men. During the 1876 famine male deaths were twice the number of female deaths, a statistic which led Sir Charles Elliott to observe "all authorities are agreed that women succumb to famine less easily than men" *(Report of the Indian Famine Commission 1898)*. An enquiry into the 1943 Bengal famine found that there had been an increse of 62.5 % in male deaths, compared with 53.2 % in female deaths from famine or associated causes *(Famine Enquiry Commission 1945)*. Women appear not only to survive but also fight famine more tenaciously than men, a supposition perhaps reinforced by the following description of one 'surviving' in the streets of Calcutta:

She was not more than 25 years of age yet there was no womanly breast. Only two nipples dangled from two parched sheets of skin from which everything else seemed to have dried up. Her hair had become matted: perhaps they were not attended since she had left home. Her eyes had sunk into the sockets, but they had not yet lost their lustre as in the case of her husband. Indeed they had an unusual glow which was the outward indication of her great determination to survive this catstrophe, most probably for her little children". (Das, T.K., 1949)

This vital role of the women is nowhere referred to in socio-economic studies of either their status or their value.

The Paradox of Status

This particular woman, had she survived the famine, would no doubt have been classified in a subsequent census as a dependent or a housewife. Because she did not fall within the definition of "labour force participant", she would have swollen the ranks of non-workers, thus leading to the "intensifying devaluation of women" *(Report of the Committee on the Status of Women in India 1975)*.

This paper has highlighted that the trends in demographic and socio-economic indicators relating to women desired by the Committee on the Status of Women (i.e., increasing female participation in the labour force, increased migration of women to urban areas, and a lower death rate than that of men) are achieved in India and in Bangladesh during famines. The policy implications of wishing for a continuation of such trends may be tantamount to wishing for famines to continue.

The paper has also referred to the deteriorating socio-economic conditons during famines which lead women to break their traditional status and role. The socio-economic conditions are, in fact, quite the reverse to those which foster economic development. Deductive logic should make us realise that by choosing the particular demographic and socio-economic indicators they have done to date, researchers have not pursued the right variables in studying the value and status of women, both key concepts in understanding the potential role of women in development programmes.

After the time and effort spent in the ten year study of the value and status of women, fostered by the World Fertility Survey, *The Status of Women: A Comparative Analysis of Twenty Developing Countries* finally concludes with a reference to Buvinic (1976):

Two crucially important questions are: which social indicators should be used to establish the ranking of the position of women relative to the position of men, and who should make this value judgement currently measures of women's status, especially those used cross-culturally, probably could be better defined as measures of *'modernity in women's participation'*.

Summarizing the relevance of this twenty nation comparative research, Curtin (1982) states: "Viewed in this light modernity the information presented in this report may be useful". Another apology that the right variables for studying the value and status of women have not been pursued.

Many of the valuable pieces of empirical research referred to in this paper (Cain et al. 1979; Chen and Guznavi 1977; Abdullah and Zeidenstein 1979), and some of the more general articles summarising research in the area, referred to the status of women and the discrimination they faced in the labour market. Unfortunately, all had one drawback: they neglected to ask the women being studied their own views of their status and which of their functions within the household and society determined their value. The value of women in India and Bangladesh has so far been examined from a perspective fostered by western ideas of development and research, an example being the exhaustive analytic discussion of women's time-allocation and function in rural Bangladesh (Cain et al. 1979) which emphasized for policy makers the need for special consideration of employment opportunities for women. Had there been some measure of the differing values which women themselves allocated to various activities (e.g. if they ranked child-care or home activities as more important than, say, trading or wage work) the authors' recommendations may well have been different. Their suggestions then may have emphasized government subsidies or incentives for women reporting their children regularly to the nearest primary health centre for immunisation and nutritional supplements, or for sending their children regularly to school. Such subsidies could be either money, food, clothing or other necessary goods such as fuel wood, or perhaps free medication for all family members, to make up for the loss of wage work in looking after their children. The example of a village in the north-east of Thailand, where research has shown that third degree malnourishment among children increased following such "development inputs" as income generating activities for women who then became busy earning incomes and did not care for their children (Valyasevi and Dhanamitta 1978−81), should serve as a lesson.

Some examples of alternative interventions (to those creating job opportunities for women) could well be: the supply of fuel wood (or other fuel) in a fixed quota per family for sending their children to school regularly, and the arrangement of creche facilities for younger siblings of school attenders. Household chores (e.g., fuel wood collection and care of younger children) are some of the main reasons for low school attendance in rural areas. Chen and Guznavi (1977), through their portrayal of the images of various women in food-for-work programmes, implicitly assume that income earning opportunities for women are the *only* answer to improving their status and quality of life. Such suggestions are essentially relevant to "the increasing proportion of women" (Islam et al. 1977) who are either widowed, divorced, separated or abandoned who need to become full-time earning members in the household. For the larger proportion of women, dependent on male incomes but needing supplementary financial support, alternative interventions to income generating activities would not only encourage them to preserve and nurture the family entity but would also lessen the drift to urban areas in search of paid work. Yet current research repeatedly proposes the creation of work opportunities for women, and continues to assess the value of women on the basis of their participation in labour. The women themselves have seldom been asked for their own ideas of "development" policies suited to their own tradition and role.

Conclusion

In this paper the status of women has been explored by documenting their roles during famine. This has exposed a paradox, because their status as presently defined for purposes of development, increases during famines. A resolution of the paradox might therefore be to consider new definitions of the status of women based upon the value systems of the women themselves.

Notes

1) Some of the variables need careful research and evalution before their effect on the status of women can be concluded. The controversy about classification of women's activities and the reporting of women's participation in the labour force (Census of India 1974) continues to remain unresolved in India. Also in a culture where work is considered a hardship rather than a privilege for women, and work for wages is associated with low status, the declining proportion of women in paid labour could, without the consideration of related economic variables, be interpreted as the increasing value of women within their own cultural system. The interrelationships among women's life expectancy, their higher mortality and their unique but risk-inducing biological role as child bearers should also be examined in greater detail before any conclusions are made about the effect of differential access to health services for men and women and the effect of this on female mortality (Chen et al. 1981). The increasing migration to rural areas could be interpreted positively as a trend in the opposite direction to urbanisation which drains rural populations and leads to deprivation of the rural sector. Taking 'development' to women in rural areas rather than expecting women to come to development in urban areas should be one of the alternatives for consideration.

2) Although famines have been known as "levelers" of social structure where class and caste barriers begin to dissolve, Singh (1975) noted that the Brahmans strongly resisted working or eating with other castes in the relief projects.

3) Currey, B.: personal communication 1982.

Note added in proof:

Two recently available articles contributing to "the differential mortality by sex during famine" controvery are:

Langsten, R.: The effects of crisis on differential mortality by sex in Bangladesh. Bangladesh Development Studies IX, 2, 75 (1981)

Rivers, J.P.W.: Women and children last: an essay on sex discrimination in disasters. Disasters 6,4, 256−267 (1967)

132

References

Abdullah, T.A.: Villagewomen as I saw them. The Ford Foundation. Dacca May 1974.

Abdullah, T. and Zeidenstein, S.: Women's Reality: Critical Issues for Program Design. Studies in Family Planning. Special Issue on Learning about Rural Women. 10, 11/12 (Nov-Dec. 1979a)

Abdullah, T. and Zeidenstein, S.: Project-Oriented Research on Aspects of Women's Knowledge and experience. Studies in Family Planning. Special Issue on Learning about Rural Women. 10, 11/12 (Nov-Dec. 1979b)

Alamgir, S.F.: Profile of Bangladeshi Women. Selected Aspects of Women's Roles and Status in Bangladesh. Prepared for USAID Mission to Bangladesh. Dacca June 1977.

Alamgir, M.: Famine in South Asia. Political Economy of Mass Starvation. Cambridge, Mass 1980.

Bang, F.B.: The Role of Disease in the Ecology of Famine. Ecology of Food and Nutrition, 7, 1 (1978)

Beteille, A.: The Position of Women in Indian Society. In: Devaki Jain (ed.) Indian Women, Part 1. Chapter 6. Publications Division. Ministry of Information and Broadcasting. Government of India 1976

Bhusan, B.: Ashani Shanket. Calcutta. Film version of novel titled "Ashani Shanket" translated into English as Distant Thunder by Satyajit Ray. India (undated).

Bongaarts, J. and Cain, M.: Demographic responses to Famine. In: Cahill, K.M., (ed.), Famine, Orbis Books, new York 1982.

Bose, A.: Social and Rural Economy of Northern India. In: Firma K.L. Mukhopadhyay, Calcutta 1961.

Cain, M., Khanam, S.R., Nahr, S.: Class, Patriarchy, and Women's Work in Bangladesh. Population and Development Review, 5, 3 (September 1979)

Census of India: Comparative Chart of Concepts and Definitions. Vol. 1, Part II − B(i) 1961.

Census of India: Report on Resurvey of Economic Question − Some Results. Census of India 1971. Paper 1 of 1974. Government of India 1974.

Chatterjee, B.C.: Anandamath. Bandyopadhyaya, B.N. and Das, S.K. (ed.), Calcutta (undated).

Chen, L.C., Huq, E. and D'Souza, S.: Sex Bias in the Family Allocation of Food and Health Care in Rural Bangladesh. Population and Development Review, 7, 1 (March 1981)

Committee on the Status of Women in India: Towards Equality: Report of the Committe on the Status of Women. Government of India, Department of Social Welfare 1974.

Chen, M. and Guznave, R.: Tentative Findings from Research: Food-for-Work; Socio-economic Implications for Female Participants. Mimeo. OXFAM and World Food Programme. Rome 1977.

Currey, B.: The Famine Syndrome: Its Definition for Prevention and Relief in Bangladesh. Journal of Ecology and Nutrition, 7 (1978)

Currey, B.: Mapping Area Liable to Famine in Bangladesh. Ph. D. Dissertation. University of Hawaii. University Microfilms Order Number 8012253, 1979.

Currey, B.: Famine Migration in Matlab: A Detailed Study of Family Structure and Movement in Non-famine and Famine Conditions. Research Progress. Department of Geography, Flinders University of South Australia, 1983.

Currey, B., Ali, M. and Khoman, N.: Famine: A First Bibliography. East-West Resource Systems Institute. Honolulu, Hawaii, and USAIOD. Washington DC,USA 1981.

Curtin, L.B.: Status of Women: A Comparative Analysis of Developing Countries. Reports on the World Fertility Survey. No. 5. A publication of the Population Reference Bureau. Inc. June 1982.

Das, T.K.: Bengal Famine (1943) As Revealed in a Survey of the Destitutes in Calcutta. Calcutta University Press. Calcutta 1949.

Dirks, R.: Social Responses During Severe Food Shortages and Famine. Current Anthropology, 21 (February 1980)

Gadgil, D.R.: Women in the Working Force in India. Asia Publishing House, Bombay 1965.

Gulati, L.: Female Work Participation: A study of Interstate Differences. Economic and Political Weekly (11th January 1975a)

Gulati, L.: Female Work Participation: A Reply. Economic and Political Weekly (9th August 1975b)

Gulati, L.: Occupational Distribution of Working Women: An Interstate Comparison. Economic and Political Weekly (25th October 1975c)

Indian Famine Inquiry Commission: Report on Bengal. Manager of Publications, Delhi 1945.

Jahan, R.: Women in Bangladesh. Paper presented at IXth International Congress of Anthropological and Ethnological Sciences, Chicago. August, 1973. The Ford Foundation. Dacca. February 1974.

Jain, D.: Indian Women. Publications Division. Ministry of Information and Broadcasting. Government of India 1976.

Kalakdina, M.: The Upbringing of a Girl. In: Devaki Jain (ed.), Indian Women Part I, Chapter 8. Publications Division. Ministry of Information and Broadcasting. Government of India 1976.

Mahalanobis, P.C., Mukherjee, R. and Ghosh, A.: Sample Survey of the After Effects of the Bengal Famine of 1943. Sankhya, 7, 4 (April 1946)

Nanda, B.R. (ed.): Indian Women from Purdah to Modernity. A Series of lectures given at the Nehru Memorial Museum and Library. Published in Bombay 1976.

Nath, K.: Female Work Participation and Economic Development: A Regional Analysis. Economic and Political Weekly (23rd May 1970)

Omvedt, G.: Peasant Movements: Women and Rural Revolt in India. The Journal of Peasant Studies, 5, 3 (April 1978)

Pearson, G.: Famine and Female Militancy in India. Paper prepared for the International Conference on Women and Food organised by the Department of Sociology, University of New South Wales, February 1982.

Reddy, D.N.: Female Work Participation: A Study of Interstate Differences. Economic and Political Weekly (7th June 1975)

Report of the Bengal Famine (1898).

Report of the Indian Famine Commission (1898–1948) (with evidence volumes). Printed for her Majesty's Stationery Office, London.

Rudra, A.: Cultural and Religious Influences. In: Devaki Jain (ed.), Indian Women, Part I, Chapter 5. Publications Division, Ministry of Information and Broadcasting. Government of India 1976.

Ruzicka, L.T. and Chowdhury, A.K.M.A.: Demographic Surveillance System – Matlab. Volume Four. Vital Events and Migration 1975. Cholera Research Laboratory. Dacca, Bangladesh, Scientific Report 12, 1978

Satter, E.: Village women's Work. Chapter II. In: Women for Women. Bangladesh 1979.

Singh, K.S.: The Indian Famine of 1967. A study in Crisis and Change. People's Publishing House, New Delhi 1975.

Sinha, J.N.: Female Work Participation: A Comment. Economic and Political Weekly (19th April 1975)

Srinivas, M.N.: The Changing Position of Indian Women. T.H. Huxley Memorial Lecture, 1976. Institute for Social and Economic Change. Bangalore 560040, India.

Torry, W.I.: Anthropolotigal Studies in Hazardous Environments: Past Trends and New Horizons. Current Anthropology, 20, 3 (September 1979)

Valyasevi, A. and Dhanamitta, S.: First Progress Report of IDRC. Health, Nutrition, Agriculture and Income Generation for Rural Development in N.E. Thailand. Institute of Nutrition. Mahidol University, Bangkok, Thailand 1979–1981.

Walston, N.: In: Daily Nation (Nairobi) 30 and 31 March 1967.

World Food Programme: Women in Food-for-Work. The Bangladesh Experience. WFP Rome 1979.

Famine as a Spatial Crisis: Programming Food to the Sahel

Gould, P., Prof. Department of Geography, The Pennsylvania State University, University Park, PA 16802, USA
and
Rogier, A., Chef de Bureau, Regie Autonome des Transports Parisiens, 13 rue Jules Valles, 75011 Paris, France

Abstract: The ability to respond effectively to severe drought conditions with emergency food supplies depends, in large part, on an effective description of the transportation system under varying environmental, political and technological conditions. Using the Sahel droughts as examples, a pedagogic introduction to linear and goal programming models is provided, and the results of several pilot models discussed. The assignments of emergency food supplies under changing conditions of network structure raise questions about contingency computer models and plans in the future, and the need for monitoring a complex and rapidly changing man-environmental system.

Introduction

There is hunger and sickness in the land
I say there is a cauldron burning on the plain
Red earth, red vengeance all aflame must it be born in vain?
I carry a ball of fire on my head and cannot put it down
I pray for rain, for vital floods to come again . . .
(Peters L: Poem 45)

It is unfashionable to be a neo-Malthusian today. Voices tell us that it is all a matter of increasing yields, genetic engineering, making contraception readily available, raising standards of living, or simply (sic) ensuring effective distribution. Yet 'green revolutions' have come and gone; genetic engineering is in its infancy; the acceptance of contraception is still limited by severe cultural, economic, religious and educational constraints; many per capita standards of living are stationary or going down; and distribution is founded upon assumptions of such idealism and ethical altruism that they surely characterize angelic, not human, behavior. Famine is an old, and all too familiar story: all the indications are that it may well be on the increase. Whatever criticisms may be levelled at the global 'Spaceship Earth' models[1]), they all point, with varying degrees of immediacy and severity, to the same conclusion − too many people, not enough food, and problems of sheer *physical* distribution in the future so immense that they startle the most concerned imagination.

During the 'Seventies, a particularly severe drought characterized the area along the southern edge of the Sahara (Fig 1), transforming the six Sahelian countries (Mauritania, Senegal, Mali, Upper Volta, Chad and Niger) into an area of acute human distress, where malnutrition, famine, despair and death prevailed. Out of the thirty million people, about one-third were severely weakened by hunger and malnutrition, and American public health experts calculated that at least 100,000 people died from the drought during 1973 alone. Most of them were children (Sheets and Morris 1974).

The severity and the magnitude of the Sahelian drought cannot be measured by the number of deaths alone. The ecological effects, the disappearance of the vegetation, and the introduction of true desert conditions also severely disrupted the economy. Indeed, the drought completely destroyed the traditional way of life for millions of Sahelian farmers and herdsmen, many of whom were obliged to migrate southwards in search of food, water and sheer survival. Demographic patterns underwent massive and dislocating change. A journalist testified:

What we have in many cases is that a city like Nouakchott, Mauritania, normal population 40,000, has been increased to something like 120,000. This means that more than two-thirds of the people living in and around there live in tents outside the city, depending upon the day to day deliveries of foodstuffs. In the city of Mopti, Mali, there is a similar situation, and there are others.

(Congressional Committee on Foreign Affairs 1973)

Many lost all their means of livelihood and were unable to return to their homes. As far as the herdsmen were concerned, their cattle had been decimated, first by the drought itself, and secondly by the diseases contracted in the new areas to which they moved. As for the farmers, their fields could not be sown, since all the seeds had been consumed as food.

There have been periods of severe drought throughout the history of the Sahel, for it is a dry zone where rainfall is marginal and subject to extreme fluctuations (Fig 1). Indeed, rainfall may not only vary greatly from year to year in total amount, but also in the times of onset and cessation. Dry years are not an unusual occurrence, but the Sahelian drought of the 'Seeventies constituted a different order of magnitude; it lasted over several consecutive years, and it was of wide geographic extent.

Although we are still uncertain about the true nature of the drought, it appears that the reduced rainfall along the southern fringe of the Sahara was due to the displacement of the subtropical high-pressure system towards the equator (Lam 1973). The displacement, which may have been caused through industrialization (Bryson 1973), was a result of the monsoon shifting southwards, away from the Sahelian region, producing a drastic, and possibly lasting, climatic change. A meteorologist has commented:

It appears that the phenomenon which is giving rise to the drought has already a long history of over twenty years of continuous development, and that it is not likely to disappear in the near future as part of any cyclic phenomena.

(Lamb 1973)

Another study found that between 1957 and 1972 the summer monsoon rainfall had decreased steadily by more than 50 % (Winstanley 1973). It is obvious that such a decrease in rainfall, in a region where agriculture depends directly on the monsoon, and where many people subsist on the very margin of existence, must inevitably bring malnutrition, famine and death.

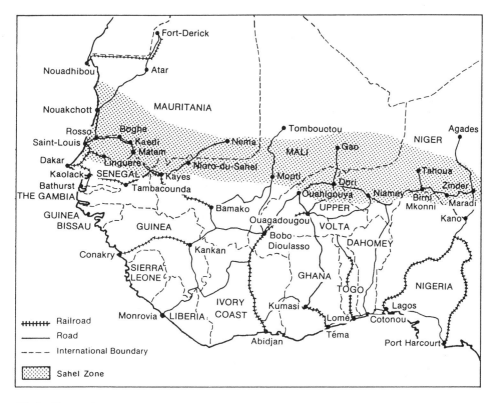

Fig 1 The road and rail network giving access to the Sahel in West Africa. (Note. The Republic of Chad is omitted from the eastern margin of the map

Unable to cope alone with such a catastrophe, the Sahelian countries called for international assistance. International organizations and various individual countries started to provide emergency aid, such as air lifts, vaccines, seeds, animal feeds, and so on, to the stricken regions. However, their actions were often greatly delayed, and sometimes the attempts failed completely due to the absence of coordination between the organizations, the lack of contingency plans, and the absence of precise and readily available data on the Sahel. In addition, the international organizations were suddenly faced with the obligation of bringing, as quickly as possible, a massive amount of aid to areas that are not only far apart, but where the transportation network is either inadequate or even non-existent. Many of the problems encountered in the relief programs began with the lack of a detailed picture of the transportation capabilities of the region. One report noted:

In the summer of 1973, for example, there was at once too little and too much grain for Mali. As shipments to Mali fell short, tons of grain piled up on the docks of Dakar. "The rats feed well at Dakar", cabled a reporter to the *Guardian* on July 24th. "Some of those stocks will still be on the wharves in November, if the rates − the only fat animals I saw in West Africa − leave any at all".

(Sheets & Morris 1974)

Many reports indicated that the failure of the rescue operations was due to the inability to bring food on time to the needed areas — an inability founded upon the gross inadequacies of the transportation network, frequently unsatisfactory even under normal conditions. Moreover, most of the afflicted states were land-locked and dependent on the coastal countries to maintain their transport links. Mauritania and Senegal were exceptions, but the ports of Mauritania were insufficiently equipped for the emergency, and Mauritania itself shared the same problems as its Sahelian neighbors. In spite of some improvements over the past thirty years, access to the sea remains precarious. For example, certain links may be disrupted for political reasons, because relationships between the inland and the coastal states tend to be unstable. For a convoy of food to arrive at its destination, it is necessary for the interior and the coastal states to remain on good terms with one another — or, in the absence of good relations, to respect transit agreements.

It must never be forgotten that distances in the Sahel are great, so that imported food must always travel over long and tenuous transportation chains. Usually, the first constraint to large shipments of food is found at the start of the supply lines: the problem of port capacity. Even under normal conditions, the poorly equipped ports are unable to cope, particularly if much of their export trade is highly seasonal, leading to severe periods of congestion.

At the height of the port congestion last month (Lagos, Nigeria), a hundred and five transports were waiting for a space at this city's fourteen berths. Shipping officials said some ships had waited for ninety days. (New York Times, 12 May 1975)

There are also problems caused by transit delays through neighboring states and the lengthy customs procedures.

It is normal customs practice that an importer's access to his goods is restricted until all customs formalities have been completed and necessary duties paid. This means that all documents must be available in the right place, at the right time — in itself a considerable logistical problem. In the case of transit goods, financial guarantees may be involved, all of which take time. (Hiling 1973)

In addition, shipments may be further delayed by deficiencies in the transportation network. Except for major arteries, most of the roads are not permanent, all-weather routes. Many have not been surfaced, and they deteriorate very rapidly under extreme climatic conditions (Gould 1960). During the monsoon season the rain washes out important links, and it is impossible to deliver food to many isolated regions except with expensive airlifts. Inadequate ferries and bridges also restrict transportation in terms of vehicle size and load, and trans-shipments are often needed, reducing the already low efficiency of these routes. Railroad traffic is also limited, with low capacities and high costs of operation. Normal transit times to the interior frequently have to be measured in weeks or even months, so that the total costs are consequently very high.

Poor transportation is obviously one of the major problems encountered by developing countries. In order to obtain greater flexibility, substantial improvements have to be made, although changing the short-term capacity of the network may be a difficult task.

In any transport system the maximum possible traffic flow will be determined by the capacity of the individual links and nodes in the network ... It follows that the short-term capacity is not easily increased and piecemeal improvements in the network may produce only marginal increases in the productivity of the through system. (Gould 1960)

Modelling the Distribution Problem

In this short, essentially instructional essay, we have several objectives:

1. To set up an optimization model that would indicate the best possible distribution of food throughout the Sahel region, assuming that the world has sufficient food surplus to fulfill the Sahelian demand.
2. To investigate the effects of changing environmental contraints.
3. To examine what would happen if the food surplus and the world transportation budget were insufficient to transport sufficient food to all the Sahelian villages.
4. To illustrate the need for long-term monitoring of large spatial systems.

It is important to note that the model has been established only as an example. Because of data limitations and time constraints, it cannot represent the 'real world', whatever we mean by that constantly changing entity. In addition, it is stressed that although the six Sahelian countries actually declared a state of emergency, we have taken into account only five of them (Mauritania, Mali, Senegal, Upper Volta, and Niger). Chad was not considered, since its problems were especially severe, particularly in the wet season.

Assuming that the world has a food surplus capable of fulfilling the Sahelian demand, we shall construct a model optimizing the distribution of the surplus to the deficit regions. In essence, we are concerned with a transportation problem which calls for shipping food to Sahelian towns with various demands. We require the most efficient solution − a solution which derives the minimum total transport cost given the unique set of network characteristics and environmental contraints.

Such a problem can be solved very efficiently with linear programming. Mathematically, linear programming deals with a set of simultaneous equations expressing the requirements which have to be met, and a linear function which represents the objective[2]. The standard computational form of linear programming is the simplex method, which determines a first, or basic feasible solution, finds new and better solutions by iteration, and then selects the 'optimal' one. In other words, it retains the solution which maximizes or minimizes the objective function subject to the conditions of the problem, which in our case refer to the set of ports and routes used by the food convoys.

Setting up an Optimisation Model

Programming Emergency Food Supplies: Am Elementary Introduction

To many unfamiliar with the wide variety of programming methods available as standard software options on today's large and fast computers, the previous paragraph will be incomprehensible. How do you get from real transportation networks, starving people, and emergency food shipments to "simultaneous equations ... iterations ... and solutions minimizing an objective function"? Programming − whether of the linear, quadratic, integer, combinatorial, geometric or goal variety − is a large and technically complex field, but like many important and useful ideas it is really quite simple in conception. In the context of distributing emergency food supplies to famine areas, it basically answers this question: How do you get surpluses of food at one set of places, to another with deficits, using whatever transportation is available, all at the least cost? We cannot give you a complete introduction to the way linear and goal programming answer such questions, but with a little patience and a bit of 'working it through' we would like to give you a 'feel' for the basic approach.

To keep things simple and manageable, we are going to take a small piece of the transportation network of West Africa (Fig 1), the railroads leading north from Lagos and Port Harcourt to Kano, and the roads to Maradi, Zinder and Agades. We are also going to make the amounts shipped, and the transport costs, simple numbers, so that we can do the arithmetic in our heads as we go along.

Suppose we 'disconnect' this piece of the overall system, and treat it in isolation just for illustrative purposes. Also suppose that Lagos has eight units to ship (+8), Port Harcourt has four (+4), while Maradi needs four (−4), Zinder needs three (−3), and Agades requires five (−5). How do we get from a verbal description of the problem, to a graphic picture so that we can 'see' what is going on, to a mathematical description that we (or a computer) can use to calculate a solution? This is the geographer's usual problem: to 'model' the situation so that the most effective solution can be found.

To start with, just to get the hang of it, suppose we ignore the actual structure of the network, how the towns are actually connected by road and rail, and simplify the problem to the situation shown in Fig 2. All this says is that both Lagos and Port Harcourt can ship their surpluses to the three deficit towns of Maradi, Zinder and Agades at the transport costs indicated in the line-breaks.

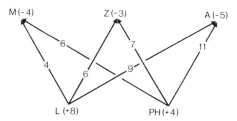

Fig 2 Graphic model of grain surpluses at Lagos (L) and Port Harcourt (PH) and transport costs on various routes to the deficit towns of Maradi (M), Zinder (Z) and Agades (A).

Now, all we are going to do is express exactly the same information in the form of a table − what a mathematician would call a Simplex Tableau − which sets up the problem in a form suitable for a computer to solve by an iterative algorithm. ("Iterative algorithm" is just a fancy name for a trial-and-error, hunt-and-peck method that will get us to the minimum solution, only in this case we are going to play the role of the computer with you, and we shall hunt-and-peck our way to the least-cost solution together.

Let us take all the information we have, and then see how it fits neatly into tabular form (Tab 1).

First of all, what are the *possible flows?* Obviously, there are six − from each of the two origins, Lagos (L) and Port Harcourt (PH), to each of the deficit areas Maradi (M), Zinder (Z), and Agades (A). These are represented by the columns in the table. Secondly, what requirements must we meet? Again obviously, L must ship +8, PH has to get rid of its +4, and M, Z and A need −4, −3 and −5 respectively. Notice that all the surpluses (+12) exactly equal all the deficits (−12). There are technical tricks to get around this required balancing act (imaginary storage dumps and so on), but we do not have to worry about them in this example. Of course, if the deficits *exceeded* the surpluses there is no way we could solve the problem, and we would have to say no feasible solution existed. People would starve, and we would have a terrible ethical problem of deciding who got food and who went without. This is a question we must touch upon again. For the moment simply notice that all the requirements, or *constraints*, are listed on the right hand side in the column which is labelled – in a great flight of poetic imagination typical of computer programmers – RHS, or Right Hand Side! So far so good?

Alright, but what about all those 1's in the other 6 columns? It turns out they are equally obvious – just follow through a couple of examples with us. Suppose a single unit (1) of the surplus (8) at Lagos is shipped from that port to Maradi. Obviously that shipment goes toward meeting the stated requirements in our model that Lagos ships out its 8 unit surplus

Tab 1: A programming (Simplex) tableau

		All the possible flows				Requirements that must be
L→M	L→Z	L→A	PH→M	PH→Z	PH→A	met (RHS)
1	1	1				L = 8
			1	1	1	PH = 4
1			1			M = 4
	1			1		Z = 3
		1			1	A = 5
4	6	9	6	7	11	← COSTS

and that Maradi must receive 4 units. (It should be noted that the number of units is *exact:* no more, no less. Programmers call this an 'equality constraint'). So, in the column L→M, we put 1's in the rows marked L = 8 and M = 4.

It follows that each time a 1 appears in any of the six columns (which, continuing to conform with the language used by mathematicians and computer programmers, we shall henceforth refer to as vectors), the constraint to ship or receive is reduced by one (1) unit. Think of it this way: the first time the L→M column "comes into solution" (more programmers' language!) with a single unit, L's constraint to ship becomes 7, and M's constraint to receive becomes 3. Similarly, each time that the PH→Z vector (a flow from Harcourt to Zinder) comes into solution, this would help to meet PH's constraint to ship 4, Z's to receive 3 . . . and so on.

The bottom row of our programming tableau simply shows the minimum cost of transporting each unit from the shipping point to the receiving city.

The question now is, what pattern of shipments will meet all these constraints at least (i.e. minimum) cost? Well, with this basic description behind us, the final step is to state the problem mathematically, like this:

Minimize: $4 (L{\rightarrow}M) + 6 (L{\rightarrow}Z) + 9 (L{\rightarrow}A) + 6 (PH{\rightarrow}M) + 7 (PH{\rightarrow}Z) + 11(PH{\rightarrow}A) = COST$

Subject to: $1 (L{\rightarrow}M) + 1 (L{\rightarrow}Z) + 1 (L{\rightarrow}A) + 0 (PH{\rightarrow}M) + 0 (PH{\rightarrow}Z) + 0 (PH{\rightarrow}A) = 8$
$0 (L{\rightarrow}M) + 0 (L{\rightarrow}Z) + 0 (L{\rightarrow}A) + 1 (PH{\rightarrow}M) + 1 (PH{\rightarrow}Z) + 1 (PH{\rightarrow}A) = 4$
$1 (L{\rightarrow}M) + 0 (L{\rightarrow}Z) + 0 (L{\rightarrow}A) + 1 (PH{\rightarrow}M) + 0 (PH{\rightarrow}Z) + 0 (PH{\rightarrow}A) = 4$
$0 (L{\rightarrow}M) + 1 (L{\rightarrow}Z) + 0 (L{\rightarrow}A) + 0 (PH{\rightarrow}M) + 1 (PH{\rightarrow}Z) + 0 (PH{\rightarrow}A) = 3$
$0 (L{\rightarrow}M) + 0 (L{\rightarrow}Z) + 1 (L{\rightarrow}A) + 0 (PH{\rightarrow}M) + 0 (PH{\rightarrow}Z) + 1 (PH{\rightarrow}A) = 5$

This is the way our mathematician, using numerals, signs and letters instead of words, has said:

"Find out the least possible cost of shipping all 12 surplus units (8 at Lagos, 4 at Port Harcourt) in such a way that they meet exactly the deficits at Maradi (4), Zinder (3) and Agades (4)".

Beneath the command "Minimize" in the text, the single line 4 (L→M) +6 (L→Z) . . . displays the single journey costs from Lagos and Port Harcourt to Maradi, Zinder and Agades.

Under "Subject to" are the constraints. Had words been used instead of letters, signs and numerals, the first line would have read:

1 unit from Lagos to Maradi, plus 1 unit from Lagos to Zinder, plus one unit from Lagos to Agades, without any shipments to these from Port Harcourt, until all 8 have been moved to where they are needed.

The second line says:

Nothing from Lagos, but from Port Harcourt one unit to Maradi, plus one unit to Zinder, plus one unit to Agades, until the available four units of surplus have been moved to where they are needed.

The next three lines say, in order, Maradi is to receive surplus units from Lagos and Port Harcourt until its total requirement of 4 is met; Zinder is to receive surplus units . . .; Agades is to receive . . . .

Now do you see why we are involved in 'optimizing a function' which expresses our objective, subject to sets of 'linear constraint equations'? Reading such material can become tedious, even boring, when it is written at such length, so we will not throw this sort of thing at you any more, but we did want you to see how it is possible to go from real problems involving starving people to rather abstract mathematical expressions. So, the real question is: what values (flows) are we going to plug in to that objective function that will minimize it and, *at the same time*, meet all the constraints we have imposed? Suppose we decided to ship the following flows:

Quantity	Flow	Transport Cost		
4 from	L→M	4	or	4 x 4 = 16
3 from	L→Z	6	or	3 x 6 = 18
1 from	L→A	9	or	1 x 9 = 9
4 from	PH→A	11	or	4 x 11 = 44
				Total 87

This certainly meets the constraint conditions that all the surpluses are shipped and all the deficits are received, but does it *minimize* the total value (i.e. the cost) of the objective function?

Let us try again. Suppose we try:

PH→M	1 x 6 = 6
PH→Z	2 x 7 = 14
PH→A	1 x 11 = 11
L→M	3 x 4 = 12
L→Z	1 x 6 = 6
L→A	4 x 9 = 36
	Total 85

So although more shipments are being made, and the constraint is maintained that all shipments are made, the total cost is lower than before. Can we do even better? Suppose:

PH→Z	3 x 7 = 21
PH→M	1 x 6 = 6
L→M	3 x 4 = 12
L→A	5 x 9 = 45
	Total 84

This is actually the minimum solution (can *you* find a lower one?), the least-cost solution that a modern computer would find in less than one thousandth of a second. But it is not a very realistic solution, mainly because we totally ignored the *structure* of the actual transportation system. This is something we can hardly afford to do: when ports or railway terminals become congested (another constraint), when roads get washed away in the rainy season and disconnect parts of the network, the whole flow system is affected and may radically alter the optimum solution. Let us try again, moving a bit closer to a realistic description. Suppose we include Kano, which seems to act as a trans-shipment point, even though is does not require any emergency food shipments itself. The structure is now:

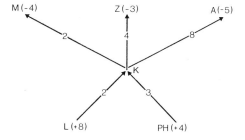

Fig 3 Graphic model of grain surpluses at Lagos (L) and Port Harcourt (PH) and transport costs on various routes via the trans-shipment point at Kano (K) to the deficit towns of Maradi (M), Zinder (Z) and Agades (A).

and again we have the job of translating this graphic representation into tabular (i.e. *mathematical*) form. Actually, it is surprisingly simple (Tab 2) since Lagos and Port Harcourt can only ship to Kano, and Kano can only ship to Maradi, Zinder and Agades.

144

Tab 2: The tableau with Kano as a trans-shipment point

L→K	PH→K	K→M	K→Z	K→A	RHS
1					L = 8
	1				PH = 4
		1			M = 4
			1		Z = 3
				1	A = 5
1	1	−1	−1	−1	K = 0
2	3	2	4	8	←COSTS

But a new twist has been added that is really rather neat the first time you meet it. We have added the constraint-requirement that K = 0. This says that since Kano is only a trans-shipment point, the flows in must equal the flows out (we do not want emergency food supplies piling up at a place where they are not needed).

Now follow through the logic of the tableau slowly and carefully with us. Suppose that the L→K (Lagos to Kano) vector comes into solution 8 times. That would obviously take care of the requirement that Lagos must ship 8 units, and we would have incurred a cost of 8 x 2 = 16 in the process. But what happens to K = 0 when this occurs? Obviously K is no longer going to be equal to 0, but will become −8. But the equality constraint says this is not allowed: come hell or high water, burning drought or massive flood, K has *got* to equal *exactly* 0. What can we do to make it so? Well, look at those K→M, K→Z and K→A vectors. For example, suppose we bring that K→M vector into solution 4 times. This will not only meet the requirement that Maradi receives the food it needs, but that −1 will change K=−8 to K=−4, which is closer to 0, and a distinct improvement.

Well, you have the hang of it now: that K=0, and the −1s are an accounting trick to make sure Kano serves properly as a trans-shipment point to the northern towns. The problem is actually quite simple (check that the solution is 88), but it allows us to introduce you to the important question of taking one aspect of the actual structure into account. For our third and last example we are going to add an additional complication, and so move towards a much more realistic and flexible description. So stay with us, reading slowly and carefully, following the description with the diagram and table in front of you.

Suppose we have this sort of situation:

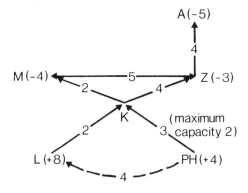

Fig 4 Graphic model of grain surpluses at Lagos (L) and Port Harcourt (PH) and deficit towns Maradi (M), Zinder (Z) and Agades (A). Transport costs are shown on the various links via the trans-shipment points of Kano (K) as well as Maradi (M) and Zinder (Z). Also shown is the sea-transfer from Port Harcourt (PH) to Lagos (L) in the event of a bottleneck on the Port Harcourt (PH) to Kano (K) link.

one much closer to actual conditions, with Maradi and Zinder as both deficit towns *and* trans-shipment points, and a capacity constraint on the railway line from Port Harcourt to Kano. This is actually very realistic: capacity constraints on roads, railways, ports and trans-shipment points are quite common, and a great deal of investment by governments and the World Bank has gone into lessening these bottlenecks over the past 30 years. But the real trick is to get from the graphic description to the tableau (Tab 3), for we must add vectors to allow shipments from more towns, including a transfer from Port Harcourt to Kano by sea via Lagos. This will mean emergency food supplies can still move northwards if the capacity constraint on the railway line proves to be a bottleneck.

Tab 3: Tableau with capacity constraints and trans-shipments

L→K	PH→K	K→M	K→Z	M→Z	Z→A	PH→L	RHS	
1						−1	L = 8	
	1					1	PH = 4	
		1		−1			M = 4	Basic requirements
			1	1	−1		Z = 3	
					1		A = 5	
	1						PH→K ⩾ 2	Capacity constraint
1	1	−1	−1				K = 0	Trans-shipment
2	3	2	4	5	4	4	← COST	

With the map and tableau in front of us, let us "think through" the problem: the L→K vector will come into solution 8 times, but the PH→K can only enter 2 times before it bumps into the ⩾ 2 capacity constraint. This means the PH→L vector must enter 2 times, *taking* 2 from Port Harcourt, and *giving* (that −1) 2 to Lagos. Now the L→K vector comes in 2 times more to send the shipments on to Kano, at which point the K=0 constraint is →12. This can only be brought back to 0 by the K→M and K→Z vectors entering the solution, and so on . . .

With a few more tricks, this is the way in which actual transportation systems, with their particular structural characteristics, trans-shipment requirements, demands, supplies, port and route capacity constraints can be modelled. For the entire West African system we need a tableau of 94 rows and 235 columns (Rogier 1975), but the *principles* are just the same as we have used here. The big advantage of such a mathematical description is not only that we can find an optimal solution, but also use the systems of equations to *simulate* different conditions. Wet and dry season conditions, for example, may drastically alter costs, or even break certain connections as bridges get washed away, or roads are flooded. Once we have a basic structural description, however, we can easily alter costs, constraints or connections, and so use our model to help us decide what to do under different circumstances. It is characteristic of complex systems that a small change in one part (a road in Mali being washed away, a bridge in Nigeria closed, a breakdown in unloading facilities, or a strike at a port), may send large ripples of effects throughout the system to change totally the optimum solution. We shall now turn to the actual problem of modelling the supply of emergency food to the Sahel.

The Structure of the Problem

During the drought, various sorts of aid were sent to the countries of the Sahel; for example, food, medicines, vaccines, feeds, and forage for the livestock. In order to simplify the model, we shall assume that only one type of commodity is going to be shipped; namely, food for human consumption. However, it would not be difficult to run the model for different commodities. For the same reason (a simplification that does not, in fact, make it at all unrealistic), we shall choose only thirteen of the major ports (Fig 1). These are the ones that are generally regarded as being most important, and although a number are insufficiently equipped, they form a set of port facilities which seem to stand the best chance of handling sudden surges of foodstuffs without becoming completely paralyzed. In addition, in the hinterlands of each port there are transportation facilities which are sufficiently developed to carry food from the coast to the interior.

We not only have to decide upon the actual ports to be incorporated into the model, but we must structure the problem in such a way that we can eventually determine the amounts that each origin point on the coast should receive. The quantities depend upon three factors:
1) the demands at the interior towns;
2) the capacities of the routes in the hinterlands of the ports;
3) the capacity constraints of the ports themselves.

The lower limit at each port is described by an inequality constraint, such that no port can have a negative capacity. Such a description has the advantage of allowing the computer to determine the optimal distribution of food along the set of coastal origins.

It is equally necessary that each port must have an upper limit, or maximum capacity, for any chosen time period. Such capacity constraints may be particularly severe in the case of west African ports. Thus, we have imposed a constraint on each port which depends basically upon wharf capacity and available unloading equipment. If a port is congested, traffic must detour to the next port which raises the total cost of the distributional problem. Such divergencies from scheduled ports are quite realistic. For example, it was reported that:

With Nigeria's normally crowded ports filled with scores of incoming vessles, some have been diverted to unload as far away as Lome, Togo, 200 miles from Lagos along the Atlantic coast.

(New York Times, 12 May 1975)

Again, to keep the model within reasonable bounds, we shall consider only the principal towns of the interior which have acted as the major redistribution points for the very small towns and villages of the Sahel, although smaller places were also included in the more remote areas of the North.

The second task is to estimate the quantity of food required at each point in the interior. Since precise information is not available, we must assume that the food requirements are roughly in proportion to the population of the surrounding regions. By setting the constraints in the simplex tableau as strict equalities, we are specifying that a particular town must receive the exact amount specified.

Because of the structure of the transportation network, we change many of the destination points into destination/trans-shipment points. Thus, they may consume locally a certain amount of food shipped to them, but they can also ship food on to other towns in the interior. We must also add four additional trans-shipment points (Kaolack, Kankan, Kumasi and Kano: four cities that have no food requirements themselves), so that the convoys of food are only passing through them on their way to their final destinations.

We must also remember that we are dealing with countries having only skeletal transportation networks, and road surfaces which are often very poor, particularly during and immediately after the wet season. Any cost over a particular route is determined by several factors: first, the length of the link, the assumption being that the transportation costs are a linear function of the distance; secondly, the means of transportation used; thirdly, the quality of the network, laterite roads not only being more expensive, but having higher risks. The network also changes from season to season. During the summer months heavy downpours will frequently wash out some of the laterite roads. When this happens, convoys must either use alternative ground routes, or the food must be shipped in by air.

Finally, it is possible to model the problem in such a way that the capacities of the various links are explicitly brought into the problem. Since a number of the routes are narrow and prone to accidents, they cannot handle large volumes of traffic. It is for these reasons, together with high congestion rates, that upper limits (or capacity constraints), were imposed on some of the roads.

Investigating the Effects of Changing Environmental Constraints

Solutions Derived by Linear Programming

With the basic problem structured as a transportation/trans-shipment model, it is now possible to obtain optimal solutions under a variety of conditions. For example, the model can be used to simulate seasonal changes in the environment (e.g. wet and dry seasonal conditions), as well as political events (such as strikes at one or more of the ports). We have chosen two solutions out of many that have been attained under various simulated conditons.

In the first example, we place upper limits (or chronic congestion effects) upon each port capacity, and also constrain some of the links in the network. Because of these constraints, the solution (Fig 5) does not simply involve the shortest paths from the ports to the interior towns, but requires that alternative routes, sometimes from more than one port, enter the optimal solution. For example, the port of Nouadhibou in Mauritania has a very limited capacity, so food supplies must be shipped over the more costly route from Nouakchott. Similarly, a capacity constraint on Lagos means that Port Harcourt must also handle some of the emergency supplies. Dori, in Upper Volta, receives most of its requirements from Tema via Ouagadougou, but constraints on the route and port mean the balance must be made up from Cotonou in Dahomey.

It is worth noting, in passing, that not only does a linear programming solution provide the most efficient distribution of foodstuffs under these contrained conditions, but something called the dual solution indicates what the probable impact would be if the capacity constraints were released. Such additional information (automatically calculated by standard computer programmes today), indicates what reduction in transport costs we could expect if the infrastructure of the network, or the port capacities, were upgraded. Thus the dual values, called the reduced costs, suggest a possible set of investment priorities. These indicate that if we treat West Africa as a whole, we would get the most return on limited investment resources by upgrading port facilities at Nouadhibou, Saint Louis, Lagos, and Dakar in that order.

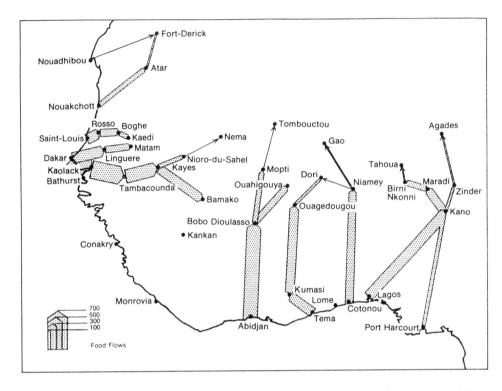

Fig 5 Food flows modelled in winter conditions with moderate capacity constraints on ports and links

A further advantage of using linear programming is that it is a very versatile and adaptable model. We can easily simulate changes in the environment by changing the constraints, and thus adapt the model to most real world situations. For example, imagine a situation where the political and economic relationships between Senegal and Mali are broken, similar to the actual situation in 1960. If the links between Matam and Kayes, and between Tambacounda and Kayes, are suddenly removed from the set of possible routes, Mali would have to find alternative routes very rapidly from the sea in order to receive its share of emergency relief. Which ports could replace Dakar and St. Louis? Certainly not Bathurst, which has no direct connection with Mali, and in any case the convoys would have to follow Senegalese routes, which would not be allowed under this particular situation. In this case, Mali would probably have to turn towards Conakry, Monrovia or Abidjan. In order to simulate such a situation, we set the capacities of the Matam-Kayes-Tambacounda links to zero, and rerun the model to obtain the optimal food flows seen in Fig 6.

The food flows in Fig 6 show that Conakry sends 400 units of goods to Bamako via Kankan, while only 110 units arrive at Monrovia to be sent on to Bamako and Kayes. Abidjan also increases its imports up to its maximum capacity (600) and this in turn allows a flow of 60 units of food to leave Bobo Dioulasso in the direction of Bamako in order to

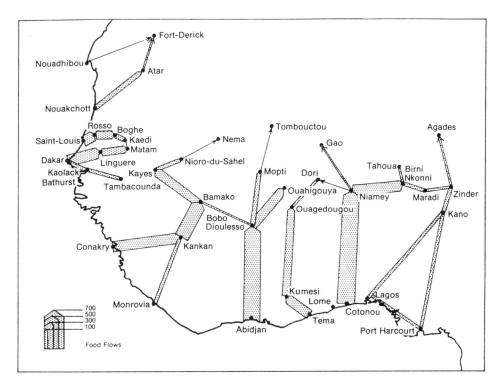

Fig 6 Food flows resulting from the model in winter conditions with political and social disruptions added.

complete the food requirements of western Mali. The price of the hypothetical Mali-Senegal disruption is severe, since the total cost has been increased greatly by using the ports of Monrovia and Conakry, which previously failed to enter the optimal solution.

As a further example of a disruption to the system, imagine that all the workers in the Nigerian ports suddenly go on strike. Thus, all incoming traffic would have to be diverted and shipped to neighboring ports. Such a situation is also very simple to simulate by setting the capacity constraints of Lagos and Port Harcourt to zero. When this happens, all the Nigerian imports are shipped to Lome and Cotonou. Because of the capacity constraint previously set on Cotonou (400 units), the food must be shipped to Lome, unloaded there, and then driven by truck to Cotonou, in order to use the route Cotonou-Niamey to get to Birni Nkonni, which is cheaper than Lome-Birni Nkonni. However, even this route, Cotonou-Niamey, has its capacity constrained to 600, so that some of the convoys must be sent to Lagos and Port Harcourt by the long detour along the coast. Thus, we can easily incorporate environmental and technological changes, as well as political and social disruptions, into the model. The new solutions could enable either the countries or the international agencies concerned, to deal quickly with new, and perhaps rapidly changing, situations.

Up to this point, we have always assumed that sufficient food supplies could be delivered by donor countries or agencies to the ports of West Africa. Suppose, however, that world supplies were insufficient to supply the devastated areas with all their requirements. We face the task of modelling such a tragic human situation − tragic, because it implies that a certain, and all too easily calculated, number of people will die of starvation. In such a situation, desperately difficult questions must be faced. For example, which countries or towns shall be abandoned to their fate, and which will be allowed to survive? This is precisely the question of triage (New York Times, 12 May 1975). Although we will consider this question in greater detail later, we shall approach it for the moment purely in cost or economic terms.

In order to simulate such a situation, we have taken one of the previous models (winter conditions with port and route constraints), and have added further limitations to represent the new situation. We have to specify first the available foodstuffs, now less than the total demanded by the devastated areas. Suppose, for example, that we only have 2800 units available to meet a demand of 3270. In addition, we must change the constraints describing the demands from equalities to inequalities. For example:

Fort Dérick $\leqslant$ 40
Fort Dérick $\geqslant$ 0

This statement implies that the quantity of food imported by Fort Dérick must be equal to or less than the actual amount (40) demanded, and that it cannot be negative.

The tragic results are all too intuitively obvious. All the emergency food supplies are distributed first to the closest points in order to minimize the transport cost. As a result, all the interior towns which needed the food the most are cut out of the solution because they are too far away. This situation might sound rational on purely economic grounds, but the humanitarian and ethical questions it raises are severe. In order to avoid such discrimination, we could change the model slightly and require that all the cities and villages situated in the interior of the Sahel receive their food requirements first. When their demands are completely satisfied, then any remainder could be allocated to other places.

In order to do this, we specify that the food demanded at the villages in the interior of the Sahel are strict equalities, and the results of the new specifications are very different. Now, all the interior towns receive their total demands, and the small amount left over is allocated to those additional places nearest the ports to minimize total costs. Four cites are without any foodstuffs at all, two in Upper Volta, Ouahigouya and Dori, and two in Niger, Birni Nkonni and Maradi. The "life boat ethics" of linear programming has designated these as the towns who will have to do without when severe shortages arise. One way these towns can remedy such a situation is by upgrading the roads leading to them so that they become the cheapest routes. In this way, the food will be allocated to them instead of other towns to the west in Senegal and Mali. Such a total dog-eat-dog situation illustrates vividly the nature of pure economic decision-making.

Examining what Would Happen if the Food Surplus and Global Transportation Budget Were Insufficient to Transport to all the Sahelian Villages

Triage as a Goal Programming Problem

We have reached the point where we are faced with problems that are basically those of establishing priorities. The traditional linear programming model sets such priorities using purely economic, or cost minimization, criteria. In many real life situations, however, these are not the only considerations. Other things intrude into the relatively simplistic economic viewpoint. A recent and more general approach, known as goal programming, explicitly allows a person to incorporate sets of priorities into the purely formal mathematical structure. Such priorities may well include political and social criteria.

We shall use such an approach to consider the distribution of food to the Sahel not only under total budget constraints, but also under constraints of political feasibility at the international level. The solutions will still represent minimum cost values, but they will be subject to priority constraints set by decision makers, as well as the now-familiar constraints of port and route capacity. Such an assumption makes the model not only more realistic, but provides a way for the decision maker (perhaps the head of an international agency), to interact with a purely formal mathematical system to simulate the various results of priority choices. Although the flexibility of linear programming is great, it does have certain limitations to represent a very complex human and environmental reality. Its use is restricted by the fact that the objective function is uni-dimensional. In other words, linear programming is unable to solve problems which take into account a whole set of contradictory constraints and objectives. In our case, the objective of distributing food to the Sahel can no longer be achieved if we place restrictions upon the resources available and the budget available for trans-shipping the food.

As a first step, we have to define a list of priority goals, and then rank them in order of importance. Goal programming will consider the low priority goals only if the higher order goals have been achieved, or if they have reached a point beyond which no further improvements are desired. The model of goal programming is somewhat different from that of linear programming, although strictly speaking the latter can be considered a more constrained subset of the former. The task of goal programming is to minimize the deviations between the goals, rather than optimizing the objective function. The technical details are beyond the scope of this pedagogic paper, but the examples are the result of actual runs specifying various goal or priority conditions[3].

In order to set up a problem in goal programming, we have to construct a constraint tableau and specify an objective function. Suppose, for example, an international organization has set the following goals and arranged them in order of importance:

1) they want to bring the food requirements to the regions in the interior of the Sahel which are undergoing the most severe crisis;
2) they want to meet both the food deficit and the budget constraints, deciding to distribute all of a limited amount of food (2800 units), while at the same priority level, they would also like to constrain the total transportation budget to 250,000 units;
3) they would also like to fulfill the food demand of all the Sahelian towns as much as possible.

Having identified the goals and constraints, we must construct the model in such a way that we can evaluate the degree to which they have been met. In other words, we must be able to check whether some degree of over- or under-achievement in each goal is satisfactory or not. Goal programming deals precisely with this sort of problem. We must also define the degree of priority we wish to place on these goals, perhaps the following:

P_1) the highest priority is assigned to the objective of getting the food requirements to the Sahelian villages of the interior.

P$_2$) the second priority factor is assigned to both under-utilization of the food surplus and of the transport budget. However, it is possible to weight the variables at the same priority level differently. Thus the international organization might decide to give greater priority to the under-utilization of food as opposed to the under-utilization of the budget.

P$_3$) the lowest priority factor is assigned to the under-achievement of each city's food requirement.

With these goals and priorities, the solution during the drier winter months indicates the first goal can be completely fulfilled. In other words, the nine cities of the interior of the Sahel can receive all of their food requirements. On the other hand, by meeting this top priority, the second and third goals have not been completely met. Because the transport costs to the interior towns are so high, the budget constraint becomes binding, and 218 units of food cannot be distributed at all for lack of money. This result is very important, and demonstrates that unless the international organization increases its transport budget, the disposable food surplus cannot be distributed, in which case more people will starve.

As for the third goal, it is hardly surprising that it could not be reached, since we have an inadequate transport budget and insufficient food supply. The towns which did not receive their share of the emergency aid were all grouped in two countries: Upper Volta (Ouahigouya, Dori and Ouagadougou, where the demand was only 29 % fulfilled), and Niger (Birni Nkonni and Maradi). To determine the exact spatial pattern of shipments, we would have to take results from goal programming, and place them as demands in our former trans-shipment problem. Thus, there is an almost symbiotic relationship between the two parts of the overall model.

In the summer months of the wet season the pattern is roughly the same, but because the summer transport costs are much higher, three new cities have to be added to the list of those which did not receive the food aid. They are Boghé and Kaedi (Mauritania) and Zinder (Niger) which only has twenty-six percent of its requirements met. It is crucial to note that under such a budget constraint, a total of 683 units of food, almost one-quarter of the total available, would not be distributed. In addition, these solutions might not appear to be very equitable at the *national* level. While Mali and Senegal get their total food requirements, Upper Volta and Niger receive almost none. Is it not possible to imagine a real world situation where an international organization would like to impose another goal on the model, in order for the food distribution to be more equitable among the nations involved?

For example, the total transportation budget could be divided into five parts, each Sahelian country receiving a share proportional to its total need. With the same set of goals and priorities, and under winter conditions, the first goals can be completely achieved. All the cities of the interior of the Sahel receive their entire food demand, and at the same time one of the five Sahelian countries has used up all of its transportation budget. As for the second objective, dealing with the budget and food surplus constraints, they have only been partially met. Again, we must make the point that by imposing essentially political constraints upon the problem, ostensibly to generate more equitable distributions at the national level, an even larger amount of food (747 units) cannot be allocated to any Sahelian city. The transportation budget has already been used up to distribute the other 2053 units of food available. Ten towns either receive no help at all, or have their demands only partially fulfilled. They are now located in all of the Sahelian countries, instead of being concentrated in only a few.

Nevertheless, we may well ask whether such a solution is more just, or whether it is, in fact, more cruel and inhumane. Indeed, the amount of food not distributed has increased by a factor of 3.4 over the previous, less-constrained model which did not incorporate national distributional priorities. At the same time, the number of cities actually receiving food has decreased, and there are now 1122 units of unfulfilled demand throughout the entire system.

Under summer conditions the situation is even more serious. The transport budget is quickly dissipated by the requirement to ship some food to each country under very bad environmental conditions. Now fourteen towns do not have their demands met, and 1154 units are left to rot on the quaysides of the harbors because of the severe budget and political constraints. In addition, and for the first time in this model, a first priority goal is not fulfilled either. Kayes, Bamako, and Tombouctou, all interior towns do not receive their full requirements.

To Illustrate the Need for Long Term Monitoring of Large Spatial Systems

In all the example we have examined, we have had to assume that the model parameters (i.e., the costs, constraints and demands) were capable of being specified with reasonable accuracy. Yet we know perfectly well that information about these things is usually very difficult to obtain in many developing countries. Moreover, this system is frequently subjected to disturbances, not only from the physical, but also from the human, environment in which it is embedded. During a crisis it might be extremely difficult to obtain accurate and up-to-date information as inputs to the model – either the more conventional linear-programming model or the hybrid goal-programming model. In a highly fluid and changeable situation, it would be essential to obtain current and fresh solutions using the best and latest available information. Such information might be difficult to acquire, and there would be considerable temptation on the part of the countries facing severe drought problems to exaggerate their plight, thus making their neighbors worse off.

Under such circumstances, it appears essential that an international agency, or perhaps a national donor country, has an independent source of accurate information. This raises, in turn, the whole question of monitoring environmental conditions closely, so that even if conditions change while ships are at sea, new solutions can be found and the carriers redirected to a new set of ports. In addition, the environmental and human disturbances may raise the total cost of effective distribution above the available budget. If these can be properly monitored and evaluated within the model, the higher-cost solutions which are simulated can serve as warning signals to loosen the budget constraint.

Enormous sums of money have been spent over the past decade on satellite monitoring systems. Such remote sensing capability should be investigated fully to determine how these newer sources of information can be used as part of an independent monitoring service. Only in this way, by using the latest and most accurate information, can the human problems be solved efficiently. We would note, in this connection, that efficiency is indeed a proper criterion to use, since it implies that limited supplies are allocated most effectively to save human lives.

As a postscript, it is worth noting that shortly after the first Sahel drought, the President of the United States sent a request to the National Academy of Sciences requesting them to examine the question of 'America's preparedness to help in large-scale famine relief. All the horror stories of transport difficulties, environmental conditions, international coordination, bureaucratic stupidity, inexperience, bribery and corruption were by that time well documented, as well as the fact that a number of aid administrators had simply broken down after serving devotedly under great stress. But by that time the publicity had gone (only to reappear during the 1978-80 famine); no funding for proper monitoring, or the construction of efficient contingency programmes was available; the usual report repeating other reports, and saying "we must do something" was written by the usual committee of 'experts' — and promptly shelved and forgotten. When the next crisis comes, little will have been learnt, the great relief efforts will start all over again from scratch, and everyone will be surprised at the 'sudden' arrival of a new famine in the Sahel, the Punjab, . . . who knows where? But as one distinguished analyst of complex systems and structures has written:

Perhaps a surprise is the answer to a question that has not been asked. (Atkin 1981)
Is it not time we asked the right questions?

Notes:

1) From the early "limits to growth" models based on the dynamic modelling of Jay Forrester, to the later, regionally disaggregated models of Mesarovic and Pestel. See, for example, Forrester, J.: World Dynamics, Wright-Allen Press, Cambridge, Massachusetts 1971, and Mesarovic, M. and Pestel, E.: Mankind at the Turning Point, E.P. Dutton Inc., New York 1974.
2) An elementary introduction is contained in R. Abler, J. Adams and P. Gould, Spatial Organization: The Geographer's View of the World, Prentice-Hall Inc., Englewood Cliffs 1972, pp. 458—475.
3) Basic introductions include Ingnizio, J.: Goal Programming and Extensions, Lexington Books, Lexington, Massachusetts 1976.

References

Aktin, R.: A Theory of Surprises. Environment and Planning B, 8, p. 365, 1981.
Bryson, R.A.: Drought in Sahelia: Who or What is to Blame? Ecologist, 366—71 (1973)
Gould,P.: Transportation in Ghana, Northwestern University, Evanston, Geography Series 4, p. 112, 1960.
Hiling, D.: West Africa's Land-Locked States — Some Problems of Transport and Access. In: Dalby, D. and Harrison Church, R.J. (ed.), Drought in Africa, p. 114, 1973.
Lamb, H.H.: Some Comments of Atmospheric Pressure Variations in the Northern Hemisphere. In: Dalby, D. and Harrison Church, R.J., (ed.) Drought in Africa. Centre for African Studies, School of Oriental and African Studies, University of London 1973.
Peters, L.: Poem 45. In: Jones , E.D. (ed.), African Literature Today, Heinemann, London, and Africana Publishing, New York 1973.
Rogier, A.: Distributing Food to the Sahel: A Pilot Study in Linear and Goal Programming, Papers in Geography, 13, the Pennsylvania State University 1975.
Sheets, H.: Morris, R.: Disaster in the Desert: Failures of International Relief in the West African Drought, Humanitarian Policy Studies, The Carnegie Endowment for International Peace, Washington, DC 1974.
The New York Times (May 12 1975)
US Congress, Committee on Foreign Affairs: The Drought Crisis in the African Sahel. Hearings before the Subcommittee on Foreign Affairs, House of Representatives, 93rd Congress, lst Session, Washington, DC 1973.
Winstanley, D.: Recent Rainfall Trends in Africa, the Middle East and India. Nature, 243 (June 1973)

The Impact of Famine Relief: Unasked Questions in Africa [1]

Snow, Robert, T., Coordinator, Africa Research, Research and Planning Dept., Maryknoll Fathers, Maryknoll, NY 10545, USA

Present adress: Oxfam America, 302 Columbus Avenue, Boston, MA 02116, USA

Abstract: Depending upon circumstances, famines may bring about large or small degrees of social change in African pastoralist societies. Relief agencies and government enter into these potentially volatile situations, often without entertaining questions about the possible consequences. They should look closely at the immediate and background causes of famine before leaping into immediate solutions which may simply complicate matters in the long term.

Indeed, disasters have consistently provided opportunities for the initiation of radical changes in poor societies that enhance development far beyond the normal pre-disaster pace.

The Protein-Calorie Advisory Group of the United Nations System (1977)

By this time, about four months after the worst of the crisis had past, it would have been impossible for the casual visitor to find any indication that the Mursi had recently experienced one of the worst periods fo food shortage in their history, and the worst in living memory.   Turton (1977)

Projections for food production in Africa during the coming decade are uniformly alarming (Christensen 1981; World Bank 1981). While there is general agreement that the primary focus of effort should be prevention of food shortages, the fact remains, at least in Africa, that famines will probably increase in frequency and severity for the foreseeable future. This paper raises a number of questions about the likely impact of famine relief on African pastoralists, a group significantly affected by famine, and relief, during the past decade. As quotations from the UNPAG *Guide* and David Turton suggest, famines and other disasters can have widely varying impacts, ushering in either rapid transformation or leaving little perceptible mark. Whatever the intentions of its donors, relief may itself become an agent of change in potentially volatile situations.

This study was prompted by attempts to respond to a request from a missionary working among the Turkana of Northwest Kenya. During 1980, he found himself more and more drawn into emergency aid programmes as cattle raids, drought, and disease created an increasingly serious food shortage. Seeking information about the best way to provide relief to pastoral nomads like the Turkana, he also asked for some indication of its likely long-term effects. While some two years' research clearly showed the existence of commonly accepted guidelines for giving relief, it was equally clear that I had been unable to find adequate answers to the latter question. This paper, addressing a number of the issues related to the potential impact of relief, particularly on African pastoralists, is based in part upon reported experiences from Turkana and elsewhere. These were supplemented by interviews with people involved in setting policy at several of the larger relief-giving agencies in the US, staff at various United Nations agencies, and with workers at the Nairobi offices of some of these groups. I have also reviewed as much of

156

the literature on the impact of famine relief as possible. Finally, a number of important additions and revisions were made, based upon information presented at the 1982 Workshop on Famines and Food Emergencies, sponsored by the International Disaster Institute and the London School of Hygiene and Tropical Medicine.

It is hoped, if nothing else, that the attention drawn in this fashion to certain consequences of famine relief and other forms of aid, may heighten the awareness of those engaged in them to the constellation of potentially sensitive issues raised by their efforts. Their reponses will, of course, depend upon the specific situation in which they find themselves.

The paper consists of three sections. The first is an enquiry into the potential impact of famine relief on pastoralists like the Turkana. It begins with what is perhaps the most far reaching and significant of the possible consequences: the impact of famine relief on 'development'. This, in practice, frequently means speeding up the transition from self-sustaining, largely autonomous subsistence, pastoral societies into market-dependent, cash and wage-labor entities incorporated into the nation state. The second poses questions about related, but more immediate and visible impacts which relief may have on the social, cultural, economic, and political structure of pastoral societies. The third section looks at these questions within the context of reports regarding the ongoing Turkana famine and relief efforts to contain it.

What Model of Development is implicit in the Actions of Famine Relief Givers? What are its Consequences for the Recipient Society?

As the UNPAG *Guide* and Turton note, famines by themselves may either bring radical change or very little apparent change to a given society. Relief efforts, whatever the giver's intentions, may become crucial variables in a continuing, and sometimes dramatic, process of change. Conversely, but perhaps less frequently, they can also facilitate a return to the status quo. Turton's observations about the rapid return to apparent normalcy among the Mursi are based upon situation in which only a very limited amount of famine relief reached the afflicted population.

"None of the measures they adopted (to cope with the famine) ... were in themselves new or unusal to them". (Turton 1977)

The likelihood that relief givers will become actively involved in the process of change within a famine-stricken society is increased by the fact that many agencies now see their role not just as providers of stop-gap aid, but also as agents of development intended to help alleviate the root causes of the famine.

For example, Oxfam states:

Oxfam's outlook as a *development agency* is also more appropriate to the needs of drought and famine situations than to the other types of disaster, because rehabilitation after a drought involves development as well as relief efforts, and worthwhile agricultural programmes may originate from this work. The very occurrence of a famine or drought-caused disaster represents a failure of development and renewed or redirected development programmes are an essential part of the response. (Oxfam 1981)

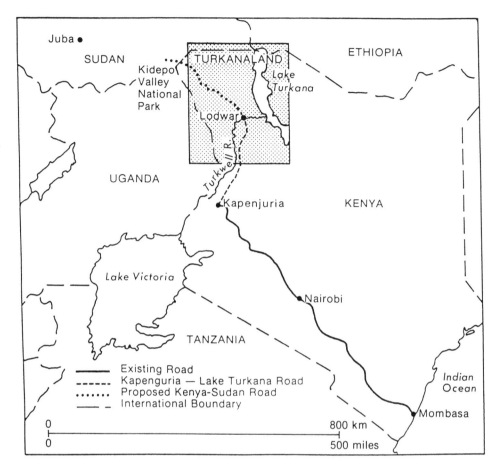

Fig 1 Turkanaland

The UNPAG *Guide* also devotes a chapter to post-disaster rehabilitation and development. While noting that such efforts will need to be coordinated with broader government plans it, too, suggests a basic strategy for the

improvement of social services, production and consumption of high-quality foods, preventive and curative health services, safe water supply and waste disposal, basic educational needs, introduction of simple energy-saving technologies.

(Protein-Calorie Advisory Group of the United Nations System 1977)

As well, it suggests ways to augment employment and income generation and to foster socio-economic development.

The *Guide* also stresses that development plans must be tailored to the requirements of a given situation, and that "promotion of community participation, with local persons providing necessary leadership, guidance, and implementation (is crucial) ... vested interests should be eliminated and the population should be kept aware of the programs and reconsulted periodically." (Protein-Calorie Advisory Group of the United Nations System 1977) These suggestions are often extremely difficult to implement. More often than not, development plans for pastoralists reflect the desires of local or distant vested interests, rather than the majority of pastoralists. The result can be an intensification of the long-term food problems, and a general undermining of the pastoralist way of life. At another level, as Mark Bowden of Save the Children Fund noted at the 1982 Workshop on Famine, development plans arising out of a time of disaster are often not well conceived in terms of the long-term, integrated development of an area. Too often, relief agencies 'slip' in to development projects because they are at the scene, rather than because the project is the most useful to do.

The heart of the problem is that no consensus exists about the origins of famine, nor on the underlying question of the root causes of Third World underdevelopment. Debate between the various sides of the argument is heated. Whatever 'development' path a government or agency elects to follow as a part of its relief effort invariably plants it firmly, if often unconsciously, on one side or another.

The matter is not, however, simply one for academic debate. Increasingly, the evidence suggests that models of development espoused in the past by colonial and neo-colonial regimes are in fact responsible for the current prevalence of famine in many parts of Africa (Franke and Chasin 1980; Ball 1976; Mamdani 1981). In Franke and Chasin's words, many current development projects are "new seeds of famine." The argument put forward by these author's work on the Sahel rejects single-variable explanations of famine and underdevelopment, using instead "history, climatic data, colonial economy and its post-colonial dependency relationships between the Sahel nations and the international capitalist system" (Franke and Chasin 1980) not only to uncover the roots of the Sahel famine, but also to critize the current thrust of much of the new, revised Sahel Development Plan. The critique focused on the consequences of integrating ever-increasing areas of Africa into the world market, a concern shared by others.

Forced production of cash crops for export by the peasantry, unequal terms of trade between Africa and Europe, and economic recessions in Europe and North America figure prominently among the causes of starvation in the former French colonies.   (Ball 1976)

This highlights the problem inherent in many development model, including those implicit in the work of famine relief agencies, some of whose plans have the unintentional effect of integrating pastoralists more tightly into world markets and the nation state.

Placing the controversy into the broader context of debates which surround the political economy of the world system may highlight what is at stake for pastoralists in the various models of development which agencies may foster. Recent literature in political economy argues the relationship between the first and the third worlds from a number of perspectives. A key argument involves the nature of incorporation of pre-capitalist societies, including those of subsistence pastoralists, into the broader capitalist world system, and the consequences of this inclusion.

From the viewpoint of writers like Wallerstein and Frank, contact with capitalist markets is the key causal element in bringing a society into the capitalist world system. Others (e.g. Laclau, Brenner, and Skocpol) disagree, pointing instead to the existence of capitalist class relations (i.e. wage labor and a pool of labor "freed" from the ties of

Fig 2 80,000 People were in famine camps in Turkanaland during the worst of the drought and famine (Photo Courtesy of Eric Wheater, Maryknoll Magazine).

feudalism and possession of land, herds, tools and other means of production) as a necessary criterion for labeling any society as capitalist. From this perspective, contact with the capitalist market does not necessarily establish capitalist class relations in less advanced societies. Brenner, in particular, points to instances where contact between a pre-capitalist society (e.g. feudal Poland) and the capitalist world market merely intensified the feudal class characteristics of that society. This debate has led other social scientists (Rey; Foster-Carter; Alavi; Taylor) to focus their attention on the relationships or "articulations" between capitalist and pre-capitalist modes of production in a attempt to determine the impact of these relationships on class structure, and on the flow of wealth and resources from less developed to more developed, or periphery and core, societies.

To date, this research has revealed considerable diversity of historical experience. While no simple conclusions have been reached, the debates have focused attention on the interaction between the forces at work in the capitalist world system, notably market dynamics and political/military competition, and those, notably class and power relations, at work in individual societies. The point to be made here is that the models of development which relief agencies pursue during and after famine are likely to draw pastoral societies into closer contact with both the market and the state, thus fostering the creation of wage-labor. These changes can dramatically, and permanently, alter the way of life of the pastoralists, often for the worse.

Fig 3 Most of the inhabitants of the camps are women and children (Photo Courtesy of Eric Wheater, Maryknoll Magazine).

What are the more Immediate and Visible Impacts of Famine Relief on Pastoralists?

Leaving aside for the moment any macro-level impact which relief agencies may have on recipient societies because of the model of development which they consciously or unconsciously pursue, the manner in which they give relief may itself have enduring consequences at the individual or community level. While it is fairly easy to understand why they have not examined their efforts in terms of the often abstract debates surrounding development, it is less readily apparent why the same agencies have not evaluated their more immediate, structural impact. The reason seems to lie in the fact that relief efforts have appropriately focussed on the nutritional and health aspects of the crisis. At such times, agencies are faced with the immediate, and often overwhelming, problems of obtaining appropriate quantities and types of relief food and other forms of relief from either local or international sources, transporting it to the famine area, overcoming interagency strife and governmental or bureaucratic obstacles, then getting the food into the mouths of those who most need it. As Masefield (1963) points out, this is not an atmosphere that promotes research. However, as this paper will attempt to demonstrate, the actions of relief givers can seriously affect the direction of a society, from which it follows that even in the midst of crisis, agencies and government should at least be sensitive to such consequences, even if no immediate alternative is possible.

In the unstable situations which famines inevitably produce, relief efforts, like any form of external intervention, can have an impact on the economic, political, social and cultural systems of recipient societies. The consequences of relief for pastoralists fall into three areas of concern:
1. the most obvious and perhaps the most serious impact is likely to be the creation of semi-permanent famine camps which can alter all aspects of pastoralist life;
2. the establishment of food for work schemes, a common occurrence in prolonged emergencies, can lay a path to the new forms of development discussed earlier, and to other changes in the economic system of pastoralists;
3. the political relationship which relief givers work out with recipient communities and their existing political leadership can reinforce or undermine the old political structure. If community participation in decision-making is both feasible and encouraged, a number of administrative problems may be avoided. On the other hand, such new styles of participation in decision-making might change the political expectations of relief recipients.

The actual impact of relief within a given setting will depend on at least five factors:
1. The nature of the famine itself;
2. the stage of the famine at which the agency intervenes;
3. the type of relief offered;
4. the structure of the society experiencing famine;
5. the structure of the national and world systems of which the affected society is a part.

How Does the Nature of a Famine Affect the Impact of Relief?

Firstly, the impact of famine relief will vary depending upon the cause(s) of the famine. Seaman and Holt (1980) argue that famine, which they define as mass starvation, may result from:
1. the loss or destruction of food by natural causes or war;
2. the lack of purchasing power by some segment of the population;
3. the failure of governments or relief agencies to provide needed food or supplies;
4. more likely than any single factor, some combination of these variables.

Famines arising from different causes will dictate different forms of relief. Situations caused by wars or involving large numbers of refugees are typically the most politically sensitive, raising complex questions about which faction the relief agency's efforts in fact 'support'.

The crisis in Somalia, exacerbated by the conflict between that country and Ethiopia and civil war in the latter, is the most recent example of such a situation which is affecting large numbers of pastoralists. In that case, the very causes of the crisis limited the type of impact which relief would have. Its origins, and the fact that many of the victims were refugees not holding Somali citizenship and therefore not permanently welcome in the country even if the agencies involve them in a development plan, means that relief work probably cannot help the recipients to develop much in the way of infrastructure for future use. They may, of course, learn skills that will later be of use wherever they are able to settle. On another level, however, the very fact that fighters for one side or the other can be reasonably sure that their families are fed and, to some degree, protected means that they can continue their struggles more readily than if there were no relief agencies on the scene. Thus, by pursuing their very necessary work among the vulnerable, relief agencies may well be affecting the larger balance of power, a fact not lost on most area governments. These governments may therefore carefully regulate the actions of relief agencies, thereby limiting the impact (for good or for ill) which these may have on food recipients.

The 1980 famine among the Turkana pastoralists was ostensibly caused by increased levels of raiding, near warfare conditions triggered by an influx of arms from Uganda following the fall of Idi Amin, cattle disease and drought. However, as discussed later, its roots may well lie much deeper, stemming from government policies which, stretching back to the beginning of the 20th century, have encouraged overgrazing. Because the more immediate causes of the famine led to a comparatively "slow onset" crisis as compared with, say, an earthquake or flood, there was at least a possibility of government or relief agency intervention fairly early in the sequence of events to mitigate the disaster. However, once large numbers of vital livestock had died, no quick or simple intervention could restore the situation, and the raiding-drought-famine crisis became a long term emergency.

Initially, the missions and relief agencies focused their efforts on feeding those most in need and only later, as it became clear that some level of feeding would be required for months or even years, did the agencies begin to institutionalize food-for-work programs designed to alter some of the root causes of the famine, viz. encouraging settled agriculture, at least as a short term source of food. Unfortunately, the agencies were and probably still are able to do little about a major and continuing causal factor of the food crisis, i.e. the large supply of guns in the area. However, in this situation, unlike the Somali refugee camps, there is at least a chance that the Turkana could receive some long term benefit from appropriate and requested food-work projects. The point being made here is that the nature of a famine (e.g. its causes, speed of onset, duration, and whether or not the recipients are refugees) sets parameters around the range of potential action of relief givers. In turn, these parameters affect the types of long-term impact which the relief may have, including involvement of relief agencies in developmental projects as well as those providing more immediate assistance.

How Does the Stage at which an Agency Intervenes Affect the Impact of Relief?

A variable closely related to the nature of the famine is the stage at which the relief agency intervenes. Dirks (1980) has reviewed the literature on the ways in which famines, as distinct from relief efforts, affect societies, noting that the response which individuals and societies make varies with the length and severity of the food shortage. In documented cases from many parts of the world, a three stage sequence emerged. First, there is usually an "alarm reaction" or period of heightened activity to seek food or to find relief from outside. At this stage, there is often a high level of social cooperation and sharing of resources. Second, if such efforts fail, individuals enter a "stage of resistance". They seek to conserve energy except to find food or other vital commodities. This individual response to famine has a range of consequences at the society level. Social ties begin to break down; families draw in upon themselves; generosity and collective action fall by the wayside. Finally, if food does not arrive, individuals enter a "stage of exhaustion" where desperate attempts may be made to survive, and chaos overwhelms the society, destroying even family ties as individuals fend for themselves.

The point at which a relief agency intervenes in this sequence will influence the type of impact which its efforts have on a society. If, as seems to have been the case in many recent famines in pastoral areas of Africa (e.g., the Sahel, Karamoja, Turkana), intervention of a significant scale arrives only in the second stage after shortages are extreme and a high degree of social disruption prevails, the relief effort may have a considerable effect on the society. In particular, because of the breakdown of normal patterns, people readily gravitate toward famine camps and, once there, accept non-traditional work and leaders. If relief could be provided at the "alarm reaction stage, it would be more possible to keep people out of camps, using at least some of their traditional coping mechanisms, and relying upon familiar leaders.

How Does the Manner in which Relief is Offered Affect its Impact?

It seems that if relief is provided over a period of months, the manner in which it is offered becomes a significant variable in a number of ways. Both the UNPAG *Guide*, and a WHO Study outline four basic types of food relief.
1. *General Food Distribution.* Dry food is distributed to people who are able to prepare their own meals.
2. *Mass Feeding.* Prepared meals from a central kitchen are served to the population.
3. *Supplementary Feeding.* In addition to the ration (dry foods or meals) for the whole family, vulnerable groups receive an *extra* meal or ration to meet their particular needs.
4. *Intensive or Therapeutic Feeding of PEM Cases (Protein-Energy Malnutrition).*

(DeVille deGoyet et al. 1978)

The choice of technique will depend largely upon the amount of food available, the degree of social disruption, the resources of the relief staff, and the seriousness of an individual's nutritional status.

As mentioned earlier, reports of experience in Africa and elsewhere seem to suggest that the main potential for negative social consequences of relief efforts lies in the unnecessary creation of famine camps. The question of how to get food to people in need depends in large part on where they live. If, as in the case of nomads, they are widely dispersed over a large area, the problem will be quite different than if they are closely concentrated. DeVille deGoyet and colleagues offer the following advice:

Wherever possible, assist people at their homes and avoid setting up refugee camps, though the latter may sometimes be unavoidable (in the case of flood victims, refugees from conflicts, etc.). Camps are very difficult to disperse. Do not create camps just because they are administratively more convenient ...

Distributing foods to nomadic groups is difficult, and no easy way of doing so has been found. Points at which people congregate (e.g., water sources may be selected as the best places at which to distribute food; alternatively, large amounts of food may be given out (100 kg) at each distribution if this avoids setting up refugee camps. (page 37)   (deVille, deGoyet et al. 1978)

Camps create health and sanitation problems, are complex to administer, and frequently difficult to break up. The latter is a particularly serious problem if, as with the Turkana, the recipients are pastoralists. The change to permanent settlement undercuts their economic base and culture. If people are fed in their homes or communities, then food is likely to be distributed according to the cultural norms of the place. This may well mean that "vulnerable groups", i.e. young children (especially girls), women and the elderly, receive less than men in the prime of life. In spite if this, from a social and perhaps even a nutritional standpoint, it seems preferable to keep people from moving into camps. While it is true that once they are settled in to them, it may become easier to monitor who is receiving which type(s) of food (particularly through the creation of supplementary feeding programs aimed specifically at vulnerable groups), these special feeding programs may also undermine traditional family roles (Oxfam 1981), while their nutritional impact is also debatable (Jackson 1982). It is commonly noted, for example, that camps all over the world are primarily occupied by women, children and the elderly Fig 2. However nutritionally useful are the supplementary or intensive feeding schemes targeted to these groups, they may unintentionally encourage this frequently encountered pattern.

Regardless of the distribution technique selected, after the initial phase of emergency feeding has been implemented, one of the most sensitive questions faced by a relief agency has to do with what the donors expect in return from the recipients. Much of the food given by aid agencies cannot be sold because of stipulations set by the donors or donor governments. This has commonly meant that the agencies attempt to require work for food in place of cash payment. The generally accepted donor position seems to be:

Where a population is entirely dependent upon relief, include tea, sugar and spices as part of the ration. In this case especially it is essential that food be given against some kind of return from the recipient whenever possible.   (DeVille, de Goyet et al., 1978)

The UNPAG *Guide* points out that free distribution of food should be relied upon only "for limited periods under special circumstances", recommending that an alternative be found as soon as possible, suggesting food as wages for work done.

Poor victims may be offered food as part of relief or rehabilitation activity; cash payments are then used to buy food for the family. The points to be noted are: 1) malnourished adult men and women should not participate in manual work; 2) the vulnerable groups in the family may fail to share in the benefits; 3) social problems may be created when adults are at work and the children are left behind; 4) if activities are not pre-planned as part of the development scheme, the work done will be wasteful and unproductive.

The program may be extended by paying wages fully or partially in kind. The staple food item can be given as part of the wages. The staple food should be sold at a reasonable price in fair price shops or ration shops, cooperative societies, etc.

(Protein-Calorie Advisory Group of the United Nations System, 1977)

The hope behind such a plan is that it will prevent recipients from becoming dependent upon handouts and that some potentially useful projects will be completed.

An alternative view criticizes food-for-work (FFW), the argument being:

of all the uses of project food aid, FFW is the only one which *has the potential* to increase local food production directly. However, the primary benefits of such programmes tend to go mainly to those who possess land.   (Jackson 1982)

It seems, then, that key questions to be asked are: what will the labor in which the famine workers are engaged lead to? who will benefit from the work that they do? and, returning to the point made earlier, what model of development is implied in the activities which agencies choose to reward with food?

For example, the digging of irrigation ditches may benefit land owners who happen to live in the vicinity, but they are not likely to benefit pastoral nomads who move frequently from place to place. Viewed from another perspective, the introduction of new kinds of crops or livestock for eventual sale on a broader market may lay the basis for a shift to a cash-crop economy. A related question has to do with the impact which food-for-work may have in societies where there has been little or no previous exposure to wage labor. Can food-for-work projects, in effect, introduce wage labor into a subsustence economy? What are the consequences of such a shift for substistence pastoralists? Additionally, a number of writers (Jackson; Masefield; Stevens) have noted that in most food-for-work projects, relatively little work is actually accomplished. If this is the case, such schemes might minimize the potential for both positive and negative impact. Again, only an examination of each specific situation can determine the likely outcome.

Finally, a key political question, which underpins all aspects of relief management, is the relationship between donor agency and the community. Two standard texts, stress the need for community involvement,

Apart from considerations of administrative coordinating structure, availability of financial resources, and personnel, the success of the program will hinge on community action. It is essential that appropriate schemes be launched for the creation of awareness amongst the community with regard to the development plans. Community leaders and officials in the area may be instructed in motivation orientation and other such training as necessary. The importance of public participation cannot be overstated. (PAG *Guide:* 129)   (Protein-Calorie Advisory Group of the United Nations System 1977)

The participation of the community in the relief program and in decision-making will help towards and orderly distribution. Holding public meetings and keeping the population informed through administrative and natural leaders is essential.   (deVille, de Goyet et al., 1978)

While involvement of the community is the ideal, it may not be possible in the on-going crisis situation of a relief camp, particularly when the relief workers are expatriates unfamiliar with the area. However, if public participation is overlooked, unnecessary problems may emerge. How to organize effective community participation will depend on the situation, and may well take a great deal of time and effort. The PAG *Guide* and deVille deGoyet *et al.* both recommend that relief agencies go through existing local leaders. However, there are often various types of leaders within a community, and identifying credible (versus formal) leaders may be difficult for an outsider. In Turkana, for instance, one would have the choice of government-appointed chiefs, or traditional elders.

A related concern is that people from the local community will be under heavy pressure to distribute food to their kin and others to whom they are obligated:

... responsible posts (store keeping, administration) must be given to reliable individuals outside the community to rule out personal bias, preferences or vulnerability to pressure. (De Ville de Goyet et al., 1978)

Masefield (1963) elaborates on this point. While it has obvious wisdom, it can also lead to the creation of a new power structure of outsiders. In Turkana, it seems that some local young men given responsibility as facilitators in the camps have become guite powerful, to the point of challenging the traditional power and respect of the elders. Alternatively, if relief distribution is through existing missionary groups, it may compromise their original goals in the sense that people begin to view them primarily as providers of food. For this reason Rowland, in a personal communication, recommends that missions get out of relief operations as soon as possible.

How Does the Structure of a Society and its Relationsip to the World System Affect the Impact of Relief?

The nature of famine, and the types of relief offered, will account for much of the variation in the impact of the relief. However, the structure and culture of the affected society together with those of the nation state and the world into which relief integrates them are also important variables. The remainder of this paper attempts to illustrate some of these influences as they affect the Turkana. These people, because they are basically subsistence, pastoral nomads, may be affected by famine relief quite differently from a group who are already highly integrated into the market-cash-wage labour system which now predominates in most of Africa. It appears that the key consequences of an extended period of famine relief on the Turkana, along with the creation of permanent camps, food-for-work programs to encourage settled agriculture, and possible undermining of the power of the elders, will be to integrate them much more closely into the market economy of Kenya, thus putting them under close control by that nation's government. The solutions which the Kenyan government and international aid agencies are proposing, for the long-term problems of the Turkana, seem to imply much greater involvement in the world system. It is not clear that the Turkana way of life can adapt to these strains. Indeed, the Turkana may be able to effectively resist those aspects of integration which they reject.

Whatever the outcome, it is useful to view the impact of famine relief on the Turkana within the context of the broad change occurring for many pastoral groups in Africa, i.e. the pressure on subsistence pastoralists to become much more closely integrated in the capitalist world system.

Famine and Famine Relief in Turkanaland

The Turkana nomads of northwestern Kenya are faced with two immediate threats to their way of life: a new highway which will pass through their lands, linking the southern Sudan with the coast of Kenya, and decimation of their livestock due to raiding, drought and famine. While these challenges are specific to the Turkana, they are also symptomatic of the deeper crisis facing pastoral nomads all across Africa.

The highway and famine relief efforts are together accelerating the process of Turkana inclusion not only into the economic, political and social systems of the nation state of Kenya, but also into the world as a whole. While this process may be inevitable, the form which it takes will determine a great deal about the future of the Turkana. The new road is being built by the Kenyan and Sudanese governments, and a consortium of foreign aid agencies. It has reached Lodwar in Kenya and will soon be pushed towards Juba in the Sudan, cutting across Turkana. At the same time that the road has been moving closer to the nomads, famine has drawn international relief agencies to the area, involving them in both the immediate and long-term future of the Turkana. The combination of raiding, disease and drought which killed large numbers of Turkana livestock in 1980 has abated. Enough grass has already returned to support a considerably larger number of animals than the Turkana currently have, and good rains in 1982 could improve conditions still further. Two immediate questions relate to the restocking of Turkana herds: should restocking be undertaken at all and, if it is done, on what basis should it be attempted by the relief agencies and/or the Kenya government? In broader terms, the questions have to do with the future of the famine camps, agricultural projects and the leadership system of the Turkana. One thing is certain: how these nomadic pastoralists respond to such changes must affect their future.

This section of the paper considers the causes and consequences of the famine in Turkana, and the results of famine relief. It next turns to the problems of ending famine relief, and looks at the future of the Turkana in light of current thinking on the changing place of precapitalist societies within the capitalist world system. The issues, simply stated are: what changes lie ahead for the Turkana because of the famine; how do the efforts of relief agencies, perhaps unconsciously, bring these changes about?

Famine and Famine Relief Efforts

Relief agencies began to receive distress signals, particularly from missionaries in Turkanaland, at the end of 1979. At the time, the Kenya government made no mention of the famine, apart from denying that there was one, apparently to avoid adverse international publicity which might affect Kenya's tourist trade. During 1980, however, the drought deepened, its effect being such that the European Economic Community (EEC) estimated some 60–70,000 Turkana (out of a total of approximately 140,000) had lost all of the livestock upon which their livelihood rested. Initially, food aid came in largely through Catholic Relief Services, although other agencies were also involved. Beginning in January, 1981, the EEC became the main provider.

Causes of Famine

Most observers agree that the root causes of the famine were external, the result of ways in which the broader world has impinged upon (or 'articulated' with) Turkana. However, there are differences in the manner in which this relationship can be viewed. The EEC and others see the fundamental origins of the famine in terms of nomadic traditions which, once viable, have now led to a cycle of overbreeding and overgrazing because of reduced land area. When droughts come, as they always have, livestock die for lack of food or water, and people then go hungry. Before the establishment of colonial and, later, national borders, the Turkana could move into areas not affected by drought during bad times. They also raided livestock from neigbouring tribes, both to survive and to restock after the drought had passed. Now, the theory goes, the closing of borders and the Kenyan government's appropriation of some of the areas which used to be dry season havens, confines enlarged herds to a smaller, dryer area. In addition, the influx of arms and munitions into the region, particularly from Idi Amin's former armies has escalated levels of violence and changed the balance of power between raiding tribes, thus accentuating even further the problem of moving herds into traditional, dry season grasslands. Indeed, the virtual certainty of increasingly violent raiding may well have been more important than the drought since it led the Turkana to concentrate large numbers of livestock around 'safe' watering sites. In turn, this led to the rapid spread of anthrax which killed many of the animals in the early part of 1980. The death of livestock then led to widespread human hunger. Grain imports from the south were slowed by the 1979 nationwide shortage, and by government regulations aimed at controlling the movement of grain to discourage its being smuggled across borders. The already weakened population was further affected by a cholera outbreak in March-April 1980, and attacks of measles. Although the missions began to respond to the need for food in February 1980, large-scale, steady supplies of relief food did not begin arriving until the EEC project got underway eleven months later. In was ironic that when their livestock first began dying in early 1980, the Turkana had large amounts of cash from the sale of the animals' skins. However, traders could not obtain permits from the District government to import grain, although they could and did bring in soft drinks. It is therefore argued that the encroachment of outside political and military forces was the ultimate cause of the famine.

This description, although widely held by relief agencies and others to present the facts of the situation does not, however, go deeply enough into the historical roots of overgrazing and famine in Turkana. As a result, solutions proposed by various aid-givers may only deepen the problem. An alternate view, while acknowledging the importance of the tightening of boundaries and heightened violence, emphasizes the detrimental effect of forced entry into the capitalist market. In a recent paper on the political economy of famine in neigbouring Karamoja in Uganda, Mamdani (1981) presents evidence that, far from being a near desert, the region was a grassland savanna at the beginning of this century. The author contends that British colonial policies and later, those of the Uganda government, not only disrupted the delicate balance between the Karamajong pastoralists and their land but actually deflected them from their gradual movement towards sedentary agriculture. These policies led to the need for cash to pay taxes; the sale of livestock for cash; overgrazing, erosion; and, finally, famine. Mamdani's analysis is similar to the Turkana scenario in at least one important way: he points to the forceable acquisition of crucial Karamajong lands by the colonial government beginning in the 1920's, arguing that without a reduction in the numbers of livestock, this led to enforced "overgrazing" of the remainder. There is, however, a key difference between Mamdani's analysis and the widely accepted Turkana scenario in that to cope with the problem of overstocking, the colonial authorities of the day implemented a policy of "destocking". In Mamdani's words, this meant that

having grabbed the people's land, the only way to restore a balance between limited grazing, pastures and livestock was to grab the people's cattle. (Mamdani 1981)

In a system similar to that devised in many other parts of Africa, where colonial governments found a need to stimulate cash cropping or wage labor, the British established a system of taxation in Karamoja which simultaneously raised revenues and reduced herd size. To obtain the cash required to pay their taxes, the Karamajong were encouraged to sell their cattle to a government-operated monopoly cattle buyer located in Karamoja. The Karamoja Cattle Scheme, as it became known, set prices below prevailing market levels. Mamdani documents that this was 'successful' in that it both "destocked" the herds and contributed to government revenue. After independence, a meat packing factory which processed the purchased cattle was moved out of Karamoja, but the newly independent Ugandan government continued the basic model with the result that 'surplus' Karamajong cattle continued to be sold for processing. This policy had the effect of making the Karamajong solely dependent upon the production and sale of cattle to meet their requirements for cash to pay taxes and to purchase goods yet, at the same time, the land available for their herds was declining in area and becoming a virtual desert. (Franke and Chassin 1981, argue that a somewhat similar pattern has been documented in the West African Sahel.) Prior to independence, the problem had been intensified for the Karamajong when the colonial government acquired land for the Kidepo Valley National Park. Commencing in 1958, this action removed still more land with fairly high rainfall from use by the Karamajong, at the same time transforming the hunting of game into "poaching" unless one had a licence. Thus, Mamdani argues that the creation of the game park on the one hand restricted access to important elements in the Karamajong food supply by taking away land suitable for agriculture, while on the other it reduced the supply of game.

In summary, Mamdani says that the net impact of colonial and neocolonial policies on the pre-capitalist Karamajong created the need for a cash income to pay taxes which could only be earned by selling cattle to sole buyer governments at a fixed, artificially low price. Cattle were raised on decreasing areas of land which became overstocked and subsequently eroded. Food from hunting and sedentary agriculture became increasingly scarce due to colonial and neo-colonial policies, with the virtually inevitable consequences of desertification, diseased cattle, increased raiding by neighboring tribes, and finally a catastrophic famine.

Are there any parallels between the root causes of famine in Karamoja and neighboring Turkanaland? The immediate response of people from several aid agencies and other organisations is, no. Turkana was always more barren than Karamoja; desertification is not new. More importantly perhaps, the Turkana, like most pastoralists, have long been relatively 'wealthy' compared with sedentary cultivators in Kenya. They would therefore have been only slightly inconvenienced by the required level of taxation and, in any case, they have not been subject to formal taxation, at least since independence in 1963. Furthermore, even when their livestock were dying in 1980, they resisted selling their animals in the hope that they would somehow survive. Presumably, if the colonial past had instilled a cash crop mentality regarding livestock, similar to that which Mamdani argues existed in Karamoja, the Turkana would have been willing to exchange their herds for cash. Finally, the perceived wisdom is that the area was relatively isolated and remains so (Bernstein 1982).

However, research in process by Odegi-Awoundo, of the Department of Sociology, University of Nairobi and that of Lamphear (1976), challenges these assumptions. First, they find that Turkana was not economically isolated from the rest of Kenya in colonial days. As in Karamoja, taxes in the form of livestock were imposed early in the twentieth century (1905−06), and were collected by force. Thereafter, these taxes were the major source of revenue of the Turkana district, and the cash to pay them came from the sale of livestock, primarily goats, to the government.

As in Karamoja, the government bought the livestock for less than the open market price. This artificially lowered price amounted to an additional, indirect form of taxation. The colonial government apparently placed the purchased animals at the disposal of the army and administration in Turkanaland, Odegi-Awuondo documenting the substantial number of goats purchased from 1905 until the mid-1940's. Lamphear (1976) estimates that between 1910 and 1915, 150,000 head of livestock were confiscated in punitive expeditions. During the bloody fighting between the British and Turkana at the end of World War I, virtually all of the livestock in northern Turkana was wiped out.

> Like other military commanders before them, the (British) officers in Turkanaland had begun to realize that it was simpler to starve people into submission than to wage costly campaigns against them. Between 1916 and 1918, an estimated quarter million livestock were confiscated from the Turkana and many more were slaughtered by various expeditions and garrisons for their rations.
>
> (Lamphear 1976)

Odegi-Awuondo feels that the British policies of taxing the Turkana heavily and of conducting "punitive expeditions" had the dual objectives of raising colonial revenue and of restricting the ability of the Turkana to obtain arms by trading livestock. Lamphear (1976), Barber (1968) and others record the history of Turkana armed resistance to British rule and taxation, especially a revolt in 1918. Turkanaland was governed as a military district from 1917–1926. Thus, the Turkana were constantly 'overtaxed', and their only way of paying these taxes was by breeding more goats to sell to the government. It therefore seems reasonable to conclude, as was the case in Karamoja, the policies by which the colonial state not only imposed high taxes but set itself up as the monopoly buyer of livestock may well have contributed to everbreeding, overgrazing, erosion and ultimately famine.

It is more difficult to trace the link between government policies and overstocking, after independence. As mentioned, the Kenyan government did not seek to tax the Turkana. However, as in the rest of the country, *harambées*[2)] were organized on a 'voluntary' basis to raise funds for necessary projects. The funds were raised by selling goats to the government for sale in Nairobi and Mombasa. Most of the revenue thus generated, left Turkana, however, making the process essentially a means of extracting surplus wealth from the region. Large scale *harambées* held during the crisis period of 1979–1980, drained a considerable number of goats and substantial wealth from the area. More recently, a Turkana Livestock Scheme has been proposed which would tax all livestock sold. Thus, while the parallels to Mamdani's description of Karamoja are not exact, there are nevertheless certain similarities for the post-independence era in Turkana. More complete documentation of the numbers and value of livestock removed from Turkana for *harambees*, together with information on Turkana views of these government efforts to raise revenues, (e.g. whether they were seen as a reason to increase the numbers of their livestock) would, of course, be necessary to make the argument more convincing.

The Impact of Famine Relief in Turkana

Colonial archives and other sources reveal that there have been a number of famines in Turkana since that of the mid-1920's, the first for which relief was provided, with those during 1960—61 and 1974—75 being among the more serious. Another, the most recent, started in late 1979 and did not ease until the rains which fell in April, 1981, Relief agencies were feeding some 60,000 people in 1981 (peaking 80,000 at the height of the crisis), of whom an estimated 30,000 were destitutes.

The administration of famine relief is never easy under any circumstance. There is always someone who, rightly or wrongly, finds fault with the efforts put into operation during an emergency. In many ways, however, the handling of the crisis in Turkana can be seen as a success story, if only because relatively few human lives were lost. Rather than praise or criticize the activities of specific agencies, it is perhaps more appropriate to examine the impact which their relief efforts have had on the structure of Turkana society. It is, of course, not yet possible to make definitive statements about their full impact, but it may be worthwhile to record certain economic, political and social effects of famine relief which people working in Turkana have noted. Again, it must be emphasized that the changes are occurring not only against the broader background of, but are contributing to, shifts in Turkana's relationship to the rest of Kenya and the world system.

Some generalizations are in order. First, relief efforts in Turkana, as elsewhere, suffered from difficulties in coordination among agencies, and between those agencies and the government. At times, this had led to food not arriving when and where it was needed. Another problem also experienced by relief programmes in other parts of the world, was that food did not always reach the people most in need — mostly women, childreen, and the old. Beyond the obvious suffering and death which this maldistribution of food caused, it also had unexpected side effects. Odegi-Awuendo, the Kenyan sociologist who spent considerable time in Turkana over a period of two years, saw an example: the increase in alcoholism due to distillation of corn, intended for relief, by people with adequate food supplies who set up stills actually inside some of the camps. (Similar experiences were reportes by missionaries working on relief efforts in Karamoja.). Such instances of corruption, confusion, and mismanagement interfering with the distribution of relief food are, however, probably no more threatening to the social structure of a famine-striken society than the succesful delivery of raid programmes aimed at its survival.

Camps and Politics

Despite strenuous efforts to avoid it, relief feeding in Turkana led to the concentration of people in camps. Missionaries, with experience dating back to the 1960—61 and 1974—75 famines in Turkana, recognized the negative impact of the formation of camps and sought to avoid them. However, the complexities of registering food recipients, coupled with the need to set up kitchens for supplementary and therapeutic feeding schemes for malnourished children, drew entire families to these sites. Once there, the possibility of receiving food at least held women and children in the camps. Attempts to move them away were thwarted by violent cattle raider attacks and the failure of food deliveries to arrive at dispersed sites. Eventually, most of the large camps which at one stage held well over 5,000 people each, were broken up. There were in 1982 some 260 "sites" with an ideal size of 45—50 families each, although at least one camp

172

still held approximately 5,000 people. About 14,000 families were still registered in the "sites" in mid-1982.

Whenever any group loses control over so vital a commodity as food, particularly for an extended period, that loss can be expected to have both interal and external political consequences. The settling of at least half the population of Turkana in feeding camps makes them more accessible to the attentions of the state. To date, however, the Kenya government does not seem to have exploited this concentration.

Indeed, one of the criticisms of the influx of foreign famine relief has been that it allows the Kenya government to continue to ignore Turkana and neglect even minimal responsibility to feed its citizens. However, the government has made clear its preference that the nomads settle permanently in villages where they can be taxed, schooled, provided with social services and, of course, controlled. Wheter the camps will prove to be the beginning of such permanent settlements remains to be seen. Many people are presently afraid to move away from the more established camps to begin cultivation, and perhaps farming, because they fear that the relief food may no longer reach them. Under such circumstances, the longer the camps remain, the more likely their continuation becomes.

Within the camps, the organization of emergency feeding has created the beginnings of a new hierarchy with at least four tiers. An analysis of this, based on interviews with a missionary and others who have worked in the camps in Turkana, shows firstly that while the Turkana do not have a tradition of strong central leadership, the elders of the community have usually been looked to for leadership in crises, a role which to some extent they still retain (Fig 4). Secondly, since colonial days, a system of government appoin-

Fig 4 While the Turkana do not have a tradition of strong central leadership, the elders of the community have usually been looked to for leadership in crises (Photo Courtesy of Eric Wheater, Maryknoll Magazine).

ted chiefs has been attempted. Often these chiefs are from different clans than the people whom they nominally govern. It seems that while they are neither widely respected nor trusted, particularly since the famine has forced many Turkana into camps, they do have some real power. Because of the increased importance of raiding between neighboring tribes since the famine began, a third group has become politically important: the middle-aged men who plan and carry out the raids. In many cases they seem to have become the real leaders in the community. They do not, however, reside in the camps. Together with the young warriors, they try to preserve what remains of their livestock and engage in raids, only returning to the sites periodically to get food from their families. Into this already complex picture, the famine camps have injected a fourth element, the facilitators. Members of this group decide who will receive food and how much, an authority which gives them a considerably measure of real of perceived power over the people in the camps. The facilitators are usually young Turkana men, often earning a cash income for the first time. Both the government-appointed chiefs and the camp facilitators owe much of their power and income to the camps and are therefore unenthusiastic about seeing people moved out of them. Many of the appointed chiefs have set up sideline businesses dependent on the camps for profit. The facilitators would likewise lose their income if relief efforts ended. If, as an alternative, the relief was simply dispersed, they would still experience a decline in income since they would the be required to accompany the aid-recipients to smaller, far flung food-for-work camps.

In these ways, at least, the perhaps unavoidable settling of people in camps to receive food-relief has already affected power structures at the grass roots level. To the extent that the settlements have reinforced certain categories of leaders who have a vested interest in staying in the camp, they have also made the goal of returning the Turkana to their nomadic way of life more difficult to reach.

Economic Impact

The style of famine relief adopted in Turkana poses several economic questions beyond the creation of new vested interests. The questions revolve around decisions regarding work, land and livestock. The first issue, inherent in any food-for-work program, is who decides what work is to be done and who will benefit from it in the long run? In Turkana, as in many other instances of relief (Stevens 1979), it is clear that little real work is actually done. However, relief agencies have decided that the work which ought to be undertaken, if people can be motivated, is preparation of land for cultivation.

This raises the question of ownership of the land which is to be improved. Lappé et al. (1980) and Jackson (1982) contend that with most such projects, it is the already affluent who benefit. In Turkana, the hope is that the local elders will meet and assign one-acre plots of land to people in the camps, land which will continue to be theirs to till after the food-for-work program ends. If the system operates in this way, then all would appear to be well. A potential difficulty, however, arises from the ambiguous status of land ownership. In Turkana, where there is no tradition of legalised, personal ownership of land, all of it being vested in the Crown, the Kenya government will eventually have to set policy on this matter. If the camps become permanent, land in and near them will become more scarce and valuable. Ownership will then become an important issue. The coming of the highway can also be expected to make adjacent land through which it passes more valuable. Resolution of the land question will therefore have an important impact on the economy and social structure of Turkana. Should land become a marketable commodity, this will further undermine the precapitalistic, nomadic way of life which relies on the shared use of large tracts, thereby pushing the Turkana even further towards dependence on wage labor for cash and on the market for necessary commodities.

Just a assignment of land for food-for-work must significantly affect the economic and social structures of the Turkana, so too will the basis on which ownership of livestock is transferred to them. The present plan, according to the European Economic Community (EEC) delegate in Nairobi, is to rely upon field coordinators in the camps to select people who deserve to receive new livestock. The terms of this restocking are not yet clear. If the livestock is given as a gift, the program may encourage people to appear as destitute as possible in order to receive the animals; on the other hand, the logistics of any kind of repayment system may be complicated to administer (Oxfam-America has succesfully used such a scheme, following on from the indigenous stock "animal of friendship" model, employed in the Sahel of West Africa). However, without new livestock, the Turkana who are destitute will necessarily remain in the camps, becoming increasingly distanced from their nomadic past. Obviously something must be done. Policy makers should therefore be aware that whatever the allocation of livestock, the basis on which such an apparently altruistic gesture is made could well have an adverse influence on the traditional economic structure of the Turkana unless the scheme is carefully planned and executed.

Social Impact

The social and psychological impacts of the famine relief efforts are more difficult to ascertain. As mentioned, the comments of those working with the Turkana suggest that most of the people living in the camps are women, children, and the elderly. One report suggests that camp life has reinforced a growing tendency for young Turkana women to seek an alternative to nomadism. Some had already gone to towns before the famine to escape the heavy work and boring routine of a nomad woman's life. The camps offer women and the young a chance to socialize, something normally limited by the frequent travel of nomadic life. The absence of husbands and other men creates certain social strains, but then the Turkana style of pastoralism frequently separates husbands and wives in any case. More serious has been the apparent abandonment of children. At the height of the famine, parents remained with their herds but felt that the children would be better cared for in the camps. How many of these families have been reunited is not known.

Relief workers in Turkana have also mentioned a type of passivity or dependence which they observed among people who had been living in the older famine camps created in the 1960's and early 1970's. They felt that these people expected, and even demanded, relief. Interestingly, most of the 'educated elite' of Turkana seem to come from this group because, as children growing up in these settlements, it had been they who had the most access to formal schooling.

There are no universal rules to guide famine relief efforts. It is therefore important to bear in mind that for a group like the Turkana, on the edge of transition from a fairly isolated, non-monetized, nomadic way of life to a much closer relationship with market capitalism and a national political system, the style in which famine relief is offered is particularly significant because it will either speed or retard this process. Relief efforts have thus created camps in which perhaps half of the Turkana now live; established food-for-work projects are leading to settled agriculture, and the traditional political power of the elders has been weakened in some parts of the region. If relief continues to reinforce political leaders with a stake in sedentary practices, hastens the creation of private land ownership and a wage-labor workforce, or encourages a new reliance on cash-based raising of goats or crop cultivation, it could both weaken the Turkana way of life and threaten the ecology of the area. As one of the anthropologists at the Norwegian Agency for International Development (NORAD) in Nairobi argued, famine relief in such circumstances may well solve the immediate problems of a food shortage but in the process aggravate longer term difficulties.

The root causes of famine in specific regions should not only be faced, but the style of relief should point the way to future solutions. This entails a careful look at the consequences of well-intentioned, but possibly counter-productive, efforts to help.

The Problem of Ending Relief Efforts: Restocking

The immediate objective of the agencies now seems to be to terminate their relief efforts in a manner that gets the Turkana out of the camps and makes them self-reliant, preferably as pastoralists.

This was never adequately accomplished after some of the earlier famines, as evidenced by the fact that several thousand Turkana still remain in famine relief villages created during the 1961 famine. Many have become permanent destitutes. (Odegi-Awuondo found that even in the 'good year' of 1978—1979, some 5,000 destitutes were being fed in Turkana. The generation which has grown up in these villages spawned by relief camps now lacks the knowledge to return to pastoralism.) In the eyes of the agencies most involved, the basic problem is to find a way of restocking the herds so that people in the camps can leave them and return to the pastoralist life-style, a desire which most Turkana seem to share.

Leaving aside the delicate issue of distributing livestock to those in the camps, restocking is itself a problem with no easy solution. The herds in Turkana were all but wiped out during the drought. Foreign species have not proved hardy in Turkana, making massive importation impractical. The EEC estimates that it will take at least two to three years to rebuild the herds, using stock from southern, less affected areas of the region. Even this estimate seems highly optimistic. Their definition of a viable level of restocking is that each extended family of 20 to 30 people should have a minimum of a male and a female donkey, a male and a female camel, and about ten goats, including at least one male. Clearly this will require considerable time and money to accomplish for the 30,000 or more people classified as destitutes in 1981. The EEC is hoping to establish three veterinary centres in Turkana to multiply livestock. They will then select families to receive the animals (the specific criteria and process of selection are not yet finalised) and recipients will be given basic training in management of this new stock. However, the EEC has had some difficulty in funding and organising the cent-

Fig 5 Attempts to rebuild the herds rest in part on the development of reliable sources of water; however, animals died of starvation and disease, not thirst, in 1980. (Photo: Courtesy of Eric Wheater, Maryknoll Magazine).

res, which form the cornerstone of thee program. In the meantime, it is trying to avoid the problems inherent in large relief settlements by running small food-for-work camps to build roads, irrigation projects, and prepare land for cultivation.

Because rebuilding the herds (Fig 5) will be a slow process, and because of the immediate need to begin shifting people out of the camps, the EEC and the Kenya government planned to set up much more rigorous food-for-work schemes through the Turkana Rehabilitation Projects, beginning in mid-1982. It is their intention that these will all be focused on irrigation for the cultivation of sorghum. Far smaller numbers of people will be fed without working, and all work will be done at six sites. It is hoped that the scheme will separate those who are actually destitute from those who have other means of earning a living. The plan, to use the cultivation of sorghum as a fall-back for the Turkana during bad years with a return to pastoralism still the stated, overall long-term objective, was, however, drawn up by the authorities without adequate consultation with the people of Turkana regarding these decisions which so vitally affect them and may thus limit its success.

The Future: Penetration by the Outside World

The EEC has been the principal aid giver to Turkana. For this reason, it is useful to examine the long-range vision which its policies reflect. The following information is based primarily on an interview in January, 1982 with the organisation's delegate in Nairobi, and talks in July of the same year with its representative for Turkana.

It is important to note that the EEC became involved in relief efforts almost by accident to deal with what was an emergency situation, and that it was only officially responsible for famine relief in Turkana for a six-month period ending in March, 1981. After that, responsibility passed to the Kenya government and to the missions, although the EEC continued to finance much of the food and contributed the vehicles for transporting it. Also, as mentioned earlier, the EEC will be funding a number of development projects in and around Turkana.

Like others with whom I spoke, the EEC delegate subscribed to an optimistic view of the increasing penetration of Turkana by the outside world. He felt that increased contact was its greatest hope for a future which he saw primarily in terms of continued reliance on pastoralism. As he saw it, however, this will probably not be traditional pastoralism of the Turkana. The delegate was quite aware that penetration will inevitably mean the transition from a subsistence economy to a monetized, market-oriented economy which he foresaw in a positive light. The Turkana would move from a society in which livestock formed the basis of security and prestige, to one based more on money which could be exchanged for food and goods in the market place.

Obviously such a shift would not occur quickly. The delegate saw it taking from one to two generations for the Turkana to learn the use of money. This would come about largely through the sale of their 'excess' livestock on the national market. This, in turn, would become possible on a large-scale once the new Kenya-Sudan highway was opened. Trucks, driven by members of Kenya's Somali ethnic minority, already make the trip to Juba by going through Turkana carrying food, cement, etc., from the Kenya coast. However, they currently return empty. The EEC delegate looked ahead to a time when the truck drivers would become buyers of Turkana skins, and perhaps live animals for sale in Nairobi and Mombasa on their return journey. At present, the high incidence of disease among Turkana livestock has resulted in a government quarantine to prevent the passage of animals from Turkana to other parts of the country. This, together with the current absence of any 'excess' livestock due to the drought, has inhibited the growth of any such trade. A key feature of the Turkana Rehabilitation Project is to be the development of a 12,000 ha holding area in Southern Turkana, where livestock can be confined for a period of months in quarantine. It is also hoped that it can become a dry-season haven for livestock during times of drought (Fig 6). If successful the scheme, in combination with the new highway, will open the way for much larger-scale marketing of Turkana livestock.

The EEC delegate and a number of other development workers hope that this new market for livestock will encourage the Turkana to sell off animals rather than overgraze the land. Furthermore, in times of drought, it will give them the option of selling their animals for cash rather than watching them die. The cash could then be used to purchase other foods. In essence, this appears to be the same basic solution which the British proposed for the problems of overstocking and overgrazing in Karamoja in the 1930's. If Mamdani's argument is valid, that policy had a disastrous outcome there. One wonders whether the Turkana and their fragile lands could survive the large-scale transition to pastoral capitalism implied by such a market-oriented strategy.

The EEC, the Kenya government, and other providers of aid, not only see the production of livestock for sale on the wider Kenya market as the foundation of the new, monetized economy, but one which could be supplemented by increased Turkana involvement in cultivation and in fishing cooperatives. The Turkwell Gorge Dam in Pokot, the cost of which will be partly borne by the EEC, could eventually create enough irrigated land to support 20,000 people. However, the transition from pastoralist to sedentary cultivator which this implies

Fig 6 Windmills have been introduced to improve the supply of water (Photo Courtesy of Eric Wheater, Maryknoll Magazine).

would require at least a generation, and a great deal of money and technical assistance, to be successful. In the meantime, the food-for-work camps are experimenting with small scale agricultural schemes. Despite current emphasis on the production of sorghum, it is not yer clear whether this attempt at cultivation, if successful, will ultimately result in the production of subsistence crops for home consumption, or cash crops for sale on the outside market. Whatever the final outcome, it will be important for the orientation of Turkana economic and social structure.

Fishing cooperatives, the other new potential livelihood foreseen by aid agencies, have a history dating back to 1961, when the Norwegian Aid Agency helped to establish them on Lake Turkana. Attempts are to be made to bring more people into these cooperatives in the future. Again, if successful, such moves will lead to a larger percentage of Turkana becoming sedentary and relying on a cash income instead of subsistence herding. The fish produced by the cooperatives will be primarily for export to foreign markets. Fish is not a food of preference among the Turkana but, in times of famine, relief workers say that people are happy to receive it. Unfortunately, even during the recent serious famine, most of the fish caught and processed by the cooperatives in Turkana was exported to Zaire and Saudi Arabia. According to one report, only when the Zaireans stopped buying, thereby creating a glut, were famine relief agencies able to obtain fish for local consumption. When the Zaireans began buying again, orders placed by relief organizations went unfilled. It appeared that the exigencies of earning foreign exchange and retaining foreign markets outweighed famine needs.

The argument of the EEC delegate that the transition to a cash economy would give the Turkana greater food security than pastoralism, because money can be used to purchase a variety of foods and goods, rests on the crucial assumption that food, even locally-produced food, will in fact be available for sale. As the example of the fish from Lake Turkana illustrates, this may not always be the case, especially when key interests rely upon the revenue to be earned from food exports. Unless the Turkana are powerful enough to demand access to food, the transition to a cash and market-oriented economy could thus pose a threat not only to their social structure, but also to their basic ability to obtain food in famine times.

Pastoral nomads across Africa are facing challenges to their way of life which has rested on a non-monetized, pre-capitalist mode of subsistence production. The Turkana, confronted by the construction of an international highway across their lands and by the changes which famine relief and development projects are bringing, face an uncertain future. The non-Turkana who are making most of the decisions which will shape the new relationship between Turkana and the outside world see the salvation of the nomads primarily in the production of livestock and, to a much lesser extent, fish and perhaps irrigated crops for sale on the national market. This may, however, undermine what is left of Turkana culture, and place stresses on Turkana land which it cannot bear. Mamdani's account of the recent history of livestock production for the outside market by the Karamajong suggests that this could happen.

Perhaps the saddest part of the current dilemma is that the people of Turkana do not have much change of reversing the current trajectory of ever-increasing penetration by outside economic, political and social systems. Given the history of colonial policies towards Turkana; its strategic position; the strongly capitalist orientation of the Kenyan state; the philosophic predilections of the aid-givers; and the absence of a strong, unifed Turkana leadership, there seems little change that they can return to traditional ways. A new articulation between the Turkana pre-capitalist mode of production and the world capitalist systeem is coming into being. However, even through much of the agenda for this transition is set by powerful external forces, it is by no means clear that they will prevail. The pull of the nomadic tradition is strong for the Turkana. They may find passive ways of thwarting the goals of outside planners, for better or for worse. Hyden (1981) finds evidence of this in Tanzania's 'uncaptured peasantry'. On the other hand, they may take positive action ro educate themselves to the challenges and organize to take whatever advantage they can of the transition. Fortunately, some efforts toward this more positive end are beginning, but the Kenya government does not seem overly committed to them, thereby frustrating the efforts of even the most sympathetic aid-givers who cannot by-pass the government to establish such programs on a large scale. Ultimately, the future will be determined by the inter-relationship between these internal and external forces and structures.

Conclusion

African pastoralists like the Turkana are among the most famine-vulnerable groups in the modern world. The long-term results of famine crises can be great or small depending, in part, on the form of relief. When famine strikes, the first problem is getting any food at all to these groups. The Turkana were among the fortunate in that the 1980 famine claimed few, if any, human lives. But the perhaps unavoidable manner in which famine relief was offered raises a number of key questions for future situations. Can ways be found to offer relief to pastoralists which discourage the formation of camps? If, for pragmatic reasons, donors or governments must institute food-for-work projects, how best can these involve the affected people in decisions regarding the objectives and beneficiaries of the work? Where the traditional political leadership is credible and respected, can relief be administered in a manner which is more sensitive to such structures, even to the point of simply giving the relief food to the elders to distribute in a locally appropriate fashion? The types of long-term development into which agencies and governments often drift at the end of a famine emergency demand close scrutiny. Development schemes posited on closer involvement in a market and cash economy, and closer ties to national government, may indeed be planting future 'seeds of famine' for pastoralists and the ecologically sensitive lands which they occupy.

References

Alavi, H.: India: transition from feudalism to colonial capitalism. Journal of Contemporary Asia 10,4, 359−399 (1980)

Ball, N.: Understanding the causes of African famine. Journal of Modern African Studies, 517−522 (1976)

Barber, J.: Imperial frontier: a study of relations between the British and the Pastoral Tribes of North East Uganda. East African Publishing, Nairobi, House 1968.

Bernstein, M.: The transition of Turkana. Suny Research '82, 6−10 (1982)

Brenner, R.: The Origins of Capitalist Development: A Critique of Neo-Smithian Marxism. New Left Review 25−92 (1977)

Christensen, C. et al.: Food problems and prospects in Sub-Saharan Africa: the decade of the 1980's. Washington, DC, US Department of Agriculture, Economic Research Service 1981.

deVille deGoyet, C.; Seaman, J. and Geijer, U.: The management of nutritional emergencies in large populations. Geneva. World Health Organization 1978.

Dirks, R.: Social responses during severe food shortages and famine. Current Anthropology 21,1, 21−44 (1980)

Foster-Carter, A.: The modes of Production controversy, New Left Review 47− 77 (1978)

Frank, A.: Capitalism and underdevelopment in Latin America. Monthly Review Press, New York 1969.

Franke, R.W.; Chasin, B.H.:Seeds of famine. Allanheld, Osmun and Co., Montclair, NJ 1980.

Hyden, G.: Beyond Ujamaa in Tanzania: underdevelopment and an uncaptured peasantry. Heinemann, London and Nairobi 1980.

Jackson, T. with Eade, D.: Against the grain: the dilemma of project food aid. Oxfam, Oxford 1982.

Laclau, E.: Feudalism and capitalism in Latin America. In: Laclau, E. (ed.), Politics and ideology in Marxist Theory. New Left Books, London 1977.

Lamphear, J.: Aspects of Turkana leadership during the era of primary resistance. Journal of African History 17,2, 225–243 (1976)

Lappe, F.M.; Collins, J.; Kinley, D.: On aid as an obstacle. Inst. for Food and Development Policy, San Francisco 1980.

Mamdani, M.: Karamoja: colonial roots of the famine. Paper presented at the Conference on Rural Rehabilitation and Development, Faculty of Social Sciences, Makerere University, Kampala, Uganda, 14–18 September 1981.

Masefield, G.B.: Famine its prevention and relief. Oxford University Press, London 1963.

Oxfam: Field director's handbook. 3. edn. Oxfam, Oxford 1981.

Protein-Calorie Advisory Group of the United Nations System: A guide to food and health relief operations for disasters. United Nations, New York 1977.

Rey, P-P.: Colonisme, neo-colonialisme, et transition au capitalisme. Paris 1971.

Rey, P-P. Les alliances des classes. Paris 1973.

Seaman, J.; Holt, J.: Markets and famines in the Third World. Disasters 4,3, 283–297 (1980)

Skocpol, T.: Wallerstein's world capitalist system: a theoretical and historical critique. American Journal of Sociology 82,5, 1075–1090 (1977).

Stevens, C.: Food aid and the developing world. St. Martin's Press, New York 1979.

Taylor, J.G.: From modernization to modes of production: a critique of the sociologies of development and underdevelopment. Humanities Press, Atlantic Highlands, NJ 1979.

Turton, D.: Response to drought: the Mursi of Southwestern Ethiopia. Disasters 1,4, 275–287 (1977)

Wallerstein,I.: The modern world system. Academic Press, New York 1974.

World Bank: Accelerated development in Sub-Saharan Africa: an agenda for action. World Bank, Washington, DC 1981.

Notes:

1) I am deeply indebted to Fr. Joseph Morris, M.M., for the motivation to write this paper and for many of the ideas incorporated in it. Although the body of the paper was completed before I attended the July 1982 Workshop on Famine and Food emergencies sponsored by the International Disaster Institute in London, the final conclusions were strengthened while others were altered or discarded after hearing the information presented by Julius Holt, the coordinator of the workshop, and other participants. My thanks also to the many relief agency personnel who were so generous with their time in answering my questions.

2) *Harambée*. The Kenyan Government's self-help programme.

Coping with Complexity in Food Crisis Management [1]

Currey, B., Dr., Food Crisis Management Group, School of Social Sciences, The Flinders University of South Australia, Bedford Park, South Australia, 5042, Australia

Present address: Robert S. McNamara Fellow, Economic Development Institutes. The World Bank, c/o GPO Box 97, Dhaka, Bangladesh.

Abstract: The causes, consequences, and management of food crises are complex. Geographers with their inherent understanding of complexity can play an important part in meshing relief measures with the long-term development of famine prone areas in developing nations. For this role, they must extend their traditional understanding of concatenation processes, phenology, semiotics, contingency approaches to warning systems, and the concept of comparative evaluation. These geographical ideas are essential elements in the training of key food crisis managers.

Introduction

Severe food crises or famines occur when the integrity of a community breaks down with the result that marginal members either have to migrate in families because of lack of access to food or die of starvation and starvation-related disease. An earlier definition of famine in terms of a 'community syndrome' (Currey 1976) sought not only to differentiate famine from starvation in that the former affects communities and the latter affects individuals, but also to emphasise the myriad causes, symptoms and consequences of the famine syndrome. All food crises whether famine, seasonal scarcity or chronic hunger are complex phenomena.

Attempts to manage food crises must cope with their complexity when seeking to understand their variable causation, to predict their occurrence, to develop warning systems for ameliorating their effects, and to prevent their recurrence. Folk knowledge (Chapman 1982) has already developed contingency models for coping with the uncertainty of the sudden collapse of the community's food system such as in the Indian proverb

If Krittika rains, grain will be dear.
If Mrigshar rains, there will be bumper crops.
But if Rohini weeps, the direst famine will follow.   (Mehta 1916)

---

1) The author is grateful to Drs. Martin R. Schaerer and Armin Kressman of the Alimentarium in Vevey for their early suggestions and to my colleagues Stewart Fraser and Dr. Lance Brennan for commenting upon the final draft.

184

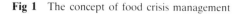

Fig 1 The concept of food crisis management

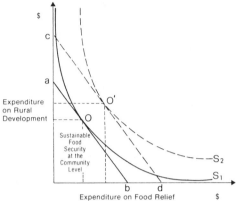

Expenditure on Food Relief

If food crisis management is to be improved, public responses to food crises should include such community knowledge of timing and the local food system within their administrative procedures (Brammer 1982). Management must also understand the complexity of community dynamics in order to enhance those on-going changes in the community which ensure sustainable food security for marginal members.

Food crisis management may be conceptualised in the abstract as a micro-economic model (Fig 1) concerned with achieving an optimal balance (0) between expenditure levels (lines a−b or c−d) and a variety of bundles of relief strategies or development strategies with different levels (S_1 and S_2) of results or effects, in order to maximise food security at the community level in regions prone to food crises. The bundles of relief strategies, like doles of food given out at gruel kitchens (Fig 2), or the air-lifting of high protein biscuits are essentially short term curative strategies sometimes called band-aids. The bundles of development strategies, like the building of canals (Fig 3) or afforestation schemes, which sometimes may be implemented because of the repeated occurrence of food crises in an area, are longer-term strategies. The longer-term strategies ought to be aimed not only at preventing food crises, but also at alleviating the more chronic hunger associated with structural poverty.

The Bengali proverb *Gacher gora kete mathai pani dhala* (watering the tree but cutting the roots) unfortunately provides an apt analogy for many of the present responses to food crises. Food crisis management attempts to improve these responses. Famine and other food crises should be managed so that the temporary watering during the crisis strengthens a tree's roots for its long-term security. As in Fig 1 food relief must be viewed in the context of rural development, and rural development, if necessary, must also play a relief role. In the interests of effective food crisis management, local government must improve its ability to respond to the unexpected and have ready appropriate rural development projects which can be implemented as relief funds become available.

Those involved in managing food crises have to go beyond the useful, but abstract theorising of micro-economics (Fig 1). The catholic view of traditional geographers with their awareness of the complexity of real world situations has a useful role to play in interpreting

Fig 2 Gruel kitchens and doles of food relieve the symptoms of food crises

Fig 3 Appropriately prepared work projects, building irrigation and communication canals stocked with fish could potentially lead to sustained development if the landless labourers were to be guaranteed long term access to the resources created by the projects.

and integrating ecological, political-economic, and community processes for the food crisis manager. Complex interrelationships have been an inherent focus to geographical knowledge at least since Jean Brunhes outlined 'The Principle of Interconnexion' in 1910.

Principe de connexite: les faits de la realite geographique sont etroitement lies entre eux et doivent etre etudies dans leurs multiples connexions. L'idee du "tout terrestre"   (Brunhes 1910)

Stoddart's articles in the mid 1960's, used organic analogies of complexity, and 'the ecosystem as a model of reality' (Stoddart 1965 and 1967) to refine the concept of a 'geosystem' and place it within the context of general systems theory. His analogies were principally drawn from the relatively simple world of the reef or island with only controlled processes and events occurring. Such control and measurement precision are the antithesis of the situation in most food crisis situations (Jodha 1975, Currey 1979 and 1980). This does not necessarily mean that the approach is invalid because understanding the concept of complexity and hence realising the limits of information increases our sensitivity to

the study of how to make decisions under conditions of irreducible ignorance and uncertainty ... it gives more encouragement than delusions of certainty, for these are eventually certain to end in disaster
(Boulding 1979)

If geographers are to apply their understanding of the concept or complexity in food crisis management, they must reappraise their level of expertise in several related areas.
1   Concatenation process models
2   Phenology of food systems
3   Semiotics
4   Contingency approaches to warning systems
5   Comparative evaluation methods
6   Food crisis manager training

Concatentation Process Models

The concatenation process is an extension of the concept of complexity. In famines it is the process in which the complex inter-relationships (from grain shipments to kinship links or from political ties to administrative chains of command) become strained and eventually rupture at a similar point or points in time and space. The process may by similar to the build up of stresses within the fabric of an aircraft wing before stresses in the decaying wing eventually reach a critical threshold and the wing distintegrates.

Reviews of the economic treatise *Poverty and Famine* (Sen 1981) have applauded its author for explaining the causes of famine. Sen's 'entitlement approach' does not, however, 'explain' the causes of famine. The work is, in fact, an elegant description using economic terminology of concepts similar to those described by Greenough (1975) and other historians (e.g. Bhatia 1975), of the reasons why some groups suffer more than others during famines. To date, the policy analyst, Sanderson (1975) at the international level, the economist, Alamgir (1980) at the national level and the anthropologist, Firth (1959) at the community level have probably come closest to an exposition of the complex concatentation processes which explain the causes of famine.

Events and processes 'concatenate', or come together in time and space, with the result that pressures on reciprocity relationships within rural communities become so great that marginal members are "sloughed off" through the deaths of individuals or the outmigration of families. As examples at the regional level, two food crises have affected communities in a northern district of Bangladesh, one during 1974−75, another during 1978−79. They resulted from two very different concatenation processes.

a) *The 1974−75 food crisis:* in the wake of the independence war, the administration was inexperienced; relations with aid donors were strained; government personnel in rural areas were left unpaid. Annual flooding was severely out of phase with the agricultural calendar in both 1973 and 1974. The dumping of sterile sand and the ponding of flood waters on the fields lessened the need for agricultural labour. The Government's initial response was minimal amidst widespread speculation, hoarding and smuggling by certain people.

b) *The 1978−79 food crisis:* population numbers had grown beyond previously estimated needs for stocks of food. The worst drought in Rangpur District's meteorological history affected internal production, particularly in the northern region. Anxiety arose after difficulties with food aid negotiations. The Government released large amounts of food stocks (already low) to urban elites because of an impending election. The cash crop, jute, was poor in quality and gave little remuneration to poorer groups so that they were then unable to purchase back supplies of rice for subsistence.

With limited data availability, a significant level of explanation for such complex concatenations is not provided by alternative models such as those of catastrophe theory (Seaman and Holt 1980); catastasis (de Freitas and Woolmington 1980); periodic cycles (Manetsch 1977); sequences (Turner 1978); continuous transformatins (Renfrew and Cooke 1979) or ecological models (Parrack 1978).

Wolpert (1980) was one of the first geographers to advocate risk analysis methods, similar to the event and fault trees used by Rasmussen (1975) in the *Reactor Safety Study,* for predicting social hazards generally. Risk analysis strategies have been questioned because of their inflexibility in dealing with complex systems where there is a lack of basic data to calculate the probabilities of individual events or faults (Lindackers 1981). The basic 'fault tree' used in these analyses tends to suggest that a single initiating event such as a pipe-fracture in a nuclear power plant (or a flood within a local food system), will eventually lead to a given probability of melt-down (or famine) if other processes such as the generation of electricity (or local food procurement) also fail. Adoption of risk-analysis methods which involve the traditional 'fault-tree' do not usually allow for the coincidental and perhaps simultaneous breakdown of several systems. Geographers could, however, usefully reverse the event trees, considering instead various "routes through the roots" or concatenations (Fig 4) as a basis for food crisis management training. These are templates for training not prediction: they seek to increase "intelligent apprehension" rather than "a too mechanical obedience to rule" (Orissa Enquiry Commissioner's Report 1867).

Both the total number of events and the individual events, which together constitute the set of critical events predisposing communities to famine, are unknown because information on past famines in different settings is limited. Similarly the mode of combining individual critical events in terms of their contribution to famine vulnerability is also unknown. It cannot be assumed that each critical event is simply added to another event to give a total probability of famine.

188

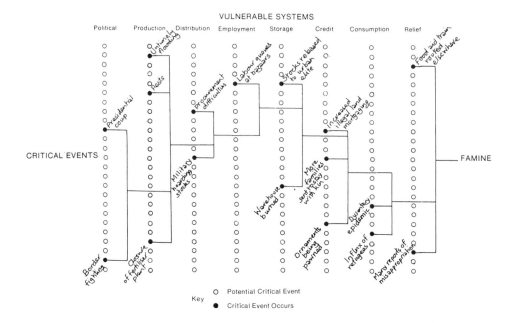

Fig 4 A template for training managers showing critical events in one famine concatenation process

Many of the critical events contributing to the probability of famine are interactive. The outbreak of a civil war alone might produce a high probability of famine; the outbreak of a civil war and a late monsoon together might produce only a slightly higher probability whereas the probability of famine from a late monsoon alone, might itself be quite considerable.

There are conditional probabilities among critical events which are poorly understood, but may be exemplified by some arbitrary examples. Two critical events may produce positive feedback thus greatly increasing the likelihood of famine: a river dumping sterile sand on farmland might have very little impact on the likelihood of famine. Similarly the breakdown of a local fertiliser plant would also have little impact on its own. Together, however, these two events might have considerable impact. On the other hand another example combination of events might produce negative feedback whereby the combination in the concatenation process actually reduces the likelihood of famine occurring. If the tardy arrival of a large food aid shipment (which itself creates a high likelihood of famine) actually occurs after a dock strike which also creates a high probability of famine, the combined likelihood of famine might be very low because the dock workers would have returned to work under improved working conditions by the time the aid shipment arrived.

The cross impact matrices (Rochberg et al. 1970) necessary to develop these intricate scenarios are again only likely to be useful for training purposes. The nuances of each particular crisis are likely to be obscured or lost for predictive purposes however many branches or 'roots' in various dimensions are modelled in any concatenation process. As MacDonnell noted over a century ago

With the lesson taught by the past before us, we may indeed hope to interpret the needs of the present but the past alone projects no certain light on a changeful future.   (MacDonnell 1876)

The food crisis manager has however to learn from past mistakes and interpret them within the context and structures of the present

Numerous lessons which should be of value to the future can be drawn from the sequence of events which led to the tragedy.   (India Famine Inquiry Commission Report on Bengal 1945)

Concatenation models illustrate the need to avoid monitoring only a limited number of parameters. The reverse 'event-tree' is a particularly useful training template because, in many potential famine situations, the data actually available to the food crisis manager are often only in the form of events mentioned in news flashes or rumours. There are seldom any series of reliable statistics. Understanding causality in terms of a concatenation process allows the manager of a food crisis to take action when he can demonstrate a consistent pattern of events or premonitory signs of an approaching famine.

An example concatenation might appear thus:

If there is no rain at the end of the month x in the planting season and if there is an attack of rice pest in months p or q as well as rice prices being over t takas in September, then we should watch for signs such as an increase in beggars, prostitutes and the eating of famine foods etc. etc. in months v or u. If months v or u do show such consistent signals, then a survey of the possible lack of access to food for particlar sub-groups should be carried out to determine the type, timing and magnitude of the interventions.

Phenology of Food Systems

Phenology is defined as the study of the timing of recurrent events. Biogeographers have already laid claim to the term in describing plant phenophases: planting, ripening, maturing. With the advent of Landsat, they can now measure the "green wave effect" of spring, sweeping polewards in the temperate latitudes around the solstice, as deciduous trees come into leaf. Although historical geographers have intensively studied 'time', the concept of 'time as timing', (Castillo 1979) or coincidence, has been given relatively little emphasis in geographical studies.

A number of geographers, writing on crop calendars and seasonal hunger, have clearly recognised the importance of seasonality (e.g. Changani 1973; Metzner 1976; Watts 1978). However, recent workshops and papers on the seasonal dimensions of poverty in developing nations have exhibited a marked absence of geographers (Chowdhury 1980; Clay 1978; Longhurst and Payne 1979).

The importance given to the synchronisation of climatic, crop and employment seasons is not merely an anachronism from subsistence agriculture although in commercial agriculture it may be a lesser constraint (Librero 1965). It is also relevant to areas where colonial rule has affected the structure of communities and where international markets and capital have altered the economy. The Collector of Rangpur District in Bengal, responding to a questionnaire from Sir W.W. Hunter over a century after British imperial markets had been established in India, reported in 1869:

The surest signs of approaching famine in the District would be the high price of grain, taken in conjunction with the events of the season.   (Hunter 1874)

190

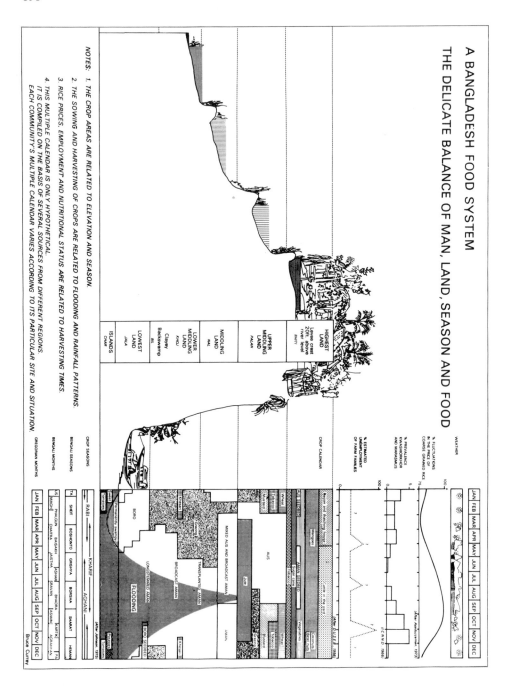

Fig 5 The complexities inherent in understanding the phenology of a food system (adapted from Currey 1979)

The complexities inherent in understanding the phenology of a food system are illustrated in Fig 5. The schematic diagram of a hypothetical Bengal: food system shows how the timing of events in an agricultural community is related not only to the seasons and months of the agricultural calendar but also to the subtle changes in elevation of the different fields. Rainfall must not only be sufficient, it must be timely. The effects of *awshomoi brishti* (untimely rainfall) will reverberate throughout the food system. Similarly, the effects of a lack of synchronisation in flood times will affect the closely adjusted cropping patterns at different land levels. If sowing or harvesting is cancelled, delayed or reduced, underemployment and unemployment of cultivators may increase, especially for landless labourers. Wages, in cash or kind, may be reduced. If harvesting is late, migrant labourers may be working in areas where they are unaccustomed to local response procedures when natural disasters strike. A distinctly abnormal seasonal regime may destabilise any or all of the relationships among food stocks, food prices, debt repayments and nutritional levels.

A food system's calendar is delicately balanced. Any ill-timed events disrupt the rural rhythm and may well precipitate a crisis from a situation of chronic malnutrition among indebted landless labourers. Two examples, again from a district in northern Bangladesh in 1974−75 and 1978−79, if read in conjunction with Fig 5, illustrate the importance of understanding food system phenology for food crisis management.

a) *1974−75:* Aid donors initially refused to respond to requests for food aid by pointing out that the flood peak of the Brahmaputra river in 1974 had reached an elevation of only 19.81 m whereas the last severe flood peak of the Brahmaputra river in 1955 which had caused minimal disruption of the food system, had reached a higher elevation, 20.12 m. Admittedly, social and economic conditions were also different in 1955, but an additional and crucial factor in the comparison was the *timing* of the 1974 flooding. There was no single flood peak as there had been in 1955. Rather there was a series of flood peaks rising above the danger level for 44 days in 1974 (compared to 26 days in 1955). The early flood peaks in 1974 interrupted the harvesting of the *aus* or summer rice harvest in June. The late flood peaks in September interfered with the three phenophases of the *aman* or winter rice, seeding, transplanting and growing. This lack of synchronisation affected not only subsistence production in the area but also the demand for labour for harvesting, transplanting and weeding.

b) *1978−79:* Officials in late August were deceptively lulled into the hope that the food crisis, following the worst drought in Rangpur District's meteorological history, was over because the price of coarse rice was falling and wage rates were high. Coarse rice prices only in the urban markets, where prices are recorded, were falling because the government had begun sales of government stocks in urban markets. Wage rates were high for that time of year because the earlier drought had meant a month's delay in the planting of the *aus* or summer rice. As a result, the *aus* was also being harvested one month later. It was being harvested together with the cash crop jute. Also the aman or winter rice was being transplanted at the same time. Wages for that time of year were temporarily buoyant, but, in early September, there was suddenly no demand for labour. This was innate knowledge for the cultivators, but not for the distant food crisis managers.

The responses to crises also have inherent phenological components which are seldom considered. Seasonality affects the importation of relief supplies: the traffic of barges full of grain for transhipment abroad may be hindered at certain times of year in the USA on the Mississippi River; roads may be impassable because of monsoon flooding in the recipient countries (Fig 6); and the imported grain, if it does arrive safely, may ferment in moist monsoon conditions.

Fig 6 A jeep is transported by countryboat as roads become impassable in the monsoon season. Seasonality is an important factor affecting responses to famines.

The successful food crisis manager also knows that seeds or fertiliser for a 'catch crop' must arrive in time to allow germination while there is still sufficient moisture in the soil. Food for work programmes are less needed for adult males at times of planting or harvesting on the subsistence plot. The apparent success of feeding programmes during famine may often be more a function of the local seasonal pattern of nutritional status than the result of the programme itself.

As geographers labour over the precise mapping of the phenology of the 'green wave effect', they should question why they do not also map the phenologies of the lean seasons in developing countries, of numbers queuing for agricultural employment or work in the bazaars, and of crucial dates by which agricultural inputs like fertiliser or seeds must arrive.

Semiotics

Semiotics is the general theory of signs. Although now claimed as the science of the linguists, the 'art' probably began when pathologists, with the best available experience of the human body's systems, attempted to interpret signs in the hope that these might lead them to intervention and thus prevent disease. The important concept is that an understanding of signs initiates action, just as a mother responds to a child's cry rather than awaiting a complete analysis of the complex processes producing the pain (Sless 1983).

Most young geographers studied semiotics when they trudged around after their professor on fieldwork and were told that the boarded-up windows in a village signified the process of rural decay, or that the crow-step gables on houses suggested earlier Dutch influence on the cultural landscape. The advent of tourism in an alpine valley was 'obvious' to students after seeing the availability of foreign newspapers in the newsstands, and the breakdown of pasture conservation practices because the farmers were busy in their new occupation as hotelkeepers. Biogeographers again have been quick to spot innumerable indicator plants (Clements 1928), signs which tell them that a particular ecosystem is deteriorating. Apart from a few errant cultural geographers and biogeographers, fieldwork and semiotics were forgotten in the mainstream of human geography as the logical positivists sat manipulating data-bases of statistical series in air-conditioned surroundings, and more recently the idealists ironically only discussed 'hermeneutics' or 'understanding' in vinyl-clad seminar rooms.

The food crisis manager facing an imminent crisis seldom has robust data series, let alone time for philosophical discussion. He needs to reach a consensus rapidly on the likelihood of a crisis and on the need to intervene. He may, however, have ample evidence from signals —

- If small farmers are suddenly selling off their goats in the market place;
- If more married rather than single men are leaving to seek seasonal employment;
- If the number of beggars around the mosque after Jumma prayer is increasing;
- If women are gathering plantain *(Musa paradisica)* saplings;
- If there is a rapid increase in activity around the land registry office.

Each of such signs alone may not be conclusive, but together, if they are consistent and interpreted by people with local knowledge, they may provide an essential complement to official government statistics which may only become available to the managers after publication several months later. Geographers must learn to observe the signs, understand the underlying processes in the food system, provide caveats against misinterpretation of the signs, and known the probable sequence of signs as the concatenation process gathers momentum in a food system with know phenophases. Such signs provide a consistent pattern to initiate ameliorative strategies.

Contingency Approaches to Warning Systems

The warning system is the decision making process by which knowledge about an imminent food crisis is transformed into action which will lessen both imminent human suffering and the possibility of future food crises. Studies of hazard warning systems, initiated by the Natural Hazards Research Group, have been principally concerned with 'dramatic events' and the dissemination of warnings by the establishment to the general public at risk in the United States (Mileti 1975).

In famine situations within developing countries, the poor know all too well that they are at risk when they are indebted and have insufficient assets and food to carry them through to the next harvest. In their case, the requirement is to get the establishment to respond appropriately. The problem then is not so much one of diffusing information down a hierarchical

Continuous Monitoring	Spatial Targetting	Special Watchfulness
First Monday of each month	On or before 1st April each year	Whenever
Police Officer in charge of Thana	District Officer	District Officer
Agricultural statistics including:	Maps of areas liable to famine based on:	records when:

Continuous Monitoring

1. The amount and distribution of the rainfall.
2. The character of the weather.
3. The progress of agricultural operations.
4. The condition of the standing crops.
5. The out turn of the crops at the time of harvest.
6. The stocks of grain, as far as these can be ascertained.
7. The retail shop prices of common (cheapest) rice (mota chaul), in respect of the district of Murshidabad, and of maize, in respect of the district of Darjeeling (quantity obtainable for a rupee).
8. The general condition of the people particularly the existence of scarcity, if any, or distress, whenever it may occur.
9. The health of the people
10. Any failure in the supply of fodder, the presence of disease, or the occurrence of any unusual mortality among the cattle.

sends to
District Superintendent
of Police and
District Officer

Spatial Targetting

1. The previous history of the tract in regard to its having been visited by famines or not.
2. The density and economic condition of the population.
3. The nature of the soil and the general capability of the tract to maintain its population.
4. How far cultivation depends on rainfall, and whether the normal rainfall is regular or otherwise.
5. How far the tract is irrigated by rivers, canals, weirs, etc.
6. The accessibility of the tract as regards importation of food grains.

sends to
Commissioner of the
Division

Special Watchfulness

Retail shop prices of the food grains rise to 20 per cent or more above the normal rates.

* * * * *

Submits explanation and reports when:
Retail shop prices of the food grains rise to 40 per cent (the scarcity rate) above normal rates.

sends to
Commissioner of the
Division

Tab 1 The sequence of information gathering prior to famines proposed in the Bengal Famine Code 1913

Danger Signals

When distress is anticipated
Weekly

District Officer
Compiles by Thana:

1. Weekly rainfall
2. Prices of cheapest rice
* * * * *
Fortnightly
District Officer
Calculates by district from
railway authorities
Imports and exports of food
grains
* * * * *
Periodically
District Superintendent of
Police
notes
danger signals:
1. Any increase in crime attributable to general rise in prices or scarcity of food.
2. Any wandering of needy, starving persons.
3. Any emigration from, or immigration into, the area.
4. Any unusual increase of mortality.
5. Any cases of starvation or severe want.
6. Any decline in the above symptoms of scarcity.
        send to

The District Officer
who if prices continue to rise, looks for indications of famine
1. The contraction of private charity, indicated by the wandering of paupers.
2. The contraction of credit.
3. Feverish activity in the grain trade.
4. Restlessness shown in an increase of crime
5. Unusual movements of flocks and herds in search of pasturage.
6. Unusual wandering of people.
7. Increased activity in emigration as seen from booking returns at stations.

A Special Report

Explaining impending famine when apprehensions of distress arise in any part of the district

District Officer
reports:

I. The grounds of his belief that distress or famine is impending, commenting upon:
1. The normal percentage of each harvest to the total harvest of a year.
2. The out-turn of each harvest of each year in cents with reference to the normal area.
3. The out-turn of each harvest of the year reduced to express the relation which each such harvest bears to the total harvests of the year (100 per cent being taken as the normal total of all three harvests).

II. The report should review:
1. The economic condition of the district or part or parts of the district affected.
2. The out-turn of recent harvests.
3. The nature and the extent of the anticipated failure of crops.
4. The probable intensity and duration of distress and the contingencies on which they depend.
5. The classes most affected.
6. The position as regards local trade, communications, food stocks, prices, fodder and water supply, etc.
7. The precautionary steps taken to organise measures for dealing with distress and the proposed measures of relief.
8. The state of the relief of programmes.
9. The probable extent to which the land revenue demand may have to be postponed or remitted.

III. The report should also show:
1. The area and population likely to be affected.
2. The extent of relief which is likely to be required.
3. The expenditure which that relief will involve.
4. The local sources from which such expenditure can be met.
5. The additional staff which will be required in the Civil, Public Works and Sanitary departments
6. Whether any landlords are likely to remit rent, and whether any concessions should be made to government estates.

The Basis of the Declaration of Famine

1. "Test relief" to find out whether the signals are real or deceptive, will be opened by the District Officer when the danger signals are clearly observable.
2. "Gratuitous relief" may be given in the villages where this is found necessary owing, for instance, to the emigration of able-bodied persons leaving their dependents unprovided for.

District Officer shall report with a view to famine being declared when:
1. Test works begin to attract workers in considerable numbers.
        or
2. Gratuitous relief appears likely to be required on a considerable scale, i.e. when one-half per cent of the population (according to the preceding census) of any Thana or larger area in the district has been on relief for two months continuously.
        to the
Commissioner of the Division and Local Government

information network, but rather getting information to move up through a hierarchy in order to have a useful response implemented. Famines are not rapid impact disasters. The concatenation process occurs over a considerable time period. Disentangling information from political fabrication during the concatenation process requires considerable skill by those operating the warning system, if the intervention is to match the distress in an area.

A contingency approach to warning systems has the flexibility to cope with such situations in famine-prone areas. Such a system operated in British India. It was the outgrowth of successive famines during the latter half of the 19th century, and was therefore built upon considerable experience amongst the officers responsible for rural administration. As can be seen from Tab 1 it was composed of a series of 'if statements' at different administrative levels.

The key manager in the warning system was the District Officer who interpreted retrospectively the price of rice against the "danger signals" (or semiotics) of famine reported from the District Superintendent of Police, viz.
● any increase in crime attributable to the general rise in the price or scarcity of food;
● any increase in the wandering of needy starving persons;
● any emigration from, or immigration into, the area;
● any unusual increase of mortality;
● any cases of starvation or severe want;
● any decline in the above symptoms.

The District Officer also interpreted the indications of famine prospectively if the price of the cheapest rice continued to rise, viz.
● the contraction of private charity indicated by the wandering of paupers;
● the contraction of credit;
● feverish activity in the grain trade;
● restlessness shown in an increase of crime;
● unusual movements of flocks and herds in search of pasture;
● unusual wandering of people;
● unusual activity in immigration as seen from booking returns at stations.

Officers at different levels in the warning system had specified tasks, predicated upon these contingencies. When a consistent pattern of signs emerged, actions were implemented. The actions were then evaluated to examine their effect on the food system: 'test relief' was opened in order to find out whether the signals were real or deceptive (Bengal Famine Code 1913).

Although the warning system of the British famine codes has been criticised for being responsive rather than preventive, and for encouraging relief dependency rather than self-reliance, some national and state governments such as Bihar have nevertheless revived and reinvigorated the system. An effective contingency approach to a warning system like that in the Famine Codes would seem to depend upon having (a) analytical and experienced rural administrators, (b) rural-development projects such as food-for-work projects (with the potential to enhance structural changes in the community in favour of the vulnerable groups) ready and in place for when a crisis is detected, and (c) a differentiated detection and response system tailored to the particular conditions of each regional food system, and flexible enough to cope with changes in that food system.

Comparative Evalution Methods

In the early 1930's Ernst Plewe made a strong plea for a strengthening of Ritter's earlier emphasis on comparative geography (Ritter 1852; Plewe 1932). Most young geographers who had endured seemingly endless lectures on soil, climate, and population comparisons of the USA and USSR, or France and Germany, were much relieved when comparative regional geography went into decline in the 1960's and 70's. Those geographers who, as students or researchers, have been fortunate enough to have first hand experience in the countries being compared, or have had the chance to visit different famine areas may have a different perspective on the value of comparative methods.

In rejecting comparative regional studies geography may have thrown the baby out with the bath water. The contents of the *Journal of Comparative Studies in Society and History* clearly indicate that other disciplines (e.g. anthropology, psychology, economics, sociology and history) now place a measure of significance on comparative studies. Fortunately, there are some notable exceptions in the geographical literature such as the Australian National University's comparative island and village studies (e.g. Brookfield 1962; Maude 1973 and 1979; Lea 1965; and Hugo, G.J. 1975) looking at the rationale for similarities and dissimilarities among processes such as migration and dependency. Some geographers studying industrial systems, for example Rogerson's study of the peripheral countries in southern Africa, (Rogerson 1978), have successfully used the comparative approach to contrast different modes of development. Nevertheless comparative studies at present hardly hold 'pride of place' in human geography, and until now little consideration has been given to their potential in food crisis management.

What other discipline has the background and training to carry out comparative evaluations of analogous strategies which affect the relationships between community and environment from one area or district to another? Just as the dashboards of some Japanese cars, where the plastic work had been initially designed under temperate climatic conditions, succumbed when the cars were first introduced to Australia because of high temperatures to which they were exposed, so most food crisis management systems must be adapted to particular local conditions when first introduced to a new locality. The preliminary famine code for all of British India was later partially, but alas imperfectly, tailored to the needs of each state (Report of the Indian Famine Commission 1898). Today, the national food crisis warning systems which are strongly supported by the Food and Agricultural Organisation must similarly be decentralised and meshed within local food systems. Comparative approaches to evaluating warning systems within different food systems are required: a warning system based on the price of coarse rice *may* be suited to another rice growing area, but not to a drier upland millet area.

Comparative approaches are required for both the detection and response sections of a warning system. In the detection section, not only may the warning signs be similar in some areas and different in others, but also the spatial and temporal patterns in which the signs of food crisis begin to occur may vary from region to region. People living in areas having a tradition of seasonal migration for labour are more likely to move with their goat herds earlier in the concatenation process than people in areas of sedentary farming who may sell their goats in the market before they migrate. Similarly, an area with a recent history of recurrent famine may be selling off land early because they had already sold off their brass and gold ornaments in a previous famine. In another region, it might still be the ornaments which are being sold off early as access to food is reduced.

In the response system, floating gardens on bamboo mats may be a response for all flood prone areas, but they would be left literally high and dry in areas prone to drought. Suggestions for improving village storehouses are excellent in localities where poorer groups traditionally have surpluses. They would, however, be superfluous if the landless groups are so bound to the debt collector that they never have a surplus to store. Involvement of women in work-relief programmes, although seen as inherently positive, is again dependent on comparative evaluation among different culture groups. If, in particular areas, women are already fulfilling a very necessary role by ensuring access to food for children, their involvement in building a village fish pond for future development must be carefully evaluated.

These comparative 'if statements' have a uniquely geographical component. Their consideration by students in developing countries should reinvigorate a new comparative geography. Ideally, such a geography would evelute famine prevention strategies in different places with similar structures, rather than continuing with the present emphasis in comparative studies examining only homologues from one time period to another when the structure of society is likely to have changed.

Training Food Crisis Managers

The involvement of geographers in training managers is neither a superficial reform nor new to the discipline of geography. Radical scholars advocating that only through revolutionary change can food crises be prevented have little supporting evidence given the high levels of post-revolutionary famine mortality in Russia (Wheatcroft 1981), China (Domes 1980), and Kampuchea (Ea 1983). In addition to the layman's every-day knowledge that the operation of bureaucracies can be significantly improved, Baker and the geographer, Heathcote, have both documented the need for greater management coordination to overcome the fragmented government approach to the complex problems associated with disasters (Baker 1976, Heathcote 1980). The possibility of better bureaucratic management defying the realities of the rural class structure in implementing rural development programmes, and thus improving food crisis management, have been outlined for Bangladesh (Blair 1978).

Traditionally, in Europe, a course in economic geography was often part of the training for commerce and business. Today, in North America, several geography departments form part of business schools in which they normally follow a spatial analysis rather than an ecological paradigm. Very few of the prestigious colleges for training lower and middle level executives for public administration now have a geographical component. If geographers in developing countries prone to food crises wish to become involved with the management of food systems, they must begin to train public administrators as part of an administrator's course.

It is difficult to know at what level of rural administrator such training should be aimed. The key level of food crisis management in South Asia certainly used to be the district.

Whatever (Famine) Commissions reported, whatever codes were written, the district officer had as usual to do the work   (Woodruff 1954)

Today, there have been a number of changes:
1) decision-making policy during food crises in South Asia may have moved up the administrative hierarchy from District Officer to Divisional Commissioner;
2) the action during food crises may have moved down the hierarchy to sub-divisional and circle officers;
3) new government agencies, such as those concerned with family planning or agricultural statistics, may bypass the hierarchy in the administrative services and channel information directly to their own ministries in the central government;
4) local members of parliament assert considerable influence in planning at the local level in some countries.

Nevertheless, the District Officer (or his equivalent) still plays a key role. They are at the only level which still has the potential to break the "administrative trap" (Baker 1976). It is a role which would be strengthened by (a) greater collation of information from different agents at the district level and (b) consideration of intervention strategies which also incorporate some of the aspirations of politicians at times of food crises.

Training of administrative officers by geographers must be interactive. District Officers who have had first hand experience in dealing with food crises must pool their knowledge and understanding of management problems. Geographers must then incorporate these pooled experiences in their conceptual frameworks and help with the training of younger officers who will later be promoted to the key functions of sub-divisional and district officers. Geogrphers should therefore assume their role in Civil Officers Training Academies and Institutes of Management.

Conclusion

Through involvement in six areas: concatenation processes, phenology, semiotics, contingency warning systems, comparative evaluation and administrative training, geographers in developing countries may help to bring the response to human suffering during food crises into line with integrated rural development.

References and Reading

Alamgir, M.: Famine in South Asia: Political Economy of Mass Starvation. Oelgeschlager, Gunn and Hain, Cambridge, MA 1980.

Baker, R.: The Administrative Trap. Ecologist 6,7, 247–251 (1976)

Bidyaratna, H.P.: Khonar Bauchon, Rauston Book Depot, Dacca 1971.

Bhatia, B.M.: Famine and agricultural labour of India: A historical perspective. Indian Journal of Industrial Relations 10,4, 575–594 (1975).

Blair, H.W.: Rural development, class structure and bureaucracy in Bangladesh. World Development 6,1, 65–82 (1978)

Boulding, K.E.: Science and uncertain futures. Technology Review 81,7, 8–9 (1980)

Brammer, H.: Disaster Preparedness Planning. Precautionary and Rehabilitation Measures for Agriculture. Department of Soil Survey, Dacca 1975.

Brammer, H.: Lessons from the 1978/79 Drought, Ministry of Agriculture and Forests, Dacca 1979.

Brammer, H.: Disaster preparedness for farmers: a methodology. Disasters 6,2, 140–144 (1982)

Brookfield, H.: Local study and comparative method: An example from Central New Guinea. Annals of the Association of American Geographers 52,3, 242–254 (1962)

Brunhes, J.: La Geographie Humaine. Felix Alcan, Paris 1910.

Castillo, G.T.: Beyond Manila: Philippine Rural Problems in Perspective. International Development Research Centre, Ottawa 1979.

Changani, A.S.: Seasonal food shortages and agricultural development. Journal of the Geographical Association of Tanzania (Special Number), VIII, 48–62 (1973)

Chapman, G.P.: Mimeo. The Folklore of the Perceived Environment in Bihar provisionally accepted by the A.A.A.G. University of Cambridge, Cambridge 1978.

Chowdhury, R.H.: Seasonal dimensions of rural poverty in Bangladesh: employment, wages and consumption patterns. Social Action 30,1, 1–27 (1980)

Clay, E.J.: Environment, technology and the seasonal patterns of agricultural employment in Bangladesh. Paper read at Conference on Seasonal Dimensions of Rural Poverty, Institute of Development Studies, Sussex 1978.

Clay, E.J.: Poverty, food insecurity, and public policy in Bangladesh. Country Case Study for World Development Report IV. Mimeo, Institute of Development Studies, Sussex 1981.

Clements, F.E.: Plant Succession and Indicators, Carnegie Institute, Washington 1928.

Currey, B.: The famine syndrome: its definition for prevention and relief in Bangladesh. Paper at Ecology of Famine Symposium. American Association for the Advancement of Science, Boston, February 20th–26th – (later reproduced in the Journal Ecology of Food and Nutrition 7, 87–98) (1976)

Currey, B.: Mapping Areas Liable to Famine in Bangladesh, Ph.D. Dissertation, University of Hawaii, University Microfilms Order Number 8012253. Ann Arbor, MI 1979.

Currey, B.: Famine Sleuthing. East West Perspectives 1,3, 6–10 (1980)

Domes, J.: Socialism in the Chinese Countryside. McGill-Queen's University Press, Montreal 1980.

Ea, M.T.: War and Famine: The Example of Kampuchea. Geo Library, vol. 4, 1984.

Firth, R.: Social Change in Tikopia. George Allen and Unwin, London 1959.

de Freitas, C.R. and Woolmington, E.: Catastrophe Theory and Catastasis. Area 12,3, 191–193 (1980)

Government of Bengal: Bengal Famine Code. National Institute of Public Administration. Sheikh Sirajuddin. Publication Officer. Dacca 1913 (Reprint 1967).

Greenough, P.R.: Famine Mortality, Destitution and Victimisation: Bengal 1943–46. 11th Annual Bengal Studies Conference, Iowa City, University of Iowa 1975.

Greenough, P.R.: The Ultimate Insurance Mechanism: Patterned Domestic Break-up During the Bengal Famine 1943–44 (Unpublished Manuscript), Philadelphia 1977.

Greenough, P.R.: Indian famines and peasant victims: the case of Bengal in 1943–44. Modern Asian Studies 14, 205–235 (1980)

Heathcote, R.L.: An Administrative Trap? Natural Hazards in Australia: a personal view. Australian Geographical Studies 18,2, 194–200 (1980)

Hugo, G.J.: Population Mobility in West Java. Ph.D. Dissertation, Department of Demography, The Australian National University, Canberra 1975.

Hunter, W.W.: Annals of Rural Bengal. Cosmo Publication, Dehli 1868 (Reprint 1975).

Jodha, N.S.: Famine and famine policies: some empirical evidence. Economic and Political Weekly, XV, 32 (August 1975)

Hunter, W.W.: Famine Aspects of Bengal Districts. Ballantine and Company, Edingburgh and London 1874.

Librero, F.: The Characteristics, Performance and the Factors Considered in the Decision Making of Various Tenure Groups of Lowland Rice Farmers in Laguna, Philippines. Unpublished M.S. Thesis, University of Wisconsin 1965.

Kunte, J.G.: Indian famines in retrospect − a challenge to administrative leadership. Indian Journal of Public Administration 13,3, 685−689 (1967)

Lea, D.A.M.: The Abelam: A study in local differentiation. Pacific Viewpoint 6,2, 191−214 (1965)

Lindackers, K.H.: A German technical adviser's point-of-view in risk analysis in the chemical industry Angewandte Systemanalyse 2,4, 172−174 (1981)

Longhurst, R. and Payne, P.: Seasonal Aspects of Nutrition: Review of Evidence and Policy Implications. Discussion Paper No. 145, Institute of Development Studies, University of Sussex, Brighton, Sussex 1979.

MacDonnell, A.P.: Report on the Food Grain Supply and Statistical Review of the Relief Operations in the Distressed Districts of Behar and Bengal during the Famine of 1873−74. Bengal Secretariat Press, Calcutta 1876.

Manetsch, T.J. On food shortage forecasting with emphasis on the South Asia case. Bangladesh Development Studies 5,3, 349−358 (1977)

Maude, A.: Land shortage and population pressure in Tonga. In: Brookfield, H. (ed.), The Pacific in Transition. Chapter 7, 163−185, Edward Arnold, London 1973.

Maude, A.: Inter-village differences in out-migration in West Sumatra. The Journal of Tropical Geography 49, 41−54 (1979)

Mehta, V.N.: Agricultural Sayings of the United Provinces, Agricultural Journal of India XI,III, 301−307 (1916)

Metzner, von J.: Die Viehhaltung in der Agrarlandschaft der Insel Sumba und das Problem der saisonalem Hungersnot. Geographische Zeitschrift 64,1, 46−71 (1976)

Mileti, D.S.: Natural Hazard Warning Systems in the United States: A Research Assessment, Monograph No. NSF − RAE−75−013, Program on Technology, Environment and Man., Institute of Behavioral Sciences, University of Colorado 1975.

Miracle, M.: Seasonal hunger: a vague concept and an unexplored problem. Bulletin de L'Institute Francais D'Afrique Noire E23, 273−282 (1961)

Ogbu, J.O.: Seasonal hunger in tropical Africa as a cultural phenomenon. The Onitcha Ibo of Nigeria and Chakoka Poka of Malawi examples, Africa, 43,4, 317−332 (1973).

Orissa Famine Enquiry Commissioner's Report 1867.

Parrack, D.W. Ecosystems and famine. Ecology of Food and Nutrition 7,1, 17−21 (1978)

Plewe, E.: Untersuchung über den Begriff der Vergleichenden Erdkunde und seine Anwendung in der neueren Geographie. Zeitschrift der Gesellschaft für Erdkunde, Ergänzungsheft 4, 1−22 (1932).

Rahman, M.M.: The causes and effects of famine in the rural population: a report from Bangladesh. Ecology of Food and Nutrition 7,2, 99−102 (1978)

Rasmussen, N.C.: Reactor Study − An assessment of accident risks in U.S. commercial nuclear power plants. USNRC. WASH − 1400 (NUREG − 75/104) October 1975.

Renfrew, C. and Cooke, K.L. (eds.): Transformations Mathematical approaches to cultural change. Academic Press, New York 1979.

Report of the Indian Famine Commission. C.−91/8, Her Majesty's Stationery Office, London 1898.

Ritter, C.: Einleitung zur Allgemeinen Vergleichenden Geographie und Abhandlungen, Berlin 1852.

Rochberg, R.T.J.G. and Helmer, O.: The Use of Cross Impact Matrices for Forecasting and Planning. Report R. 10, Institute for the Future, Connecticut 1970.

Rogerson, C.M.: Industrialisation in the shadows of apartheid: a world systems view. (Draft) Seminar Paper, Research School of Pacific Studies. the Australian National University 1978.

Sanderson, F.H.: The great food fumble. Science 188,4188, 503−509 (1975)

Seaman, J., Holt, J.F.J.: Markets and famines in the Third World. Disasters 4,3, 283−297 (1980)

Sen, A.K.: Poverty and Famines: an Essay on Entitlement and Deprivation. Clarendon Press, Oxford 1981.

Sless, D.: In Search of Semiotics. Croom Helm, London 1983.

Stoddart, D.R.: Geography and the ecological approach: the ecosystem as geographic principle and method. Geography 50, 242−251 (1965)

Stoddart, D.R.: Organism and Ecosystem as Geographic, Models in Geography 511−548, Eds. Chorley, R.J. and Haggett, P. Methuen, London 1967.

Turner, B.A.: The development of disasters − a sequence model for the analysis of the disasters. Sociological Review 24,4, 753−774 (1967)

Watts, M.J.: Seasonal Hunger and Poverty in Northern Nigeria. Paper delivered to the Conference on Seasonality and Rural Poverty. Institute of Development Studies, Sussex 1978.

Wheatcroft, S.G.: Soviet Famines and Food Supply Problems before the Second World War. Paper read at Famine in History Colloquium. The Alimentarium, Vevey 1981.

Wolpert, J.: The dignity of risk. Transactions, Institute of British Geographers 5,4, 391−401 (1980)

Woodruff, P.: The Men who Ruled India: the Guardians. Jonathon Cape, London 1954.

8. Malthus and famine
28. Lack of geog. analisis